CAUGHT OUT

Foreword by Darrell Hair

CAUGHT OUT

Shocking Revelations of Corruption in
International Cricket

BRIAN RADFORD

JOHN BLAKE

Published by John Blake Publishing Ltd,
3 Bramber Court, 2 Bramber Road,
London W14 9PB, England

www.johnblakepublishing.co.uk

www.facebook.com/Johnblakepub facebook
twitter.com/johnblakepub twitter

First published in hardback in 2011

ISBN: 978 1 84358 384 4

British Library Cataloguing-in-Publication Data:

A catalogue record for this book is available from the British Library.

Design by www.envydesign.co.uk

Printed in Great Britain by CPI Mackays, Chatham, ME5 8TD

3 5 7 9 10 8 6 4 2

Papers used by John Blake Publishing are natural, recyclable products made
from wood grown in sustainable forests. The manufacturing processes conform
to the environmental regulations of the country of origin.

To my wife, Jill, for her remarkable patience and support,
and Toby, Rebecca, John, Emili and Faye

CONTENTS

FOREWORD
By Darrell Hair

I t is not often that a book about sport, and cricket in particular,
delivers on all its promises and publicity. This book is one of
those exceptions.

My career in cricket umpiring, and a lifetime in the game, has time
and time again, told me that many people within it have an
opinion about its dark side – the cheating and under-performing
for financial reward, which provides a fraudulent contest for those
who genuinely believe they are watching a match that is being
played, and won or lost, on its merits.

But when push comes to shove, few players, if any, are willing to
say exactly what they know, or think, for fear of retribution from
apathetic and ignorant administrators, or fearing that they will be
ostracised by team-mates and driven from the game.

It is a shame when cricket administrators treat allegations of
corrupt behaviour with apathy or absolute fear. One reason for this
attitude could be the thought of their game being dragged through
the mud and may, in the eyes of the public, ruin the values and

spirit of the game that have been inherent in the culture of cricket for more than 280 years.

Cricket's unique appeal has always been the willingness of players to accept an umpire's decision, show respect for the laws of the game and its traditional values, and to believe that cheating has no part in it.

In the modern game, this spirit has sadly often been abused by unruly behaviour from players, open dissent towards decisions by umpires, and the advent of much more sinister behaviour in playing corruptly by manipulating the game for financial benefit.

It is this corrupt behaviour, and there can be no other words for it, that Brian Radford's book exposes, and cuts to the bone. The very core of the game has suffered because a greedy few have exploited cricket and, in doing so, produced a fraud on the public – the very people whose support the professional player of the 21st century relies upon so heavily.

On the pages of this book, you will discover how the Anti-corruption Unit, which is run by the International Cricket Council, was continually frustrated by a conspiracy of silence, even though overwhelming evidence existed of illegal betting on such mundane things as the outcome of the toss for choice of innings.

The depth of unsavoury behaviour also extended to information being divulged to bookmakers, as to who would open the bowling in a particular match, and from which end of the ground.

Further startling revelations emerged as to how pitches were doctored midway through a match to ensure certain results, and how the ever-present metal bottle top was used by some players to scratch the ball to make it swing even more.

Corrupt behaviour and blatant cheating are to be abhorred. Immoral behaviour strikes at the very heart of our game. I took a stand in trying to stamp out such behaviour, and my reward was to be ostracised by the International Cricket Council, which later watered down its rules on ball-tampering, and dissent at an umpire's decision.

Cricket should be sacrosanct. But it never will be, unless participants and administrators band together to stamp out corruption.

Brian Radford's book goes a long way to exposing the manner in which the game has been infected. His exposé about the past may, hopefully, ensure that the game is cleansed of the greed and corruption, so that its future, and the future of its players, is beyond reproach. We must certainly hope so.

Darrell Hair,
Executive Officer,
NSW Cricket Umpires & Scorers Association Inc.

Darrell Hair is a distinguished Australian umpire who reached the peak of his profession when the International Cricket Council appointed him to its Elite panel. He officiated in 73 Test matches and 135 One-day Internationals before he retired in 2008, and was highly acclaimed for his fairness and integrity.

CHAPTER ONE

PANIC AND PRAYERS AT CONDON'S ANTI-CORRUPTION UNIT OFFICES

Lord Condon's highly expensive Anti-corruption and Security Unit was set up in a plush office in south-west London in September 2001, funded by the International Cricket Council (ICC) to a reported £2 million. Condon, a former Commissioner of the Metropolitan Police, had been appointed three months earlier as Director of the Unit with a remit to recruit the best team of available investigators to mastermind and launch a worldwide search for the cheats and crooks who were corrupting international cricket matches, and had being doing so systematically for at least 20 years.

A former chief superintendent from New Scotland Yard was appointed senior investigator, and two other former high-ranking detectives were added to the team, along with a security adviser, a systems manager to establish an intelligence database, and a full-time secretary, who acted as office manager.

Condon was directly accountable to Malcolm Gray, President of the ICC, and he began his mammoth task by stressing that confidence in world cricket would be restored only if there was

1

open and frank analysis of past problems, and a resolve to confront the challenges which continued to threaten the integrity and reputation of the game.

No punches were pulled as Condon lashed out at corrupt practices and deliberate under-performing by players that had permeated cricket at all levels across the world, additionally emphasising that a full-blown resurgence was a real and probable threat.

Silence, apathy, ignorance and absolute fear greeted Condon's clean-up squad as they quickly realised that allegations in the public domain were merely the tip of a titanic iceberg, and that a vast number of people had not reported attempts to corrupt them, or come forward about other people they believed were corrupt.

A diabolically frustrating conspiracy of silence was soon evident among players not wanting to be seen as informants and risk being ostracised by colleagues, while other players and officials justifiably feared that whistle-blowers would be penalised rather than supported.

Condon had to concede that players were afraid of having their international careers brought to a swift end should they dare express anxieties about corruption. And in this he was spot on, as it sadly turned out when Pakistan's prolific opening batsman Qasim Omar – the only player ever brave enough to provide Condon personally with specific evidence of corruption – exposed the frightening scale of it, and candidly named names, no matter how big they were in world cricket and idolised by millions.

Omar was subsequently 'rewarded' for his courageous whistle-blowing assistance with an outrageous seven-year ban by the disgraceful Pakistan Cricket Board (PCB) that totally destroyed his international career and alienated him from players of all cricket nations.

I accompanied Omar to the office of the Anti-corruption and Security Unit (usually known just as the Anti-corruption Unit, or ACU, in matters relating to cricket corruption) on two separate occasions and took copious notes while he sat directly opposite Condon and a couple of senior investigators, who struggled with their own note-taking to keep up with an avalanche of explosive revelations, though they knew that everything that he disclosed was being taped-recorded to ensure that not a word was lost in transcript. Later on I shall recall precisely what Omar told Condon and his startled squad behind closed doors on those private visits.

Players, former players, umpires and others have been understandably shocked, angered and embarrassed to discover that they have taken part in matches that were scandalously rigged. Murder, kidnapping, and alarming physical threats to individuals and their families were also immediately linked to cricket corruption as Condon's squad went into action.

Many players and officials were genuinely frightened of the consequences if it ever became known that they had cooperated with the Anti-corruption Unit, and some were too scared to stop for fear of being attacked by ruthless bookmakers and gambling gangs, and had no choice but to continue.

Great concern arose after several insiders alleged that a major criminal had access to a particular national team to such an extent that he could influence who was selected to play and decide how each member of the side would perform – and under-perform.

It was feared that a contract killing in South Africa resulted from a dispute between rival corruptors from other countries. With its easy profit and simple money-laundering, proceeds from cricket corruption have been sufficiently large to attract organised crime.

Investigators soon collected overwhelming evidence that illegal betting could take place on international cricket matches anywhere in the world, and in some areas it was perceived that players under suspicion of corruption had been tolerated by their governing bodies because they were too important to the national team to be exposed and excluded from selection. Condon made it clear that blame for the spread of ugly cricket corruption should not be placed on the Indian subcontinent alone, and he conceded that corrupt practices were so deeply ingrained in cricket culture that major criminals could be involved.

Some terrified informants agreed to be interviewed only after absolute guarantees were given that all such meetings would be held in safe and secret surroundings, but many rejected even these assurances, declining to provide evidence in a formal and public form. One such person was Indian bookmaker Mukesh Gupta, who alleged that he had paid several highly respected players for crucial information – and named them.

Condon's crime-busters received allegations that corrupt betting was taking place on:

- the outcome of the toss at the start of a match
- the end from which the fielding captain would select to bowl first
- a set number of wides or no-balls occurring in a specified over
- players being placed in unfamiliar fielding positions, like someone who usually stood on the boundary being put in the slips
- top-order batsmen scoring fewer runs than their opponents who had batted first
- batsmen being dismissed at a specific point in their innings
- total runs when a captain would declare
- the timing of a declaration
- total runs scored in a particular innings, and particularly the total in the first innings of a One-day International.

Several umpires had admitted to being approached by shady people who wanted to know at which end they would stand at the start of a match. Groundsmen had also confessed to fixing pitches for bookmakers to ensure that a match ended in a positive result, and tampering with a pitch overnight to change the predicted course of a game.

Another area of immense worry was the consummate ease with which corruptors were gaining access to players, especially through the total absence of accreditation on tours that allowed undesirable people to mix freely with teams, which provided the perfect breeding ground for improper approaches and corruption.

Condon and his investigators were eager to interview Pakistan batsman Qasim Omar who had courageously broken the strict code of silence among players and officials and had become the first – and only – well-informed insider to go public and lift the lid on the phenomenal extent of corruption swilling around in cricket's international cesspool.

The ebullient and likeable Omar had telephoned me at the London office of *The People* newspaper where I worked as a sports and news investigator and offered to blow the whistle because he could no longer bear to see his game destroyed, and the general public deceived and derided by a growing band of greedy crooks in a world of corruption.

After much negotiating about dates and times, Condon's wish was finally granted when Omar and I arrived at the ACSU office, where he and his two senior investigators, Alan Peacock and Martin Hawkins, both former Scotland Yard officers, greeted us warmly.

Omar had played with, and against, the world's very best cricketers, many of them absolute legends in the game, and Condon and his aides were openly grateful to him for his explosive revelations about players linked to betting, drugs, prostitution and money-laundering. At one point Condon leaned forward and stressed: 'Qasim Omar's revelations are a very important part of the jigsaw. My terms of reference are that we support criminal investigations anywhere in the world. A huge amount of work is under way. There are not enough hours in the day to cope with it.'

That first riveting meeting between Omar and the ACSU was still very much the appetiser, and it was only when Omar returned to their London offices that the main meal was put on a plate for the investigators in a dramatic ten-hour session.

Again I went along with him and again I listened and scribbled as he disclosed, almost without taking a breath, stark details of players who were making a fortune from cheating – and he named them all, clearly and confidently.

Omar, who wanted the investigators to know that he was a devout Muslim, began by recounting a recent visit to Pakistan to talk to cricketers about the value of religion. He recalled arriving at the Gadaffi Stadium in Lahore and meeting three of the country's best players: bowlers Abdul Qadir and Wasim Akram, and batsman Saeed Anwar.

Becoming noticeably emotional, Omar said: 'When I was talking to them, people in the Executive Room were wondering who I was, and Rameez Raja [Pakistan's brilliant opening batsman, and now a popular television commentator] recognised me, and told them that it was Qasim.'

General Tauqir Zia, then President of the Pakistan Cricket Board (PCB), was with them and he told Rameez that Omar should go up and speak to him. Omar was with a former Olympic hockey player, and they both went up to the Executive Room.

'On my way up, I kept thinking that as General Zia had lots of bodyguards, and was very powerful, he might tick me off [for going public about cricketers and corruption],' said Omar, 'but he got up from his chair, and said he was pleased to meet me.'

Omar said he told Zia that he was working in religion, and Zia said: 'You are in the news again.' Omar replied: 'Yes, and I am speaking the truth,' to which the General responded that if he was now in religion, he should stay away from controversial issues.

'I told him that if the Pakistan Cricket Board had listened to me many years ago, it would not have got caught up in drug scandals and match-fixing,' said Omar. 'But people took no notice of what I was saying.' Then General Zia had said: 'When there was a gambling inquiry, why didn't you come?'

Omar had replied: 'First of all, you people dragged it on for years and years, but not a single player was mentioned. If you had invited me over [from England, where he lived with his family in Durham], I would have come.' Omar told Zia that he was going back to the ICC's Anti-corruption Unit and would tell them what he had seen other players doing, and they should not expect him to keep quiet.

'I asked him if he was saying that no one knew about these people, when *I* knew,' Omar told the ACU, 'and I asked him: "What about my problem when you banned me? Don't expect me to stay quiet. If I see anything, I'm going to speak out." I admitted to him that I'd been involved [in cricket corruption], and that I'd apologised for that, and that I was young and naïve when it happened.'

Zia had asked Omar how they could eliminate things like match-fixing and players under-performing and taking money from bookies. Omar said he was amazed that Zia didn't know what match-forecasting meant, and had to explain it to him.

'I told him that players, and captains in particular, took money from bookmakers for letting them know whether they would bat if they won the toss, and what the batting order would be, and who was in the team. And if the captain decided to field, he would tell the bookmaker which player would open the bowling and which end of the ground he would bowl from. This was all new to him. I was shocked that he could be so badly out of touch.

'I told him that if any money was on offer, certain cricketers would grab it, as lots of them have a short career and didn't earn a great deal, so they would take risks to earn a bit extra.'

(Condon was due to meet Zia sometime shortly after his chat with Omar, so Omar's advice to the General was perfectly timed –

without that information he would have been highly embarrassed and would have looked stupid.)

With the ACU tape-recorder still whirring, Omar then named a prominent Pakistan player who had said privately that Pakistan matches in New Zealand had been fixed, and that a Pakistan bookmaker, who ran a catering business in Karachi, had assured him that a leading Pakistan batsman had pocketed the equivalent of £100,000 from fixing matches in New Zealand. Omar named this dodgy player, and said that he also knew the bookmaker extremely well, and that he had stayed with him at his home near Karachi airport.

Names of alleged crooked cricketers cascaded from Omar's relentless tongue as the ACU interview gained momentum, and the next player to be identified was yet another hugely successful Pakistan batsman who, according to Omar, had regularly called at the home of a leading bookmaker in a village near Peshawar, and that the player and bookmaker had gone to tournaments together where matches were fixed.

Omar then switched his fusillade of disclosures to Australia, where he claimed that 23 'stunning' girls had worked as high-class hookers for a bookmaker to provide additional perks for players who fixed matches. Apart from one Pakistani model and a Chinese doctor, the girls were all attractive Australians, and Omar named them all, and even provided their telephone numbers and addresses.

He said the network had been set up in the mid-Eighties and stretched right across Australia, from Brisbane to Perth. Over the years the hookers had included a nurse, a schoolteacher, a travel agent and a glamorous television presenter. Two madams ran the sleazy operation from their homes in Sydney. Omar named them both. He also assured Condon and his team that an identical 'girls-as-perks' scandal was being run by a bookmaker in New Zealand, and he named him.

Omar listed some of cricket's biggest Test stars as having had sex with the go-anywhere hookers, in addition to pocketing large sums of money from bookmakers, both in Australia and New Zealand. Most of the deals were struck secretly in team hotels, with the Sheraton in Sydney a popular rendezvous, plus a restaurant in Sydney's seedy red light district and a McDonald's in Melbourne.

One leading Asian bowler was named as having deliberately under-performed in several matches because he desperately needed money for a house he was building. Another bowler was alleged to have faked injury straight after Test matches in order to be paid big money by a bookmaker for not playing in friendly four-day games. This information enabled the bookmaker to land large bets on forecasting who would not be in the Pakistan team.

Omar also revealed that players were pocketing big money for deliberately dropping catches – information that would have infuriated spectators if the truth had ever got out. Omar told Condon and his investigators that the New Zealand hookers usually went to a player's hotel room for sex, and that one grateful bookmaker also provided porn movies as an additional perk. Specific incidents in Auckland, Wellington and Christchurch – the country's three main cricket centres – were graphically recalled.

At the time Condon was receiving this astonishing information, ICC President Malcolm Gray was warning that the match-fixing scandal could get seriously worse. Alarmingly, he stated: 'I can assure you that it has been a lot deeper and broader than anyone realised or expected, and I suspect we might get hit with more bad news.'

His disturbing prediction was spot on, which Omar soon confirmed, pointing out that teams from England, the West Indies, Pakistan and India were all in Australia when the sex perk was at its peak.

Yet another shock hit the ACU's investigators when Omar revealed that an apparently squeaky-clean director of a large company with its headquarters in Western Australia had masterminded the 'hooker rewards' operation that was organised with such military precision.

Omar admitted that several of these hookers had been sent to him, but he insisted that he always rejected their sexual favours, though he did enjoy an occasional massage from them and went out for drinks and meals – but that was as far as it went.

Focus was placed on the elusive 'Mr Fixit', who was described by Omar as the 'smooth wealthy director' whom he named, and he provided business and home addresses. Omar described the director as 'tall and smart' and said that he always called him 'son'. 'He would say "Hello, son!" or "Thank you, son!" and "Well done, son!" He never called me Qasim, or Omar. He would come to see me before the start of a match, and sometimes during the lunch or tea breaks.

'We got to know each other well after I scored 48 in the first innings of the First Test against Australia in Perth when I was caught by Graham Yallop off bowler Carl Rackerman. That innings impressed a lot of good cricket judges, including the great Richie Benaud, the Australian bowling legend who was commentating on the match for a TV channel. These people, like Benaud, could not believe that a young newcomer could play such fast bowling with so much courage.

'When I returned to the team's hotel, I found that a T-shirt and a nice pen, with the name of a company stamped on it, had been left at reception for me, and later in the evening a man rang my room and praised my innings. He invited me to dinner and, after saying who he was, he handed me an expensive Rado wristwatch, which I later sold in Karachi because I found it too heavy to wear.'

Omar recalled that the mystery man introduced himself as a director of a large company, which he named, and said that he could use money from the company to bet on cricket. He also mentioned the name of a leading Pakistan bookmaker, and said that he knew him well.

Omar was shocked that the director knew this bookmaker, and he recalled: 'He then said that a number of leading Pakistani batsmen had taken money from him for throwing their wickets away, and that he would "look after me" if I threw my wicket away in the second innings, preferably without scoring a run.

'I told him that I couldn't do it, but I promised to do something for him in a three-day match in Sydney, and later on in Brisbane.'

In the second innings of that Test match, wicketkeeper Rodney Marsh caught Omar when he was on 65, and Rackerman was again the bowler.

Proud of his performance, Omar said: 'People in the media rated my innings the best seen in Australia for many years, as I was so young and had no experience of facing such fast bowlers on such a fast wicket. My innings was played over and over again on television.'

Omar recalled that the Pakistan team travelled straight to Sydney after that Test match, and that a woman called Wendy was waiting for him in the lobby of the Sheraton Hotel when the team arrived. She handed him an envelope containing a letter and A$500.

Omar told the investigators: 'The letter said that a woman called Wendy would "look after me" and I knew exactly what that meant. Wendy told me that the company director had asked her to hand it to me, and she invited me to dinner at a different hotel, where she said that I had to score less than 50 in my first innings. She also predicted that Pakistan would be dismissed for a low score, and she was right. Greg Matthews took lots of wickets and bowled me for 25.

'Wendy rang my room again in the evening and we went to a restaurant in Sydney's famous red light district, where we both dined on kebabs.'

Wendy joked with Omar that he should not eat too many kebabs, and claimed that she had been smart and slim before she put on lots of weight from eating this type of food.

According to Omar it was all very relaxed, and he and Wendy got on really well. She knew a lot about cricket, and she surprised him when she named a leading Australian batsman who had worked as a match-fixer for the company director, who had paid him big money for letting him know the team, which bowler would open the attack, and from which end of the ground.

She also named two other Australian players who had 'taken lots of money from the director to throw their wickets away'.

One of Pakistan's biggest bookmakers, who travelled all over the world to Test matches, had told Omar that one of these two Australian players had been offered as much as 25,000 dollars to lose his wicket deliberately. Omar told the investigators that this disappointed him a lot because this very popular player had been his hero.

Wendy also told him that a lot of money was being bet on a certain Australian player ending up in an unusual fielding position for him in a Test match during the series.

Holding nothing back, Omar admitted: 'I was offered 1,000 dollars if I scored less than 25 in the first innings of the Test match in Brisbane, and 2,000 dollars if I did exactly the same in the second innings. Kim Hughes caught me off Geoff Lawson's bowling in the first innings when I was on 17, and I was on 11 in the second innings when it rained heavily and the match was drawn.'

Next day a number of local newspapers published a quirky picture of Omar standing on the outfield in wellies, and holding a brolly over his head.

He then recalled that one Pakistan bowler was paid by a bookmaker not to play in a number of domestic games, so he faked injuries after Test matches, took big money for doing it, was able to stay out late at discos and casinos, and ended up with a girl who got pregnant.

Adelaide was the team's next stop and Omar was surprised to find several girls lining up to see him when the team coach arrived at the hotel. He recalled: 'My director friend had sent them. Wendy was not there this time; a girl called Jill Gabriel had taken over. Just like Wendy had done before, she took me out for a meal in the evening and offered me cash to throw my wicket away. I refused and told her to explain to the director that my place in the team was not guaranteed yet.'

Omar, however, did promise her that he would let them know where certain Pakistan players would appear in the batting order, and who would bowl and from which end. It turned out to be a terrific Test match for Omar, who hit a brilliant 113 in the first innings before he was caught.

Omar told the investigators that when Wendy returned to the cricket circuit she introduced him to a Chinese girl called Kit Wong who controlled betting outlets for Chinese bookmakers and gamblers, and that they discussed plans for him to throw his wicket away, and that she offered him 800 US dollars to do it.

Wendy tried hard to persuade Omar to introduce her to his famous captain, Imran Khan, a legend in world cricket, but he refused, insisting that he never introduced girls to players or dealt in drugs.

He said: 'Wendy even sent an attractive escort called Tara to Imran, but a security guard spotted her in the corridor just as she was about to knock on his door, and she was marched out of the hotel because she looked too young to be visiting him.

'When we reached Tasmania, yet another girl, this time called Janet, had left a message for me. I met her at a bar close to the hotel, and I agreed to score fewer than 50 in both innings. She said that big bets had been placed on me to hammer the Tasmanian bowlers. Money and gifts poured in throughout the rest of that Australian tour and I earned around 8,000 US dollars in total for doing what I was asked.'

It was close to 3pm in Condon's office when Omar suddenly broke off from his conveyor belt of startling revelations and asked, with some urgency, for a mat. Peacock, Hawkins and I were bamboozled. Condon was not present when this commotion was taking place.

'What on earth are you talking about?' I asked Omar. 'What's your problem?' He didn't say a word, didn't even look across at me but raised his voice, threatening to walk out and never come back unless someone found him a mat.

With time running out, Omar explained that as a devout Muslim he prayed up to five times a day, and as he was now too far from the nearest mosque, he had to have a mat to kneel on for prayers at three o'clock. Desperate not to lose him, Peacock and Hawkins darted from room to room in search of a mat, but could find nothing suitable – until Peacock came up with an idea. 'What about a newspaper?' Peacock asked, gingerly. 'Will that do? Can you manage with that?'

'Yes,' Omar replied. 'Where is it?'

Trouble was, there was no newspaper to be found in the office, so one of the investigators rushed into the street and returned with a pristine copy of the London *Evening Standard*, which Omar folded neatly, placed on the floor in front of him, and knelt on for 15 minutes, saying his prayers while the rest of us waited silently in an adjoining room until he had finished.

With his prayers happily out of the way, Omar returned to plying the investigators with yet more information, vividly recalling an evening in Wellington when two young prostitutes went to the hotel where the Pakistan team was staying and offered Omar 'a massage that he would never forget!'

Suddenly chuckling, as the memorable occasion crossed his mind, Omar said: 'I told them "No thanks, please go away," but I was told later that the hotel was swarming with high-class hookers who had been sent along by a bookie in return for our team batting and bowling badly. Lots of players might have under-performed on the field, but I'm pretty sure they did their best when the girls arrived! They were terrific!'

Omar admitted to the investigators that he threw his wicket away in the first innings of a three-day friendly match in Christchurch, but scored a century in the second innings to secure his place in the Pakistan team for the First Test in Wellington. He recalled that soon after Pakistan arrived in New Zealand, two of his team-mates introduced him to a hotel owner who also operated as a bookmaker and provided hookers and cash in return for 'inside' information.

'This man offered me 1,000 US dollars to score fewer than 50 in my first innings in the Test in Auckland,' Omar said. 'It was very tempting and I said yes, though on this occasion I had no intention of doing it. I took a chance and accepted the money and, as it turned out, I was caught for 33. It was a genuine bat-pad catch, though it seemed to the bookie that I did it deliberately, just as he had asked me to.'

Omar remembered vividly that his paymaster was ecstatic about what he had apparently done, and in the evening he took a 'gorgeous' girl round to his hotel and asked Omar if he would like to invite her to his room, and was stunned when Omar turned him down with a polite 'No, thank you...'

Before the start of the final Test match, Omar said that he arranged with this bookmaker that if he managed to build a big score in the first innings, he would consider deliberately losing his wicket for very few runs in the second innings. He promptly hammered an impressive 96 in the first innings, and had scored 75 in the second innings when 'someone' in the team told him that a lot of money had been bet that he would not reach a hundred.

Omar was caught out on 89, and he was deeply disappointed as he desperately wanted to score a century against New Zealand. Again, the bookmaker thought that he had deliberately given his wicket away, and paid him 1,000 US dollars.

He had also played in two One-day matches before that Test – the first in Hamilton, where he chased a wide ball and was caught for two; and the other in Christchurch, where he carelessly ran himself out for nought. Both times he was paid 1,000 US dollars.

Omar also named a prominent England bowler who accepted 1,000 US dollars from an illegal bookmaker to send down a full-length ball that was wide of the leg stump in his first over so that the Pakistan batsman could hit it to the boundary for four, which he did.

Continuing to bare his soul, Omar told the investigators that he personally acted as the bookmaker's agent in this deal, that he handed the money to the bowler in an envelope at the Continental Hotel in Lahore, and that they later became good friends.

While disclosing the vast scale of international cricket corruption, Omar claimed that some captains were pocketing up to £1,000 simply for telling a bookmaker in advance whether they would bat or bowl should they win the toss. And that captains were earning even more for telling bookmakers who in their team would open the bowling, and from which end of the ground.

Some of the best-known stars were reportedly raking in at least £5,000 a match. The biggest fees were being paid to players who deliberately got themselves out for nought, and to those who let themselves be clean bowled or run out, especially in the first over.

Distance was no problem to many Asian bookmakers, and Pakistan players were personally contacted while on tour in England, Australia, New Zealand and the West Indies. Omar named a leading Pakistan batsman who suffered a string of low scores on a dreadful tour of England when the fans and media were convinced that he was suffering a bad run of form.

Omar, who played alongside him and socialised with him, knew the truth. He clearly recalled: 'He was not off form at all; that was rubbish. He was working with the bookies and he made big money from them. He also threw his wicket away in a Test match in Australia for a huge fee. I was there when he did the deal and I heard him accept the bribe.'

A spokesman for Condon's investigating team later confirmed to me that they had traced and spoken to the elusive 'Wendy' in Australia, and that she had admitted to them that she was a regular spectator at the Sydney Cricket Ground and that she knew Omar, but categorically denied that she ran hookers for a bookmaker or had paid cricketers to cheat.

Plainly not put off by this predictable reaction, the spokesman added: 'Our purpose will now be to find her friends. We are going to try to locate as many of the girls as we can.'

When told several weeks later that Wendy had denied that she had organised the hookers for players and paid players to cheat, a tetchy Omar replied: 'What did they expect? She paid players, and she found girls for players. That's the way it was. That's the truth. I've met these girls, and I've already given their names to the investigators. It was a very big gambling operation.

'If necessary I will go to Australia and meet her face to face. Players from every cricket country were involved. She paid me for throwing my wicket away. She offered girls to me. They were beautiful girls. I never got involved, but I did have a massage once or twice. So how can she say it never happened? It *did* happen! Sexual favours were being provided to players for fixing matches and giving information, and it came on top of cash payments.'

A grateful Condon said: 'Qasim Omar's revelations are a very important part of the jigsaw. We are strenuously pursuing his allegations. We are very grateful for the information we have received.'

Condon and his sleaze-busters made several trips to India, where they met the Minister of Sport, the Law Minister, officials of the Central Bureau of Investigation (CBI), Delhi police, the country's Board of Control for Cricket, and special investigator M Mahaven.

What never became clear was whether Condon's investigators ever interviewed Uttam Chand, who had admitted using codes when making telephone calls to players, and that bets had been placed on what a particular player would score in a certain innings and on what the team would score. A strong rumour went around dressing rooms that the highly confidential code had been cracked and that a large number of star players were shaking in their boots, waiting for a knock on the door.

There was also no hint, let alone confirmation, that Condon's investigators had interviewed Sanjiv Kholi, a well-known ferocious gambler who ran a chain of smart restaurants and boasted about being close to Indian bowler Manjor Prabakhar, and who had admitted that he had asked him for information during England's 1993 tour of India. There was even further doubt about whether the ACU had spoken to Piloo Reporter, the Test umpire whom leading Indian bookmaker Mukesh Gupta had claimed was paid for information during England's same tour of India.

There was no apparent record, either, of an interview with Daleep Seth, who ran the exclusive telephone exchange with 120 private lines for a gang of illegal bookmakers, gamblers and players, or with Rajesh Kalra, who had told the CBI that Prabakhar had placed bets through him.

It was beyond doubt, however, that Mukesh Gupta had twice met investigators from the ACU and had repeated to them what he had told the CBI inquiry – that he had paid England batsman/wicketkeeper Alec Stewart £5,000 for weather, wicket and England's team composition during the 1993 tour. Stewart was subsequently cleared of any wrongdoing whatsoever by the ECB's Disciplinary Standing Committee.

Mark Harrison, the ICC Communications Manager, issued a statement on behalf of the ACU in which he said: 'Mukesh Gupta has been seen twice in India by the Anti-corruption Unit and he verbally confirmed his allegations to investigators from the Unit.' The Indian authorities also stated that they totally believed what Gupta had told them.

Condon confirmed that he had interviewed Prabakhar, whom

Gupta said he had paid to be introduced to Stewart, but 'was not at liberty to say at this stage what his position is'. What was particularly intriguing was Condon's adamant comment that 'for anyone to say, or give the impression, that Alec Stewart would be cleared should Gupta not provide legally binding evidence is quite wrong'.

He went on: 'It would not mean that the inquiry is at an end. Gupta's evidence is not the only evidence we have gathered. It does not all depend on Gupta. Those who might think so are ignoring the fact that the inquiry team has interviewed certain players, and members of our team will form a judgement about what the players have said to them.

'I am not in a position to name those players. Everything has been done on a strictly confidential basis. But let us not get carried away with thinking that this inquiry collapses if Gupta does not go on record legally.

'The position with Gupta is fairly straightforward. My team has seen him twice. The latest occasion was in March when he verbally confirmed to two investigators all that he had said in the CBI report. It was then important to build on that, and to see whether he would repeat his words in disciplinary or criminal proceedings. He is extremely difficult to pin down, and we are the only people who have seen him, apart from the CBI.

'I have two investigators in India at the moment doing a number of important things. Part of their role will be to remind Mr Gupta that we are looking to him to fulfil his responsibility. I have invited him to make up his mind by 1 July. If he does not respond by that date, then we must assume that he won't be doing so. But that would not mean it's the end of the inquiry because there are many things going on.'

Condon expressed serious concern about the possibility of extreme violence and even murder having been part of the squalid match-fixing world, and said: 'A number of people have referred to murder. They have reported the fear that some people have been involved. We have no doubt that certain individuals have received personal life threats.'

He was aware of Mukesh Gupta's statement to the CBI that the Pakistan team had been close to a bookmaker called Hanif Cadbury who was killed in South Africa. Gupta had said that they were most probably 'doing' matches for him. Boldly sticking his neck out, Condon predicted: 'If players are found guilty I am confident that all these countries will apply the appropriate penalty. No one involved in this inquiry is going to let the guilty go free, no matter how good a player he might be.'

Sadly this was totally contradicted by an ICC spokesman, who said: 'Our brief is not to catch players but to stop the culture of corruption. As soon as our inquiries become criminal we will do our best to get the relevant police to take it on.'

The ICC has no powers of arrest, so everything is very much in the hands of the players and their cricket boards to decide what action is taken, which is why it is so easy for the guilty to have a good laugh and walk away scot-free.

Indeed, Prabhakar told me from Delhi: 'We've been punished over here, so why are players not being punished by the cricket boards in other countries? Why are they being treated with kid gloves?'

Condon's comments were so strange at times that I wondered whether he was the right man to be heading such a vast inquiry into a sport with which he had so little empathy or knowledge, and his qualification for the job as a former Metropolitan Police superintendent seemed seriously insufficient for the task in front him.

I imagine that the statement he made in May 2001 kept flashing back as the number of cricket corruption inquiries and allegations grew to a crisis level, and that Pakistan's despicable match-fixing tour of England in summer 2010 caused him untold nightmares and embarrassment. Should anyone have forgotten, Condon's fateful words were: 'My ambition is to make it so tough for the few bad guys still left that the risks are not worth it.'

Players too terrified to bowl a deliberate no-ball, drop catches, give their wickets away in return for fat brown envelopes? Hardly! The truth is that cricket's legion of crooks know too well that the ICC and the toothless independent cricket boards have as much bite as a mouse with dentures. Absolutely nothing will improve until cricket's leaders forget about trying to preserve the 'we are absolutely clean' image and burn the brooms that brush the dirt under their carpets.

Silence is golden, as the old saying goes. Never could those words have been more joyfully said than in world cricket, in all languages from Bombay to Brisbane, Lahore to Lord's, and Colombo to Cape Town. Test cricketers across the world have united in a conspiracy of silence, and key informants have refused to speak to the ICC investigators.

Condon encountered the frustration first-hand when he and a senior investigator flew half way round the world to Sri Lanka to interview two former Test heroes who had been named in the CBI report as players who had accepted money from an Indian bookmaker, but they declined to answer the questions he put to them.

Undaunted by their silence, Condon and his investigators battled on with little success, and he despairingly disclosed that only two countries had responded 'satisfactorily' to an ICC request for confidential knowledge and details of involvement in corrupt practices.

The trouble was that the proverbial wall of silence did not end with tongue-tied players, officials, managers and administrators. Not a single new name was mentioned in Condon's 77-page tome. He referred only to those exposed in the CBI report, the King

Commission in South Africa, and the Pakistan Cricket Board inquiry.

To be fair to Condon, he accepted that he faced a gigantic problem in getting people to speak to him and his team. He made the point that 'although the Anti-corruption Unit has a vital role to play, its members do not have the powers given to judicial inquiries and police forces'.

India's cricket leaders were fully satisfied that bookmaker Muktesh Gupta had told the truth. Indeed, they named, warned and banned players on the strength of his evidence. An official statement confirmed: 'The CBI felt that their principal witness, M K Gupta, a bookmaker, had not been disproved in respect of *any* allegations that he had made, and they did not think he was lying.'

Corrupt cricketers, illegal bookmakers and crooked gamblers are a curse to the game at every level, and it is critical that the ICC does not help them tarnish the sport even more by staying mute when drastic action is needed.

It is imperative that the ICC tears off its gag and names and shames the guilty individuals, and it is just as important that every individual governing body provides maximum support to rid the sport of the insidious silence that is threatening to undermine all those genuine efforts that are being made to clean up the sport.

CHAPTER TWO

HOW ENGLAND SWEETLY LICKED THE AUSSIES!

I t seemed that everyone in Britain was suddenly being gripped by Ashes fever in the summer of 2005 as England tried every imaginable trick – legitimate and otherwise – to lick the mighty Australians in a cricket contest that had the country practically grinding to a standstill.

Even those who knew nothing about the game, and the ones who hated it, were magically transformed into trembling fanatics desperate to follow every ball that was bowled. Some people confessed that the tension often became too much for them, and that they hid behind settees and under tables, unable to suffer the suspense of looking at their television sets. It really was that riveting.

Australia entered the series as holders of the prestigious little urn that theoretically contained those specks of dust that matter so much to players and supporters of both nations. It was a powerful Australian squad that was top of the world ratings. Their brilliant pace bowler Glenn McGrath, along with many, many others, were predicting a possible 5-0 whitewash.

In a series that was subsequently hailed as the 'most thrilling ever', there were countless shocks and surprises – and, sadly, it is now officially known that there was quite a bit of cheating and chicanery, too.

England won the series 2-1, with the outcome decided on the very last day amid immense drama and excitement. It was a sweet success in more ways than one. Some fanatics were trumpeting that England had actually licked the Aussies. And how right they were. In fact they had *literally* licked them! Reverse swing had played a major part, with England's pace bowlers constantly bamboozling Australia's strong batting line-up. Andrew Flintoff, Simon Jones, Steve Harmison and Matthew Hoggard all generated enormous swing, and were unplayable at times.

Towards the end of this truly unforgettable series I was telephoned by a reliable England insider and assured that there was a lot more to this extraordinary reverse swing than just physical skill or playing conditions. 'It's all down to Murray Mints!' was the astonishing claim. 'Someone is sucking Murray Mints to get sugar into his saliva, and then when he licks the ball he gets more shine on it, and this helps it to swing all over the place...'

To be honest, I was shocked and disappointed. Other cricket nations had been pilloried for ball-tampering – one country in particular – and now I was being told with absolute certainty that England had succumbed to doing the same. Winning at all costs was universal, it seemed, and I resented it. I thought of all those millions of ecstatic British supporters, including thousands new to Test match cricket, who genuinely believed that what they were watching was absolute skill and nothing more.

The name of England's marathon Murray Mint chewer was also disclosed to me, and I found it hard to believe that he was involved, especially as he was someone I had admired as an exceptionally gifted batsman.

Though working as an investigative reporter for a Sunday tabloid at the time, I resisted the temptation to tip off my sports editor and reveal to him and the nation that England's powerful left-hand opener – Marcus Trescothick of Somerset – was virtually licking the Aussies on his own.

Every England player, and presumably the entire management, would have known that a pocketful of mints was being used to try to change the course of the Ashes by changing the condition of the ball, and it was incredible that they all managed to keep it under wraps right through to the end without anyone letting the secret slip.

It was long after England's triumphant Ashes series that Trescothick eventually confessed, in his candid autobiography *Coming Back to Me*, though it must surely have crossed his mind that a revelation of this magnitude might just help to sell a few extra books.

Opening up in his customary full-blooded manner, Trescothick admitted: 'I was firmly established as the man in charge of looking after the ball when we were fielding. It was my job to keep the shine on the new ball for as long as possible with a bit of spit, and a lot of polish.

'And through trial and error I finally settled on the type of spit for the task at hand. I had a go at Murray Mints and found they worked a treat. It was common knowledge in county cricket that certain sweets produced saliva which, when applied to the ball for cleaning purposes, enabled it to keep its shine for longer, and, therefore, its swing.'

Trescothick, seemingly fully supported by his captain Michael Vaughan and the rest of England's management, was illegally altering the condition of the ball, and so breaching one of cricket's strictest rules.

Law 42, Subsection 3, states categorically that any fielder may polish the ball, provided no artificial substance is used and such polishing does not waste time. Any fielder may also remove mud from the ball under supervision of an umpire, and any fielder may dry a wet ball with a towel.

But it is 'unfair for anyone to rub the ball on the ground, interfere with any of the seams or the surface of the ball, use any implement, or take any other action whatsoever which is likely to alter the condition of the ball'. Law 42 further stresses that it is the responsibility of captains to ensure that play is conducted within the spirit and traditions of the game.

Umpires are expected to check regularly that the ball has not been scuffed with a fingernail or sharp object, and that illegal substances such as sugar from sweets, lip balm or hair gel have not been applied to it. Pace bowlers regularly use spit and sweat to help the ball swing. It is a legitimate method of polishing the ball, as is rubbing the ball hard against the thigh.

Players tamper with cricket balls specifically to achieve more favourable bowling conditions. In England's case it was to enhance the shine for its four seam specialists – Flintoff, Jones, Harmison and Hoggard – and the experiment evidently played a substantial part in the ball swinging so violently. Flintoff captured 24 wickets in the series, followed by Jones (18) and Harmison (17).

Once Trescothick had let his explosive cat out of the bag, shocked Australian newspapers displayed headlines such as 'England cheated to win Ashes' and wrote that: 'England's ability to get the ball to reverse swing early in the Australian innings regularly led to the downfall of the top order. Simon Jones and Andrew Flintoff regularly swung the ball inside the first 20 overs.'

As Trescothick had publicly confessed to sucking the sweets, the International Cricket Council (ICC), the game's governing body, had to respond responsibly when challenged and could not brush the matter aside as simply gossip and rumour, even if it wanted to.

The ICC has acquired a disappointing reputation for keeping controversial issues as low key as possible, often to avoid potential conflict between cricket-playing nations, which is fantastic news for anyone thinking of breaking the rules and wondering what type of punishment he would get if caught. Maybe a rap on the knuckles, if he happened to be unlucky!

In Trescothick's case, an ICC spokesman said: 'According to the laws, this is illegal. But we won't outlaw sucking sweets. It depends on the evidence and circumstances, so if something is brought to our attention it would be dealt with. But where do you stop, for example, if you try to stop everyone who is chewing gum?' He promised that the matter would be investigated should it be 'appropriate'.

As Trescothick, Vaughan, Flintoff, Hoggard and the rest of England's belly-laughing squad did not think it wise to queue up to give evidence, yet another rule-breaker walked away without facing a single question.

In addition to scoring stacks of runs for Somerset, the aggressive Trescothick amassed 5,825 runs in 76 Test matches, and a further 4,335 runs in 123 One-day Internationals. He retired from international cricket in March 2008, but committed himself to continuing his career with Somerset, and captained them in 2010.

Australia won the opening Test of the 2005 series by 239 runs at Lord's, with Kevin Pietersen on top form as England's highest scorer in both innings, hitting 57 and 64 not out. Steve Harmison emerged as England's best bowler, bagging 5-43 and 3-54, and cut Australian captain Ricky Ponting on the cheek with an absolute flyer. One memorable delivery from Matthew Hoggard swung between Matthew Hayden's bat and pad and knocked back his off stump.

England's hopes of quick revenge soared even before the start of the Second Test at Edgbaston when Australia's legendary pace bowler Glenn McGrath tore ankle ligaments when accidentally standing on a cricket ball while playing rugby in the match warm-up.

Michael Kasprowicz was called up to replace McGrath, but he

didn't possess the star bowler's guile or control, and England took full advantage by hammering 407 in the first innings, brilliantly led by Marcus Trescothick who clattered 90 runs, including nine boundaries off a lacklustre Brett Lee.

Australia responded well with 308, England then grafted to 182, and Australia were asked to score 282 for victory that would secure a two-match lead and a huge psychological advantage.

Despite a fusillade of short-pitched bowling from the fired-up Flintoff and Harmison, just two runs were needed for victory when last man Kasprowicz faced yet another vicious bouncer from Harmison, which he tried desperately to fend off. The ball flew down the leg side, and the athletic Geraint Jones flung himself towards it, held it, and appealed so loudly that he was probably heard in Birmingham city centre.

Umpire Billy Bowden, the flamboyant, gesticulating New Zealand official, had the unenviable responsibility of deciding whether Kasprowicz's bat had touched the ball on its way through to Jones. The short, agonising wait for Bowden's decision seemed to last many minutes. The tension grew and gripped. Finally he raised his crooked index finger, his unique trademark that all batsmen dread, and Kasprowicz was given out and England had scraped home by an incredible two runs in a breathtaking finish.

Even then, justice had not been done. Film footage suggested – and that is very much a euphemism – that Bowden, so rarely wrong, had slipped up this time and that the ball had struck Kasprowicz's glove while it was not on the bat handle, making it technically not a legitimate catch. England's two-run triumph was the narrowest in Ashes history.

The Third Test ended in a meaningless draw at Old Trafford, so it was now crucial for England's management 'think tank' to mastermind a vital victory in the next battle at Trent Bridge beginning on 25 August. England were entering this Test at 1-1, and knowledgeable commentators were already predicting a 'no result' on the traditional Oval flat bed in the final encounter in early September. The reality was that, if England did not succeed at Trent Bridge, it was hugely likely that this pulsating series would end all-square, with Australia retaining the Ashes, and England having nothing to show for their exceptional skills.

Over the years, Trent Bridge pitches had acquired a reputation for greatly helping seam and swing bowlers, and Nottinghamshire county cricket club, which played there, had always taken full advantage by importing the best bowlers from all over the world to exploit these conditions, including New Zealand star Richard Hadlee and South Africa's brilliant Clive Rice.

England had the perfect 'swing' quartet to make the Aussies dance! Surely there was no better anywhere in the world than Harmison, Hoggard, Flintoff and Jones to get the right tune from this pitch. Not to mention Trescothick, the marathon mint-sucker, secretly licking his lips and ensuring that the ball retained a shine bright enough for captain Vaughan to comb his hair in.

Nothing would be left to chance. Every available means of winning this Test match had to be grasped if England were to earn the urn. Tactical discussions continued well into the eve of the first day's play, with the think tank plotting and planning every strategic move, including one that was to cause an ugly row between England's coach Duncan Fletcher and Australia's captain Ricky Ponting in full view of the shocked crowd, and the millions of viewers transfixed to television sets all round the world.

England welcomed a major boost when Glenn McGrath, potentially the best bowler in the world on a traditional Trent Bridge pitch, was again ruled out through injury, this time to his elbow. Australia dropped the out-of-form Jason Gillespie, leaving them with a seam attack of Brett Lee, Michael Kasprowicz and Shaun Tait, who was playing in his first Test.

Winning the toss, England elected to bat, and openers Andrew Strauss and Marcus Trescothick raced to a 100 partnership before

Strauss, on 35, swept Shane Warne onto his boot and Matthew Hayden took a straightforward catch in the slips. Lucky Trescothick escaped when bowled by a no-ball from Lee, and England went to lunch at 129-1.

Rain washed away all but 3.1 overs in the afternoon, and England immediately lost two wickets when they resumed after tea, with Tait exploiting heavy cloud cover to swing the ball and cause serious problems. Michael Vaughan and Kevin Pietersen each survived a dropped catch, and were moving along smoothly when Ponting did the unthinkable and brought himself into the attack with gentle medium pacers.

But the brainwave worked and Ponting incredibly removed Vaughan for 58, and England ended the day on 229-4. Pietersen edged a Lee out-swinger to wicketkeeper Adam Gilchrist next morning, but Andrew Flintoff and Geraint Jones took England to 344-5 at lunch, so there was much to smile about over a full-blown salad and crisps. Trent Bridge apparently serves up exceedingly good food!

Evidently well nourished, Flintoff went on to complete his century before Tait trapped him lbw for 102. Geraint Jones continued undeterred and looked all over another centurion when Kasprowicz destroyed his ambition on 85, taking a comfortable return catch. England's innings ended on 447 at tea, boosted by a stubborn last-wicket partnership of 23 between Hoggard and Simon Jones.

Now the real testing time had arrived. How much serious swing could England's dynamic quartet find to destroy the Australia top batsmen? Hoggard soon provided the answer. He was devastating. How he managed to achieve so much more swing than any of those highly rated Australian bowlers was a magical mystery. Surely sucker Trescothick was not making such a mammoth difference so quickly?

Australia's best batsmen found him embarrassingly unplayable, and three wickets fell in 11 balls as Ponting's baffled top order found themselves in disarray at 99-5 at the close of the second day. Next morning Simon Katich and Adam Gilchrist decided that attack was the only way to emerge from their deep hole and progress, and they had added 58 in 8.5 overs when England burst into life and grabbed four wickets for a measly 18 runs, leaving Australia quivering on 175-9.

Simon Jones was now literally in full swing. He removed Katich and Warne in successive balls, and then bowled Kasprowicz. But Lee remained unperturbed and clouted 47 in 44 balls, including three colossal sixes, to lift Australia to 218 before he was caught to give the devastating Jones his fifth wicket of the innings.

Australia trailed by 259 runs, and Vaughan promptly asked them to bat again. It was the first time that Australia had followed on in 17 years. Little went right for England as Australia strove to bring some crucially needed authority and composure to their second innings. Strauss dropped Justin Langer on 38, Geraint Jones missed a stumping chance, and the dynamic Simon Jones left the field and was taken to hospital for a scan on an ankle injury.

Yet all these troubles were soon completely and dramatically eclipsed by a furious public confrontation rarely seen on a village green let alone in the middle of a key Test match during an Ashes series.

It had become apparent that the England think tank had devised a shrewd way of improving their all-round fielding skills, which meant taking players off at regular intervals and replacing them with far more athletic, and fresh, substitutes. It seemed, too, that pace bowlers in particular were being rotated for rest periods, and that the unflattering cliché 'win at all costs' had sprung to mind again.

By now, many highly respected commentators were voicing strong disapproval of fielders being switched so frequently, and the more critical even accused England of not playing in the spirit of the game. Trescothick's mints were plainly not enough to secure victory, and England unashamedly sent the practically unknown Gary Pratt onto the field as their latest tactical substitute.

Pratt was not England's official 12th man, and he had never been considered good enough even to figure in their international squad at any time. In truth, he was a promising young batsman, learning his trade with Durham in the first-class championship, and was light years away from being a Test match candidate.

Hardly anyone among the crowd packed into Trent Bridge that day had heard of him, and questions buzzed around the ground, like 'Who is he?' and 'What's he doing here?' In a short time they would find out… and witness one of the most dramatic and bitter moments in world cricket.

At the Durham club, colleagues and fans knew all about the mercurial Gary Pratt, whom they rated as one of the best fielders in championship cricket, and they praised his speed, agility, and a throw that was fast as lightning and straight as an arrow.

Pratt incensed the Australians when he sprinted out as another weary bowler trudged off, though it was ironic that when the proverbial bomb exploded, he was genuinely on the field for Simon Jones, who was in an ambulance heading to the local hospital for tests and treatment.

It all took off when batsman Damien Martyn prodded the ball into the covers and called Ponting for a quick single. Ponting is world renowned for being one of the sharpest batsmen between the wickets, and he and Martyn had played together often enough to know each other's running capabilities.

Maybe in most cases the single would have been achieved. But this time the ball was heading to the nimble Pratt, who swooped and threw in one amazingly swift move. The ball smashed into the stumps before Ponting, sprinting at his fastest, could reach the crease and ground his bat. In the context of the match it was a gigantic wicket for England, as Ponting looked secure and in fine form and ready to steer Australia to safety, and ultimately to retaining the Ashes.

Pratt was an instant hero. Some presumptive optimists were hailing him as the man who had won the Ashes for England, even though there were still two days left of this Test, and The Oval game still to come.

All eyes were on Ponting as he stormed off. He was blatantly livid, though not with himself or with his partner Martyn, but with the England think tank for using the quicksilver Pratt as a specialist substitute. Ponting deliberately looked towards the England dressing room as he charged up the pavilion steps and launched a ferocious verbal attack in the direction of coach Duncan Fletcher. At close of play, Australia were still 37 adrift but had six wickets in hand.

Ponting's tirade inevitably took the focus away from the actual match situation, and later in the evening he released a statement to apologise for his conduct, saying: 'I was disappointed with my dismissal, given that it was at a crucial stage of the game and I'd worked hard to get to that position. I let myself down with my reaction, and for that I apologise to those who see me as a role model. My frustration at getting out was compounded by the fact that I was run out by a substitute fielder, an issue that has concerned us, and one we raised before the series.'

Fletcher, who was on the dressing-room balcony when Ponting was dismissed, said: 'I don't know what he said. I haven't spoken to my players about it, but there's always some sort of chat out there. I don't say "Hold on, what are you talking to the Aussies about?" I saw him [Ponting] mumble about something, but I don't know what he said.'

Referring to England's use of substitutes, Fletcher said: 'What we try to do is... every game we go to a county which doesn't have a county game, and say "Can you supply your best fielders to us?" Australia brought it up with the match referee during the One-day series, but nothing has been said. It's part of the series. There's a lot of pressure. Things are getting tight. It's about who can handle the pressure.'

Both Ponting and Fletcher were eager to get back to the match. Extreme pressure was building on both sides and day four began with Clarke and Katich circumspectly taking Australia into the lead. Patience was essential if England were to regain command, and when Hoggard took Michael Clarke's wicket before lunch, and Gilchrist's straight after it, there were jubilant smiles all round.

Australia continued to lose wickets in rapid succession. Only Warne showed any diligent resistance, and when he went for a hard-worked 45, the end was in sight. A modest 129 was England's target for victory. Trescothick began with typical enterprise, bludgeoning 27 runs from 22 deliveries. The Australian attack was being made to look woefully tame and ordinary.

Then, crash! England lost three wickets in a flash. Warne dismissed Trescothick (27), Vaughan for a duck, and Strauss (23), and Lee sent back Ian Bell (3). England were rocking at 57-4. The victory dream was suddenly a nightmare.

Ironically, the demand for a cool head fell on Andrew Flintoff (26) and Kevin Pietersen (23), two of the game's most aggressive batsmen who hardly knew the meaning of patience and calmness. On this occasion they performed with maximum care and responsibility, and added an invaluable 46 together before Lee dismissed them both.

Warne then removed Geraint Jones (3), before the unlikely lads Ashley Giles (7 not out) and Hoggard (8 not out) edged England to a three wicket win and a 2-1 Ashes lead. All those who still had nails to chew, and there couldn't have been many, anxiously waited for the final Test to begin at The Oval on 8 September.

Vaughan won the toss for the third time in the series and chose to bat, and England went to lunch at 115-3. The first day belonged exclusively to opener Strauss, who struck 129 for his second century of the series.

England were 319-7 at close of play and partisan weather-watchers were excitedly predicting heavy showers for London over the next few days, and very much hoping that they would be torrential to make it impossible for the match to continue. Giles and Harmison frustrated the Australians in the early stages of the second day before England were dismissed for 373.

Langer and Hayden responded confidently with a century partnership and surprisingly walked off immediately after tea when offered the light, even though England had decided to bring gentle Giles into the attack. The light never improved and drizzle drifted across the ground, so the Australians retreated to their hotel for the night on 112-0, still a hefty 261 runs in arrears.

Wet ground conditions limited play to just 14 overs before lunch next morning; Langer and Hayden added 45 runs, with each surviving a confident lbw appeal. Langer had just reached his 22nd Test century when Harmison finally broke the partnership, but Hayden continued to bat resolutely and he, too, completed his hundred.

Fiery Flintoff then nudged himself into the record books. Strauss caught Ponting at slip, so Flintoff had equalled Ian Botham's 300 runs and 20 wickets in an Ashes series. Only 45.4 overs were possible during the day, and Australia again took advantage of a bad light offer and left the field early with eight wickets intact, and 96 runs behind.

Australia had reduced the deficit to 17 runs by lunch on the fourth day and were finally dismissed for 367 in mid-afternoon, still six runs short of England's first innings score. Flintoff finished with five wickets, and Hoggard four. England had built a 40-run lead for the loss of Strauss before bad light again ended play prematurely.

Tension was high on the last morning of the series. England surely could not let the precious urn slip through their fingers at this late stage. For 40 minutes Vaughan was bold and brave and in complete command. But no one is ever really set against McGrath, a truly great medium-pace bowler, and right on time he produced two magnificent out-swingers to send back Vaughan and Bell with consecutive deliveries.

England stuttered to 133-5 at lunch and Australia were clearly scenting victory, with cricket's most menacing duo, McGrath and Warne, already sharing four of the five wickets to fall and looking deadly dangerous.

Everything was set up for a titanic finish. Pietersen had his 'I'm a responsible batsman' helmet on, and evidently a rabbit's foot, a four-leaf clover and a lump of coal tucked in his trouser pocket. How else could Australian fielders, famed for having the safest hands in world cricket, drop him three times in one session?

Of course, Pietersen said 'thanks' in the most effective way by tip-toeing through the minefield to his maiden Test century before he was dismissed for a memorable 158 that included 15 fours and seven sixes. Giles stubbornly stumbled to 59, and Australia were left with around 19 overs to score 341 runs – rather like trying to climb Everest in bedroom slippers. Impossible.

The situation became even more absurd when the Aussie openers almost immediately accepted the offer of bad light and walked off. Restless spectators called for umpires Koertzen and Bowden to remove the bails and pull up the stumps to declare the match over, and to end a magical series that had captivated the country and had given Test cricket an unprecedented boost.

At precisely 6.17pm the umpires laid the stumps to rest. The match was a draw and England had won the series 2-1. Those priceless, mythical Ashes were back in Britain. It was time to celebrate. For the record, Australia scored just four leg byes in their second innings, making it the only innings in Test history in which every run was an extra. Australia's coach John Buchanan had the honour of selecting England's player of the series and chose Andrew Flintoff, while England's coach Duncan Fletcher named Shane Warne as his top Australian.

England's ecstatic entourage barely had time to open the champagne before a message arrived from the Queen: 'My warmest congratulations to you for the magnificent achievement of regaining the Ashes. Both sides can take credit for giving us all such a wonderfully exciting summer of cricket at its best.'

Similar congratulatory messages poured in from political leaders, led by Prime Minister Tony Blair, who said: 'By bringing the Ashes back after so long you have given cricket a huge boost and lit up the summer.' Michael Howard showered equal praise for the Conservatives, and Charles Kennedy for the Liberal Democrats.

Even in defeat, Australia's Prime Minister John Howard did not want to be left out, and considered the Ashes so important that he broke away from a United Nations summit in New York to say: 'There's natural disappointment, but it's a situation where you give credit to the team that won.'

Euphoria swept the nation and tens of thousands of people lined the streets of London on 13 September to cheer the proud England squad and its backroom staff as they waved joyously from an open-top bus that took 90 minutes to crawl from Mansion House to Trafalgar Square, where the crowd suddenly burst into a proud rendering of 'Jerusalem'. Close behind was another open-top bus carrying England's equally thrilled women cricketers, who had also beaten the Aussies to complete a colossal double.

Gary Pratt, the dynamic run-out specialist, was spotted among the England players, which clearly showed how much Vaughan and his team-mates valued his controversial dismissal of Ponting that essentially helped to win that Test match, and ultimately the whole series.

Pratt said very little at the time, but four years later – and after being dumped by Durham – he finally broke his silence and said: 'In a way what happened [in the Test match] hampered my career. All of a sudden I was renowned for my fielding, even though I felt I offered a lot more than that.

'I had averaged 35 in One-day games for Durham, but that piece of fielding went against me because suddenly clubs didn't look at me as a middle-order batsman. They saw me as a fielder who had done something in the Ashes. It was disappointing.

'I was more renowned as 12th man than even someone like Paul Collingwood, who played at The Oval, but isn't really associated with that Ashes win. That run-out was just one of those things where everything clicked. It's still a bit of a blur. I know it was a turning point in one of the greatest series of all time. I sat down with Ponting after the game. He was great. There were no hard feelings. I even got him to sign a photo of us, and he gave me a couple of pairs of his boots and a shirt.'

Ponting inevitably managed a wry smile in July 2008 when the ICC announced: 'Substitute fielders shall only be permitted in cases of injury, illness, or other wholly acceptable reasons. Wholly acceptable reasons should be limited to extreme circumstances, and should not include what is commonly referred to as a "comfort break".'

So England's highly successful 'revolving door' strategy was finally officially closed. Yet, curiously, there was no mention of the mints that had indisputably helped to change the condition of the ball, and which many genuine cricket followers considered to be cheating at its worst.

Once Trescothick had retired from international cricket, England's search for a discreet 'sucker' became a confidential priority, but no one, it seemed, had been appointed up to the end of England's triumphant 2010/11 Ashes series in Australia, where there was no sign of a player slipping something furtively into his mouth and then polishing the ball furiously to enhance the shine.

In some ways 'spot the sucker' could be the perfect panacea for drowsy spectators to stay awake in dull moments of Test cricket. But if all Test matches are as riveting as the 2005 series, there never will be a dull moment, and that would be tremendous for the game.

CHAPTER THREE

BOB WOOLMER: POISONED OR NATURAL CAUSES?

It was on 23 March 2007 that Lucius Thomas, distinguished head of the Jamaican police force, released the chilling announcement that Bob Woolmer, one of the world's most popular cricket personalities, had been brutally murdered. Woolmer had died suddenly in his Kingston hotel room six days earlier.

Thomas made his shock public statement after receiving the official post-mortem findings of the Jamaican government pathologist who had reported that the highly respected coach of the Pakistan cricket team had died from asphyxia caused by manual strangulation.

In a calm and measured tone, Thomas told the world: 'Mr Robert Woolmer's death is now being treated by the Jamaican police as a case of murder.' It was such a categorical statement of fact, based wholly on the official autopsy result, that it totally removed any conjecture that Woolmer might have died from natural causes, or any other means.

The police chief immediately appealed for 'anyone with information that would help us to identify Bob Woolmer's killer, or killers, to come forward in order that his wife, Gill, and his family, can begin the process of healing'.

A murder in Jamaica was hardly something new for its busy police force to deal with, as serious crime and killings were a constant issue in a country with massive drugs and gang problems. Even so, this was a murder case that went way beyond anything that the Jamaican police had encountered before, as Woolmer was a high-profile visitor who had died in mysterious circumstances just hours after Pakistan had been eliminated from the 2007 Cricket World Cup by Ireland.

Once the Jamaican police chief had so confidently stated that Woolmer was murdered, the floodgates were automatically opened for conspiracy theorists to point accusing fingers in all directions, which included players and officials in the Pakistan tour party, all of whom were on the island for the World Cup.

It was Dr Ere Sheshiah, the government's chief forensic pathologist, who concluded that Woolmer had been strangled after he had carried out a microscopic examination of the coach's body at the local mortuary. The highly experienced Dr Sheshiah was in his 18th year in this specialised forensic field, and it would have taken a brave, or ignorant, person to accuse him of not knowing what he was talking about. He was a complete and reliable professional.

Once Dr Sheshiah had produced his official post-mortem report it was generally expected that the police would launch an immediate full-blown murder hunt to ensure that crucial evidence was secured before it was deliberately removed or lost by accident.

A swift and methodical investigation was imperative to apprehend the person or persons responsible, but, incredibly, the anticipated course of action slowed up, and Dr Sheshiah's findings were suddenly challenged and questioned, and the reason for Woolmer's death curiously developed more twists and turns than an Austrian mountain pass.

Without doubt it was the most macabre mystery ever to befall world cricket, and from the outset the shocked public was desperately hungry for every morsel of information, and millions of amateur detectives in homes and offices and bars around the world instantly set about trying to separate fact from fiction.

Thoughts went back to when Woolmer was last seen in public on Saturday 17 March, as he tried to come to terms with Pakistan losing by three wickets to lowly Ireland at a stunned Sabina Park in Kingston. It was Pakistan's most humiliating defeat of all time, and Ireland's first World Cup success. Even allowing for all sorts of unpredictable sports upsets that never cease to baffle fans, this was exceptional on every conceivable level.

Woolmer had not been able to hide his distress as he told reporters: 'We batted abysmally. Just made mistake after mistake. It just compounded, and eventually we were 40 to 50 runs short. We made some very injudicious shot selections. Mohammad Yousuf, Kamran Akmal and Azhar Mahmood are three, off the top of my head, who played shots that weren't necessary.

'That's sad. Two-and-a-half to three years' work has gone into this, and to fall out like this is very disappointing. I don't really know what to say, apart from apologising for the team's performance.'

Woolmer was then asked about his plans for the future, and he gloomily replied: 'My contract runs out on June 30 anyway. So I'll sleep on my future. I'm reluctant to continue in international cricket, purely from a travelling point of view. But I'll stick to coaching at a different level. I think a decision's probably been made for me... I'll talk to the PCB [Pakistan Cricket Board] and see what they want me to do. If they want me to go, I'll go. If they want me to stay, I'll stay until June 30th. I'm not going to break my contract, but if the PCB want to get rid of me, that's their business.'

Plainly distressed and concerned, Woolmer then released an alarming cryptic comment: 'A number of extenuating circumstances in the past six months have made coaching Pakistan [cricketers] slightly different from normal sides, so those are things that I would have to consider. A lot of those things would have to change if I were to continue with Pakistan.'

At no point did Woolmer offer or try to explain what he meant by 'extenuating circumstances' or his puzzling remark 'coaching Pakistan [is] slightly different from normal sides'. Any number of interpretations could have been made to try to make sense of this apparently coded message, and some cynics inevitably concluded that betting and cheating were what he had in mind.

Whatever Woolmer was bothered about, however, it did seem that he had virtually decided that his Pakistan career was close to coming to an end – either by him resigning and walking away, or being sacked by the PCB. He even teasingly admitted that he would like to do consultancy work in England. 'I want to continue coaching,' he stressed. 'I think it's time for me to start coaching coaches.'

It was at this point that he took everyone by surprise when he suddenly revealed that he 'had been writing about the game recently, so I'd like to continue to do that...'

But writing about what? And whom? It was a dramatic disclosure that provoked considerable conjecture in the sad days ahead, and probably will forever, as many well-informed observers were convinced that he was about to expose the full extent of corruption among international cricketers and officials. Woolmer ended what turned out to be his final interview with, in hindsight, the incredibly ironic words: 'I have not made up my mind. Let me sleep on it...'

Every piece of available evidence indicated that Woolmer never even got to bed that night, let alone fall sleep in his room on the 12th floor of the 17-storey Pegasus Hotel in the heart of Jamaica.

What *was* known was that Woolmer sent a number of late-night e-mails to his wife, Gill, at home in Cape Town. Several weeks later she said: 'He was really depressed, and could not believe how this could have happened.' It was generally assumed that those highly emotive words referred to Pakistan's appalling defeat.

Exactly what Woolmer said in those private e-mails to his wife that night has mostly remained confidential to the family, and it is highly unlikely that their intimate details will ever be put in the public domain, in which case there will be no definite way of knowing his exact state of mind while he sat alone in his hotel room pondering his present position, and the future.

It was around 10.45 next morning when hotel staff found Woolmer lying unconscious on his bathroom floor. He was rushed to hospital but died an hour later. Police chiefs quickly stressed that there was no sign that anyone had made a forced entry into Woolmer's room, or of a physical struggle, and that his possessions seemed to be undisturbed.

Consent for a post-mortem came immediately from Woolmer's family, who said that he had been suffering from stress, and they thought it was this that might have caused a heart attack and killed him. The first post-mortem was deemed to be 'inconclusive', so extra tests were ordered, followed by Jamaica's deputy police commissioner Mark Shields (who had been recruited from Scotland Yard in 2005) announcing that Woolmer's death was being treated as suspicious, although there was nothing to suggest murder at that stage.

As many as ten forensic science officers were soon on the scene, and they meticulously combed Woolmer's hotel room amid rumours that traces of blood and vomit had been found on the floor and walls, and that a blood-testing device for diabetes had been discovered.

Further speculation suggested that scratches were found on Woolmer's neck, as well as blood on his cheek. All this escalating gossip was putting huge pressure on the police to admit, or deny, what was being alleged, but a wall of silence was being built up, and lips were suspiciously sealed.

Suicide was another inevitable consideration, bearing in mind Woolmer's apparently profound distress, but his distraught wife, Gill, who knew him better than anyone else, completely rejected this possibility, although she would not rule out murder.

Fingerprints and statements were taken from every member of the Pakistan playing squad, plus officials and backroom staff, although the police carefully emphasised that no one in the party was a suspect in their inquiries, and that they were free to leave at any time. CCTV footage from the Pegasus Hotel was flown to Scotland Yard in London for examination by technical experts with the help of the most up-to-date analytical equipment.

Then, four days after Woolmer's death, and completely out of the blue, the police suddenly announced that further post-mortem tests had shown that the popular Pakistan coach, and former England Test batsman, had been strangled.

But by whom? And how? And why? The media erupted, a major guessing game began, and conspiracy theorists conjured up all sorts of frightening possibilities – so it was no surprise when the Woolmer family leapt in to stress that they knew of no threat that had been made on his life, and that they had no knowledge of him being involved in match-fixing.

A number of Scotland Yard detectives then arrived in Jamaica just as several reliable media outlets were reporting that Woolmer had actually been poisoned by a deadly plant, or even snake venom, before he was strangled. Another gruesome rumour was that Woolmer had visited a player's hotel room and had innocently picked up a bottle of champagne that had been spiked with poison. Even *Panorama*, the BBC's foremost television documentary programme, claimed that a powerful drug had been found in Woolmer's body that would have rendered him helpless.

Woolmer's remains were flown to Cape Town, where he was cremated privately at a family service in a funeral parlour close to his home, but a large number of incredulous journalists were still not satisfied that the entire truth had been disclosed to the public. Britain's largest-circulation daily tabloid, *The Sun*, even claimed in a startling headline that 'Potter drug did kill Woolmer'.

The newspaper maintained that Woolmer had been poisoned by the drug aconite, also known as wolfsbane, which is mentioned in the bestselling J K Rowling book *Harry Potter and the Philosopher's Stone*.

'Toxicology tests have confirmed "significant" traces of it in the Pakistan coach's body,' alleged *The Sun*. 'The tests were ordered following an anonymous tip to Jamaican police eight days after Woolmer died that aconite had been used. Aconite, which paralyses the nerves, normally takes only 30 minutes to kill. Victims suffer vomiting and diarrhoea before collapsing, unable to breathe, to die in agony. A neck injury which caused police to say Woolmer had been strangled is now thought to have followed a fall when he collapsed.'

The newspaper continued: 'Detectives believe the drug, in the form of white powder, could have been tipped into whisky Woolmer was drinking in his room, or sprinkled over sleeping tablets and diabetes tablets that he was taking. The ancient poison, also known as wolfsbane, is said to be perfect for concealing murder, and has been used in several high-profile assassinations in Pakistan. Its use fuels suspicion that Woolmer was murdered to stop him exposing match-fixing.'

Nothing came of the tabloid's claims, but Home Office pathologist Dr Nathaniel Carey, who had flown in from London to examine autopsy 'material', agreed that Woolmer had *not* been strangled – leading to confusion and widespread frantic cries of 'cover-up'.

Dr Carey was aided by pathologists Dr Michael Pollanen from Canada and Professor Lorna Jean Martin from South Africa, and a short time later a Scotland Yard spokesman announced that Woolmer had died from natural causes. He explained that this conclusion, which was totally different from the original official post-mortem report by Dr Sheshiah, was based on what Dr Carey and his colleagues had discovered. No specific medical definition of 'natural causes' accompanied this conclusion.

It was then left to police chief Lucius Thomas to make an official statement on 12 June that the Jamaican police force had accepted the findings of the three overseas pathologists, and bluntly added that it had 'closed its investigation into the death of Mr Bob Woolmer'.

Although this terse statement brought a sharp and official conclusion to the complex mystery of Bob Woolmer's demise, sceptics around the world would be seeking a more detailed explanation for this sudden, and what some regarded as suspicious, verdict.

A highly experienced government pathologist had originally reported that Woolmer had died from asphyxia caused by manual strangulation, but now we were being asked to believe that he got it wrong, and that Woolmer's death was really due to natural causes.

A series of extraordinary allegations later came from more than 50 witnesses at the coroner's inquest into Woolmer's death, which opened in front of an 11-member jury in the Jamaican Conference Centre in Kingston on 16 October. The inquest was originally arranged for 23 March, five days after Woolmer was pronounced dead at the University Hospital of the West Indies, but inquiries and conflicting theories had forced the seven-month delay.

Over the next three months, witnesses would tell the inquest jury that Woolmer was seen with a stranger putting bundles of money in a bag shortly before he died; of pesticides being found in his system during the autopsy; and of an admission to his wife in an e-mail that he was depressed.

The first witness, hotel maid Bernice Robinson, recalled seeing blood on a pillow and smelling alcohol and vomit when she entered Woolmer's hotel room to clean it, before finding him unconscious on the bathroom floor. Yet another major twist in this incredible case came when a janitor stepped into the witness box and alleged that she saw Woolmer counting 'coils of United States dollars' in the company of another man inside a private area of the dressing room at the Sabina Park cricket ground.

She told the jury: 'Mr Woolmer was checking it [the money] and putting it away in a big bag, similar to bags carried by cricketers. The money was in a thick coil. I saw lots of money on the table.' The janitor worked as a senior superintendent for a maintenance company and, although she did not know the man who was with Woolmer, she believed that 'the person was an Indian' but couldn't explain how she came to that conclusion.

She said that the incident happened on 12 March, six days before Woolmer was found unconscious, and that the dressing-room door was closed when she arrived, and that she was allowed in after she identified herself. According to the janitor the two men spoke in a language she did not know. She replaced the dressing-room toiletries and left.

Government pathologist Dr Ere Sheshiah told the inquest that he stuck by his conclusion that Woolmer was poisoned by the pesticide cypermethrin and then strangled. He stressed that he had served his profession for 18 years, which seemed to be a deliberate attempt by him to reassure everyone of his professional knowledge and experience.

Cypermethrin is a manmade chemical that was first synthesised in 1974 and first marketed in 1977 as being highly effective against a-wide range of pests in agriculture, public health and animal husbandry. It is a mixture of several closely related chemicals. Excessive exposure to cypermethrin can affect the brain, digestive system, eyes, lungs, peripheral nerves and skin.

British forensic specialist Dr John Slaughter told the jury that he had analysed toxicology tests on Woolmer, and found no traces of a potentially deadly pesticide in samples that were provided.

It could be significant that Dr Slaughter did not categorically state that no pesticide was found, but used the words 'potentially deadly'.

A principal witness, who had worked for 26 years in the Forensic Laboratory in Jamaica, told the jury that tests carried out on blood and urine from Woolmer's body had shown evidence of cypermethrin, and that the tranquilliser chloropazne was found in his stomach. Alcohol was also found in blood specimens.

Chief investigating officer Mark Shields read to the jury an e-mail that Woolmer had sent to his wife, Gill, from his room on the evening after Pakistan's shock defeat. It said: 'Hi darling, feeling a little depressed currently, as you might imagine... I am not sure which is worse, being knocked out in the semi-final at Edgbaston, or now in the first round. Our batting performance was abysmal, and my worst fears were realised. I could tell the players for some reason couldn't fire themselves up... I hope your day was better, but I doubt it, as you were probably watching. Not much more to add I'm afraid, but I still love you lots.'

Mark Shields told coroner Patrick Murphy that former Pakistan captain Inzamam-ul-Haq was one of four Pakistani people who had refused to attend the inquest to give testimony and be questioned. He said that medium-pace bowler Rana Naved-ul-Hasan, assistant manager Asad Mustafa, and former media manager Pervez Mir had also refused to travel to Jamaica. Requests for them to attend had been made through the Pakistan Cricket Board.

The shock-filled inquest lasted an intriguing 31 days before it closed on 28 November, by which time 57 witnesses had given evidence and a further seven witness statements had been handed to the jury, who took just three hours to return an open verdict, being unable to decide whether Woolmer died from natural causes or a criminal act. The jury foreman explained: 'We came to an open verdict because the evidence was too weak. There were too many "ifs and buts" and "what ifs". It was not conclusive.'

For conspiracy theorists it was the ideal result that would allow them all sorts of extravagant conjecture with little risk of official contradiction or denial. One immediate new theory was that Woolmer had died of heart failure brought on by chronic ill-health and possibly diabetes, even though as national team coach he was physically active every day and he had not talked about or shown any worrying health problems. Another more alarming theory was that he was going to name people involved in cricket betting in a book that he was writing.

Many crucial questions had still not been answered. For instance, did he send e-mails to his wife that fateful night that were not read at the inquest? What exactly was meant by 'natural causes'? What did the death certificate state in detail, and who signed it?

At least one person was allegedly seen in the corridor near Woolmer's room in the hours shortly before he died, and CCTV footage was sent to Scotland Yard for its experts to identify any images. Police chief Mark Shields confirmed that the Jamaican police were also working hard to identify everyone captured on security footage from the hotel.

So what exactly happened to the tell-tale film that was sent to Scotland Yard and to the Jamaican police? It is a matter of some concern that it was never disclosed whether the experts who studied the CCTV footage drew a blank, or whether they were indeed able to identify clearly an individual lurking in the corridors close to Woolmer's room, and decided, for whatever reason, that silence was the best option.

Professor Tim Noakes, of the University of Cape Town, later came forward to say that he and Woolmer were writing a cricket coaching manual together which was due to be published by the end of the year. Woolmer was hardly taking a physical risk in compiling a tame coaching manual, but it would have been different if he were writing an explosive autobiography recalling shady dealings in the international cricket world.

Many well-informed journalists believed Woolmer was bringing his autobiography up to date, and that it would include his time in Pakistan, exposing scandals and naming perpetrators. Woolmer was coach of the South African team when captain Hansie Cronje, a close friend, confessed that he had accepted money from Indian bookmakers to fix matches, although it is stressed that there was nothing whatsoever to suggest that Woolmer was personally involved, or even knew what Cronje was up to.

Woolmer's wife, Gill, has repeatedly said: 'I don't see any conspiracy in his death. He had nothing to do with the match-fixing controversy, and we've never had threats, as far as I know.' She also said: 'My sons and I were relieved to be informed officially that Bob died of natural causes, and that no foul play was suspected in his death.' Woolmer's son, Russell, added: 'There was a lot of stress in his job, and it might have been stress that caused it.'

Yet it was the inquest jury's failure to confirm what the three overseas pathologists concluded in direct contradiction of the initial findings by a highly competent government medical expert – with 18 years of experience in a fiercely volatile country – that was the great worry, and which means that the mystery remains as impenetrable now as it was when Bob Woolmer was found unconscious on his hotel bathroom floor.

No one was better placed than former Warwickshire all-rounder Paul Smith to provide a reliable and profound analysis of Woolmer the man, and Woolmer the coach. For several years Smith and Woolmer were close friends and colleagues, both at Edgbaston and in South Africa, where they often met up to coach and chat during the English winter months when there was no cricket.

Smith had the highest admiration for Woolmer, and in his explosive autobiography stressed that, as far as he was concerned, any accusations directed at Woolmer that alleged match-fixing would be a load of garbage. He was convinced that Woolmer was killed 'precisely because he was so clean and so determined not to allow any of that seedy world to enter the sport he loved. He was certainly no match-fixer.'

Smith was aware that at the time of the 'murder' in the Caribbean, Woolmer was in the process of starting an academy in Cape Town, and was absolutely sure that his good friend and colleague would never have done anything to damage the game he loved. Quite amusingly, Smith said: 'He might have found it hard to say no to Thai food, but he wasn't greedy when it came to money. Very few top coaches would have been prepared to live in the basic one-bedroom flat in the National Stadium in Pakistan that Bob made his home for so long.'

Smith had the same welter of praise for Woolmer as an individual, and said that he would always be grateful for the part this special coach played in his education as a person. He recalled that what immediately stood out with Woolmer when he joined Warwickshire as coach in March 1991 was the time he spent trying to get his point across.

'We would debate anything and everything, talking cricket for hours in an attempt to understand what could turn our fortunes,' said Smith, admiringly.

'It was time well spent. The four years he was with us at Edgbaston took the club to a different level. He was superb. A father figure, keen as they come, and with a professional approach and attention to detail that were allied to excellent communication skills and a healthy portion of common sense.'

Smith praised Woolmer in particular for his inventive skills and for not being afraid to be different, and recalled how this gifted coach judged fast bowler Allan Donald's rhythm by listening to the noise his feet made on the ground as he ran to the wicket, and the exact sound when he passed the umpire.

Again with a touch of humour, Smith said: 'Under Bob we learned that chewing extra-strong mints helped the ball to swing more. We even worked out that spices in curry lingering in our saliva helped with shining [the ball].

'Bob showed that if you worked hard, thought positively, and backed yourself, anything was possible. He put smiles back on faces at Edgbaston, creating an environment in which everyone wanted to be involved. He taught us how to assess and correct things within games, and taught us about the importance of imagination and affirmation. He was miles ahead of other coaches at the time.'

Bob Woolmer was born in 1948 in a hospital in Kanpur, India, which was aptly situated directly opposite the town's cricket ground. He came to prominence as a stylish stroke-playing batsman in the successful Kent side in the 1970s. He also took wickets with his accurate seam bowling.

Woolmer made his debut for England in the Second Test against Australia in 1975, and on his second appearance later in the series doggedly accumulated 149 runs in more than eight hours at the crease to save the match, bravely defying the fiery fast-bowling pair of Dennis Lillee and Jeff Thomson. Two further centuries against the Australians established Woolmer as a dependable international batsman, but his escalating career was suddenly halted when he joined the maverick Kerry Packer World Series Cricket revolution in 1977.

His return to Test match cricket was disappointing, and he quit as a top-class player in 1981 to join a rebel tour to South Africa. Woolmer played in 19 Tests, and scored 1,059 runs at an average of 33.09.

Eventually, he started to use his talents as a coach in South Africa, and returned to England in 1991 to take charge of Warwickshire – a role in which he was enormously successful, steering the county club to four trophies in two years – and it came as no surprise when he was beckoned back to South Africa in 1994 to coach the national side. Again he performed brilliantly and helped South Africa to win ten out of 15 series of Test matches, and prepared a squad for One-day Internationals that was just as strong.

Woolmer was a pioneer of cricket technology. He used video cameras, laptops and other electronic gadgets to identify and correct flaws in his own players, and to spot and exploit weaknesses in the opposition. He lost his South African job in 1999 after a World Cup defeat by Australia, and he changed course completely and became a high-performance manager for the International Cricket Council, where he helped to develop the emerging cricketing nations in skills and strategy.

Woolmer returned to top-flight coaching in 2004 when he surprisingly accepted an invitation from the Pakistan Cricket Board to undertake what turned out to be the hardest job in the game. Amid all the horrendous political and playing problems that erupted in his three years in the post, Woolmer remained courteous, diligent, never avoiding awkward questions, always offering honest explanations, and never once tainting his own, or his team's integrity.

It was only in the last few months of his impressive reign that traumatic off-field problems, splits in the team and political undermining began to get under his skin and cause him to lose his cool and react aggressively. A blazing row with Shoaib Akhtar in South Africa, the ball-tampering walk-out at The Oval, and shameful drugs bans for Akhtar and Mohammad Asif were just a few of the many disturbing incidents that piled on the pressure.

But above all else, Bob Woolmer was a placid person who was passionately dedicated to his work, although he could be fiercely outspoken if the occasion demanded it, and was especially forthright on issues such as poor pitches, indifferent umpiring, and the congested international fixture programme.

Ironically, his frankness was never more in evidence than in his last hours when answering a barrage of blunt and awkward questions after Pakistan's humiliating drubbing by Ireland.

He left the ground a sad and embarrassed man, never to return...

CHAPTER FOUR

DISGRACED PAKISTAN TRIO PUT THEIR FEET IN IT

Two money-grabbing Pakistan pace bowlers were exposed as blatant cheats in a classic tabloid sting brilliantly supplemented by a dossier of close-up photographs that destroyed all hope of any logical defence. Dodgy duo Mohammad Amir and Mohammad Asif were firmly trapped bowling deliberate no-balls as their contribution to a million-pound international spot-fixing scam.

Television viewers and spectators had no reason to doubt that the no-balls delivered by Asif and Amir in a Test match against England at the immaculate Lord's cricket ground in late August 2010 were mistakes that bowlers often make when trying too hard, or when rain or dew have left the grass too slippery for them to keep their feet. But nothing like that could be blamed on this occasion.

Their slippery (in a different sense) London-based agent Mazhar Majeed had earlier predicted to undercover reporters – masquerading as front men for a Far East gambling syndicate – precisely when those no-balls would be bowled, and had accepted £150,000 in exchange for his cast-iron inside information. It was further reported that Majeed had claimed that Pakistan captain Salman Butt was also heavily implicated.

A sting team from the *News of the World* – a robust Sunday tabloid with no rival in exposing corruption – had executed yet another masterclass of investigative journalism. To leave no one in doubt about Majeed's shameful involvement, the reporters filmed him with hidden cameras, and the newspaper played a video of the explosive interview on its website for the world to see.

Majeed is shown in close-up confidently guaranteeing specific deliveries in specific overs when umpires would call the two Pakistani players for bowling a no-ball, and with equal certainty he correctly named Asif and Amir as the guilty pair. Sitting totally relaxed, Majeed assured the sting team that Amir would bowl the first over and that his third delivery would definitely be a no-ball. His prediction was spot on, and Amir overstepped the line by such a big margin that it caused gasps of great surprise among former players now working as television commentators.

Majeed then predicted that the sixth delivery of the tenth over would also be a no-ball and that Asif would be the bowler. And it all happened just as he said it would. Seen speaking clearly in the video, Majeed claimed to be working with a total of seven Pakistan players, but decided to name only Amir, Asif, Butt and wicketkeeper Kamran Akmal.

Cameras then zoomed in and captured Majeed gleefully laying out blocks of bank notes on a large table. At one point he stopped and carefully took the notes from a bundle and counted them individually to ensure that he was not being ripped off. These astonishing foolproof pictures, and Majeed's alarming revelations, hit the cricket world with the ferocity of a cataclysmic earthquake, and the stunned hierarchy scrambled around, desperately seeking the best response to protect the game's integrity.

Without losing a minute, the *News of the World*'s editorial bosses and legal staff again did their public duty and handed the bulging dossier, which contained superb photographic evidence, to senior Scotland Yard detectives for them to launch an immediate and widespread investigation.

Majeed plainly loved the sound of his own voice, and he talked freely and assured the sting team that he could arrange for 'his' players to do what he wanted them to do in return for substantial payments. The journalists had reported in detail that they had met Majeed on several occasions, including sessions at the Copthorpe Hotel in west London, the Hilton Hotel in Park Lane, and the Bombay Brasserie restaurant in central London.

Majeed believed that he was discussing potential business with a gambling syndicate that could earn him and his crooked associates vast sums of money. Having pocketed £10,000 as a deposit at one of their early meetings, and a further £140,000 at a subsequent session, Majeed had successfully assembled the £150,000 deal he had demanded for providing exclusive inside information.

To pull off such a huge sting, a newspaper would usually hire a room at a famous London hotel for at least two days before the actual showdown meeting in order to conceal a host of listening devices and covert cameras, so that every word and every move could be captured clearly and conclusively.

Little did the hapless Majeed realise that while he was counting out his £140,000 in bundles of crisp £50 notes, hidden cameras were recording him on film that would be produced as evidence to leave no one in doubt that he had made his claims, and had accepted the money.

Majeed boastfully promised: 'I'm going to give you three no-balls to prove to you firstly that this is what is happening. They've all been organised, okay? This is exactly what's going to happen. You're going to see these three things happen. I'm telling you, if you play this right, you're going to make a lot of money, believe me.'

The damning video footage showed Majeed guaranteeing the specific delivery of the specific over when the no-balls would be bowled, and Majeed clearly naming Asif and Amir as the bowlers who would overstep the line.

In his marathon boast, Majeed claimed that he had several top cricketers in his care who were banking huge sums of money from bookmakers and betting syndicates, and that accounts had been opened in Switzerland where corrupt players could hide their ill-gotten gains. He also alleged that Pakistan captain Salman Butt was the ringleader.

Majeed promised the sting team that he could make them 'millions' if they paid him up to £450,000 a time for information on matches, as all their bets would be placed on what had been fixed. With great delight, Majeed said that he worked closely with the Pakistan Cricket Board, and that he had landed large sponsorship deals for a number of players and had helped them to negotiate contracts.

To get Majeed on side, the sting team had convinced him that they would like to be involved in a Twenty/20 tournament in the Middle East. He swallowed the bait like a hungry shark – as he was – and guaranteed them that he could supply all the players they needed, provided they paid the right fee. He backed up his boast by claiming that he had spent seven years with a number of players who were involved in gambling.

He said these players had made 'masses' of money through him, and that they trusted him because he was highly professional.

Majeed let slip that a group of Indian gamblers was a vital part of his operation and that they paid him generously for exclusive inside information, and that it was because of their involvement that the scams could work and be profitable. These scams had included international batsmen deliberately scoring quickly at first and then slowing down to accumulate fewer runs in a specific time that had been carefully planned for their gambling connections to make a killing. In the same way, bowlers would deliberately concede runs in a pre-planned number of overs and bowl no-balls exactly where they had agreed to deliver them. Everything was meticulously plotted long before the teams went out on the field to play.

Haroon Lorgat, Chief Executive of the International Cricket Council (ICC), was angry and shaken by allegations that Asif, Amir and Butt had conspired with bookmakers to bowl no-balls deliberately in return for money. Plainly outraged, Lorgat admitted: 'In terms of corruption in the sport, this must rank as the next worst after the Hansie Cronje case.' (See Chapter Nine.)

There was no suggestion, however, that the Pakistani players had conspired to affect the actual result of the match, which Pakistan lost by an innings and 225 runs in their worst ever Test defeat.

Scotland Yard detectives questioned Amir under caution for five hours about claims that no-balls were deliberately bowled during that Fourth Test on the orders of Majeed as part of a spot-fixing scam, and Majeed was arrested on suspicion of conspiracy to defraud bookmakers. But Amir, Asif and Butt all left the police station without any action being taken against them.

Questions about Majeed's family background and business connections were soon part of the media's interest in this ubiquitous broker who was calling himself a 'sports agent' and lived in a £1.8 million home in Surrey, owned a property company in London, and was co-owner, and major shareholder, in Croydon Athletic FC (which played in the national Ryman League).

Many of cricket's best judges had praised the highly successful 18-year-old Amir during the 2010 Test series between England and Pakistan, and predicted that with his enormous talent he had the potential to become a major bowler in world cricket.

It was not long before the ICC charged Amir, Asif and Butt with multiple breaches of its anti-corruption rules, and suspended them from every level of cricket with immediate effect. All three were warned that they faced lengthy expulsions and even life bans if the allegations against them were proved, and they became the first players from any country to be suspended under the ICC's strict new rules to try to protect the game's integrity, which appeared to be under serious threat.

After protesting their innocence, all three returned to Pakistan, as there was no prospect of them taking part in the remaining matches in England. Asif had even been earmarked for his debut in a film, playing the part of a cricket coach with high ethical standards, which now looked ridiculous, and he was instantly dropped from the cast. The film's Indian director was deeply disappointed and said: 'Asif agreed to take the role, but then there was this scandal in London, so it was very difficult to have him in the film, so I removed him.'

His obvious concern was that cinema audiences would not want to see a professional cricketer associated with a major spot-fixing scam playing the part of a role model for young people. Asif had passed a screen test in London after being handpicked to play a clean-living Pakistani cricketer who visited India to run a coaching school.

Not entirely deterred by the spot-fixing scandal, the Indian film director said he would continue to look for a prominent Pakistani cricketer to play the part, and revealed that he had 'two to three in mind' though he took great care not to name them.

It had been reported that the police found £50,000 in cash in Butt's hotel room, some of it in foreign currency, which he insisted was to pay a dowry for his sister. A spokesman for Scotland Yard said: 'Following information from the *News of the World*, we have today arrested a 35-year-old man on suspicion of conspiracy to defraud bookmakers.' Scotland Yard were referring to the elusive Mazhar Majeed, who was also being linked to an HM Revenue and Customs inquiry, supported by claims in the media that his telephone had been tapped during this investigation.

It was further reported that Majeed had made 'suspicious' phone calls about cricket matches to people abroad, and that 'officials' had been told about them. There was no clue as to who these officials were, or where they were based. Pakistan team manager Yawar Saeed openly disclosed that police officers had confiscated mobile telephones that had been used by Butt, Asif and Amir.

At first the ICC gave the impression that it would not take action until the police had interviewed the three Pakistani players, but after it had examined some of the evidence already gathered against the trio it decided to go ahead and duly charged them. The ICC's code rigidly prohibits 'fixing or contriving in any way… the result, progress, conduct or any other aspect of any international match', which categorically covers the deliberate bowling of no-balls.

To suspend the players pending the outcome of the disciplinary action reflected how seriously the ICC was treating the case. Until now players had always been allowed to continue to take part in matches while waiting for the result of a disciplinary hearing to come through.

Sir Ronnie Flanagan, Chairman of the ICC's Anti-corruption Unit, said he would congratulate the *News of the World* if its allegations resulted in convictions. Flanagan also admitted: 'We are not a police force. We cannot arrest, and we cannot engage in undercover operations. They [*News of the World*] brought it to light in ways the ICC would not want us to engage in. You can never be 100 per cent foolproof. There will always be cases of wrongdoing.'

Neither Lorgat nor Flanagan would comment on media reports that marked notes used in the sting had been found in a player's locker, believed to be Butt's, and at Lord's cricket ground. Flanagan added: 'The players are aware of the charges against them, and it is up to them and their legal representatives whether they want that to be made public. We are determined to be scrupulously fair.'

Lorgat stood shoulder to shoulder with Flanagan, and stressed: 'We will not tolerate corruption in cricket. It's as simple as that. We must be decisive with such matters, and, if proven, these offences carry serious penalties up to a life ban. The ICC will do everything possible to keep such conduct out of the game, and we will stop at nothing to protect the sport's integrity.'

Pakistan's High Commissioner, Wajid Shamsul Hasan, did not agree with Lorgat's views, insisting that the ICC should not have acted until the police investigations, and investigations by its own Anti-corruption Unit, had been completed. Hasan protested that the suspension of the three players was 'unhelpful, premature, and unnecessary', and he revealed that he had attended a three-hour meeting with the three players in London, and concluded that they were all innocent, a seriously flawed judgement that made him look grossly foolish several weeks later when a disciplinary panel found them all guilty and banned them.

Thankfully the ICC had more sense and totally disagreed with him, a decision that was forcibly endorsed at a two-day hearing in Dubai in late October 2010 when it rejected appeals from Butt and Amir, and stated that both players remained provisionally suspended on charges of spot-fixing. Asif had chosen not to appeal.

Michael Beloff QC, the ICC Code of Conduct Commissioner, chaired the hearing and stressed that the players could not appeal against this decision, explaining that they would next appear before an independent anti-corruption tribunal that would look into the actual charges and decide whether they were innocent or guilty.

In a forthright statement, Beloff said: 'Having considered every aspect of the case, I dismissed their appeals, and they remain suspended. The players have denied the charges, but they will remain suspended until a Code of Conduct Commission is formed to hear the case. It was not up to me to decide whether they committed any crime – the Commission will establish that – and if they are found guilty they will be given punishment as per the ICC code of conduct.'

It was made clear that there was no time limit for when the tribunal should take place, and the ICC would only say that it would happen 'in due course'. Butt was represented by Aftab Gul, a former Test cricketer, along with Khalid Ranjha, a law minister, who seemed to think that there was a 40-day timescale, and said that the decision had 'left us unhappy'. Lawyer Shahid Karim represented Amir.

Both players wasted no time in lashing out at the ICC, and within 24 hours of leaving Dubai and landing in Lahore they were claiming that they had been treated unfairly. Butt went straight to a television studio and told the nation that he believed there was a 'conspiracy' against the players, and against Pakistan.

He raged: 'They listened to us, but it felt that their decision had already been made from before. It was not based on a single piece of evidence. There was no evidence that established that we had some agreement with Mazhar Majeed. After a 12-hour hearing, the only so-called evidence they had was the same as the *News of the World* article, and the same video everyone has seen.'

When invited to comment about what was said in the video, Butt replied: 'You are asking me questions, but tell me where am I in this video? These things have to be proved when you talk about such charges. You cannot base it on suspicions. It is supposed to be innocent until proven guilty. I am not here to convince you. Did he say on video that I had done something? Of course I am denying all this. I feel like I am talking to the English media!'

Equally aggressive, Amir said: 'Before we left for Dubai we felt the case would be in our favour. But when he gave the decision it looked as if he had written the decision before. We went for the truth, but this could be a conspiracy against Pakistan to tarnish Pakistan's reputation.'

What was especially noticeable was that the Pakistan Cricket Board (PCB) was emphasising that it was distancing itself from what Butt and Amir were alleging, and said that it was up to the players, and their lawyers, to settle the matter. A legal adviser at the PCB condemned outright the attack Butt and Amir had made on the ICC decision, and said: 'It was hugely inappropriate of the players to cast doubts on the impartiality of the tribunal after the order had been announced.'

Lawyer Aftab Gul, who represented Salman Butt at the ICC hearing, made a shock statement several weeks later when he said: 'Corruption is rife in world cricket. I have so much evidence. I could tell you names that would make your hair stand on end. It has now become spot-fixing. It is much easier to do.'

At the same time, Butt continued to protest his innocence, and while referring to money that police officers found in his London hotel room, he said: 'People can have their opinions, but I actually know where the money came from. The Pakistan Cricket Board pay us daily allowances on tours, and it was a long tour. So about £11,000 of the money was my daily allowance. Being captain, I had extra entertainment allowance, which amounted to about £4,500. The rest of the money was an advance payment from my bat sponsors for which I was under contract. I also picked up £2,500 for opening an ice-cream parlour in south London, along with Mohammad Amir. That's what we were paid for.'

A short time after the police had quizzed the Pakistan trio in London, an ugly incident erupted on the outfield at Lord's cricket ground while the England and Pakistan players were warming up before a One-day Test match. Tensions over the spot-fixing scandal had reached boiling point, and England batsman Jonathan Trott and Pakistan pace bowler Wahab Riaz had to be physically pulled apart as their verbal squabbling threatened to develop into an unseemly brawl.

Detectives had questioned Riaz and other Pakistani players during the previous week, and Trott was alleged to have joked: 'How much are you going to make from the bookies on this game?' After a fiery exchange of words, the angry pair began to throw cricket pads at each other, and former England opener Graham Gooch, now the team's batting coach, stepped in and separated them. Trott and Riaz were instantly summoned to face match referee Jeff Crowe, the former New Zealand star batsman, who admonished them on the spot, and warned them about their future conduct.

It had become clear that Trott and his team-mates were incensed by extraordinary comments made by Ijaz Butt, the Pakistan Cricket Board Chairman, who had rashly claimed that England players had 'taken enormous amounts of money' to fix the previous One-day International at The Oval, which they had lost by 32 runs.

Ijaz Butt had talked of a 'conspiracy' against Pakistan, and in a television interview had alleged, without a grain of evidence, that: 'There is loud and clear talk in bookie circles that some English players have taken enormous amounts of money to lose the match.'

It was absolute poppycock, of course, and former England captain Ian Botham was so angry over what Butt had said that he thought Pakistan should be banned from world cricket until allegations about their spot-fixing had been fully investigated. Botham asserted forcibly: 'We keep sweeping things under the carpet. The public pay money to come and watch the games... What do they do if a catch goes down, or if someone bowls a no-ball? What are they thinking? Enough is enough!'

In a television interview with Sky Sports News, a clearly enraged Botham went on: 'I would like to know how Ijaz Butt knows what the bookmakers are doing. Maybe he should tell us something. It's appalling. It's farcical. It's gone on for too long. It needs to be stamped out. If it means giving guys an amnesty, saying "Come clean, guys, tell us what happened," then we'll move on. Whether they would have to serve a ban, that's for the ICC. The ICC needs to wake up. It needs to get off its backside. From what I can see, it hasn't done very much at all.'

Another former England captain, Nasser Hussain, also thought a temporary ban on Pakistan might have to be considered, adding that: 'There may come a point when removing Pakistan temporarily from world cricket might be the only way to preserve the game's dignity.'

Pakistan High Commissioner Wajid Hasan also felt it was time for him to step in, but let himself down badly by supporting the erratic Ijaz Butt when insisting: 'Mr Butt made a very innocent argument. He said that it is very strange that, when Pakistan lose a match, people describe it as spot-fixing, or fixing of the match. When Pakistan win a match, the same allegations are levelled against it.' Hasan naïvely remained convinced that Amir, Asif and Butt were all innocent, stressing: 'I still maintain that they are innocent until proven guilty.'

From the House of Commons, a plainly agitated Sports Minister, Hugh Robertson, leapt to the defence of England's smeared players, saying: 'I can absolutely understand the emotion involved in all of this. They have had their integrity questioned in the most fundamental way.'

No one was remotely surprised a few days later when Ijaz Butt came to his senses and withdrew his fatuous remarks about England fixing The Oval match, although cynics mischievously concluded that it was the fear of legal action from the ECB rather than a change of heart that was behind his embarrassing U-turn.

England's players had unanimously deemed Butt's ill-chosen words to be defamatory, and the Pakistan supremo had evidently been advised that he could be facing a sizeable libel bill if he did not retract and apologise.

Butt said that he was withdrawing his allegation on behalf of himself and the Pakistan Cricket Board, adding sheepishly: 'It is regrettable that there was a misunderstanding arising from my comments. I would like to make it quite clear that in the statements which I made I never intended to question the behaviour and integrity of the England players, nor the ECB, nor to suggest that any of them was involved in any corrupt practice, or in a conspiracy against Pakistan cricket.' Butt's grovelling apology was instantly welcomed and accepted by the ECB and the England players, who stressed that the matter was now closed.

The Pakistan media was brutal in its attack on Amir, Asif and Salman Butt, with one newspaper claiming the no-ball allegations were the 'final humiliation to a cricket team that has lurched from disaster to disaster for several years'. A damning editorial in another prominent daily newspaper called for the entire team and management to be sacked, insisting that they had 'stabbed the country in the back'.

And yet another highly respected daily newspaper blasted the Pakistan Cricket Board for failing 'to clean up the game after years of rumours, innuendo and infighting'. It went on: 'Some critics are of the view that most of the time it was because of the players' power that exists in Pakistan cricket that the Pakistan Cricket Board did not take action against the alleged players, and the situation has come to a head in England.' And Prime Minister Yousef Raza Gilani said the scandal had made his country 'bow its head in shame'.

Former Pakistan captain and wicketkeeper Rashid Latif, who once admitted to cheating, had no sympathy for Amir, Asif or Salman Butt, and was especially hard on Amir, the youngest of the three. Latif demanded: 'Whatever was done by Mohammad Amir is a crime, and stern punishment should be handed out to him if he is found guilty. Apart from a life ban I would award him a two-year gaol sentence – a harsh sentence to Amir would send a powerful signal to other players. I was not expecting such a thing from Salman Butt, which tarnished the image of the country.

'I would urge Salman to apologise and reveal what he knows about fixing. He should not hesitate in taking [sic] names of past and current players involved in the malpractice. This move would ultimately benefit Salman and the ICC, and perhaps end the game of the menace to a large extent, and I am not talking of Pakistan only. Salman should also expose any wrongdoing that he has witnessed elsewhere, especially in the Indian Premier League.'

Latif was also particularly critical of how the Pakistan Cricket Board chairman, Ijaz Butt, had handled the spot-fixing scandal, arguing that the PCB should have suspended the trio without waiting for the ICC to do it. Shortly after making his outspoken comments, Latif resigned from his high-ranking position as Pakistan Academy wicket-keeping coach, and accepted the job as head coach to the Afghanistan national team.

Latif has campaigned vigorously for several years to fight corruption in international cricket, and has admitted that he appealed for a catch while wicketkeeper in a Test match against Bangladesh, although he knew that the ball had actually struck the ground first before it ended up in his gloves. He confessed: 'What I did was intentional. The ball dropped from my gloves as I rolled over, but I picked it up quickly and claimed it as a clean catch, and the batsman was given out.'

The crucial ICC anti-corruption hearing for which the cricket world had patiently waited for more than two months finally opened in Qatar in early January 2011, when a three-man tribunal panel set out to decide the fate of the three Pakistani players charged with various offences under Article 2 of the ICC's anti-corruption code. Michael Beloff QC sat as its Chairman, along with Justice Albie Sachs from South Africa, and Sharad Rao, a highly respected Kenyan lawyer.

After six days of interviewing players and witnesses, and examining a mountain of oral and written statements, listening to tapes, watching video recordings and analysing forensic submissions, the panel, not surprisingly, decided that it needed at least two weeks to consider the evidence and promised that it would announce its verdict on 5 February, which piled even more pressure on the three defendants, who knew that the worst outcome was a lifetime ban from all forms of cricket anywhere in the world.

True to its word, the ICC released its findings right on time, and stated that it had found all three defendants guilty of the charges laid against them, and banned Butt for ten years, with five of them suspended; banned Asif for seven years, with two suspended; and banned Amir for five years, with none suspended.

In effect all three had been banned for five years, which brought a storm of protest from present and past players in virtually every cricket-playing nation, who believed their punishment was far too lenient.

Even former Pakistan Cricket Board chairman Sharayar Khan considered the penalties 'too light' and said: 'It's a shameful thing for Pakistan cricket that three of our players were found guilty. I thought Asif and Butt might have got life bans, and Amir a lesser punishment.'

Senior staff at the *News of the World*, the Sunday tabloid that exposed the scandal, blasted the ICC with a headline 'No balls for a band of idiots' and slammed the length of suspensions given to the players as 'appalling'.

Both Asif and Amir were found guilty of deliberately bowling no-balls in the Lord's Test against England in August 2010 under Article 2.1 of the ICC's anti-corruption code, and Butt, as captain, was found guilty of being involved with them.

Butt was also found guilty under Article 2.42 of failing to disclose to the Anti-corruption and Security Unit that he was *approached* by bookmaker Mazhar Majeed to bat out a maiden over in the Oval Test match against England from 18 to 21 August 2010. The charge that he agreed to this was dismissed.

It had been a horrendous 24 hours for the disgraced trio, who on the previous day had been stunned when the Crown Prosecution Service in London suddenly announced without any warning that all three players would be charged in a criminal court with accepting corrupt payments, plus a charge of conspiracy to cheat.

Accepting corrupt payments is an offence under the 1906 Prevention of Corruption Act, and carries a maximum sentence of seven years in prison and an unlimited fine. Cheating is an offence contrary to Section 42 of the 2005 Gambling Act, and carries a maximum sentence of two years in prison and an unlimited fine.

Majeed was also informed that he, too, would be charged when the case opened at the City of Westminster Magistrates' Court in London on 17 March 2011.

Simon Clements, head of the Special Crime Division at the Crown Prosecution Service, stressed that extradition orders would be requested should the three cricketers refuse to return from Pakistan to face the charges, and added: 'We are satisfied that there is sufficient evidence for a realistic prospect of conviction, and that it is in the public interest to prosecute.'

In particular it was yet another mammoth black mark on Asif's troubled five-year international career, having:

- tested positive for a banned steroid in 2006, and banned for a year, but overturned on appeal.
- failed a drugs test at the 2008 inaugural Indian Premier League tournament (IPL) and having been banned for two years.
- been arrested at Dubai airport for possessing a banned drug and detained for 19 days only to be deported after police found that the quantity of the substance in his possession was 'insufficient' to pursue a case.
- now been banned for seven years – two suspended – for deliberately bowling a no-ball in a spot-fixing scam, and facing the prospect of a long prison sentence if found guilty in a criminal court.

Explosive evidence was given to the ICC tribunal by Khawaja Javed Najam, a former security manager of the Pakistan cricket team, who revealed that Butt and wicketkeeper Kamran Akmal had constantly violated rules and regulations in order to remain close to bookmaker Mazhar Majeed and his brother Azhar.

Najam testified that he had regularly seen the Majeed brothers with Pakistani players during different tours, and that he had warned them many times, but they continued to stay close to the brothers.

He recalled that the brothers were seen in the West Indies during the Twenty/20 World Cup [in 2010], and that the players were again warned to stay away from them.

Najam further claimed that he was present when the police raided Butt's hotel room in London [during their spot-fixing inquiries] and found valuables worth 5.9 million rupees.

He resigned from his highly responsible security job shortly before Pakistan's tour of New Zealand in December 2010, when he cited 'issues' with certain Board officials as his reason for stepping down.

Quite incredibly, during the time the panel was studying the evidence following the six-day hearing, Amir, who was still banned from all cricket anywhere in the world, put on his cricket whites and incensed the ICC by bowling for the Pakistan Army against Rawalpindi in a domestic match at the Rawalpindi Stadium.

To make matters worse, it was reported that a team coach, who was employed by the Pakistan Cricket Board, was actually at the match and made no attempt to stop the suspended bowler from taking part.

A bitterly angry ICC official said: 'It is a clear violation of the tribunal order. After the hearing, the tribunal chief made it clear that the trio could not participate in any cricket activity, and that order should have been respected.'

He then similarly blasted the PCB and said: 'The ICC cannot monitor the three players. It is the PCB's responsibility to ensure that the [tribunal] order is being implemented.'

A spokesman for the PCB tried frantically to claim that the governing body had not failed in its duty, insisting that Amir had not played in any tournament that came under its control, though it did admit that he had played on a ground that came under its jurisdiction, and promised an immediate inquiry.

It was greatly encouraging for everyone in the game when the PCB promptly announced that it fully supported the bans on Butt, Asif and Amir, which strongly suggested that it was now genuinely interested in dealing effectively with cheats rather than looking for ways and excuses to see major offenders exonerated.

Chairman Ijaz Butt accepted that the three guilty verdicts were 'regrettable and a sad reality, which must be faced', and he promised that his Board would help the shamed trio with their education and rehabilitation programme, and that it would work with the ICC on this 'sensitive matter'.

Just five days after receiving his ten-year ban, disgraced captain Salman Butt must have enjoyed a good chuckle when a Pakistan television station signed him up – no doubt on a fat fee – as an 'expert' to provide commentary during the World Cup in India, Sri Lanka and Bangladesh from 19 February to 2 April.

Doing brilliantly not to burst out laughing, Butt crowed: 'As I was not playing in the event, I thought it was worth participating as an expert.'

Butt, Mohammad Asif, and Mohammad Amir were committed to stand trial at Southwark Court on May 20, 2011 when they appeared on spot-fixing charges at Westminster Magistrates Court in London on March 17. All three, along with their agent Mazhar Majeed, were charged with conspiracy to cheat, and conspiracy to obtain and accept corrupt payments. They denied the charges and were given unconditional bail.

The court heard that the charges related to an alleged plot to bowl deliberate no-balls in a Test match between England and Pakistan at Lord's in August 2010. The cricketers gave their addresses as being in Pakistan. Majeed lives in London.

As this book was going to Press, it was revealed that the three players were planning to apply for legal aid to pay their defence lawyers which, if granted, would land British taxpayers with hefty legal bills.

Shortly after the spot-fixing scam at Lord's in August 2010, it was sensationally revealed that cricket's highly infectious 'fixit' disease had spread to Sri Lanka, where the country was reeling from allegations that a prominent player was suspected of rigging matches for an illegal bookmaker in return for big money.

Rumour was rife that several team colleagues were so appalled at what they had learned that they had named the player in a protest letter sent urgently to the International Cricket Council's anti-corruption officers, and that they had branded him a 'traitor' and demanded an immediate inquiry. Certain members of the backroom staff were also reportedly under suspicion.

Several senior Sri Lankan players were concerned that their dubious colleague had missed important squad meetings in the team hotel during the Twenty/20 World Cup tournament in England in 2009, and that he had been absent from other bonding sessions, and had not provided an explanation.

Most damaging of all the allegations was a claim that the player, and some support staff, had been seen with 'dodgy-looking' people in a casino in England, and that this incident had been reported to the Sri Lankan officials in charge of the team.

Information that leaked from inside the Sri Lankan camp claimed that tour manager Brendon Kuruppu was so concerned by certain issues that he had hurried through a confidential report to ICC headquarters, but was sacked when he returned home because he had not alerted the Sri Lankan hierarchy to the incident, or told them of his report to the ICC. One official on the tour resigned immediately he landed back in Sri Lanka.

Within a few weeks of receiving Kuruppu's report, investigators from the ICC flew to Sri Lanka and carried out a series of interviews, but the customary silence followed and no details emerged of what – if anything – was uncovered.

Concern continued to escalate, especially after an 'internal' petition was sent to the island's Criminal Investigation Department, which subsequently questioned several players as well as a number of Sri Lankan cricket officials.

A series of high-level meetings then ensued as panic spread, and one of the team's coaching staff was fired with no explanation – and mysteriously reappointed several weeks later on condition that he never again accompany the national team on a foreign tour.

Sri Lanka's captain Kumar Sangakkara also spoke frankly to the media after an English national newspaper had named batsman Tillakaratne Dilshan as the player being investigated on suspicion of links with an illegal bookmaker.

Sangakkara said: 'We have no reason to suspect any of our team members of being involved in any such thing like fixing. We encourage players to report any suspicious behaviour they observe. Players should not be afraid of reporting this.'

In the fierce question-and-answer exchange that followed, Sangakkara remained firm and candid:

Q: What was your first reaction to Tillakaratne Dilshan being under the ICC scanner for his alleged involvement with bookmakers?
S: I can only give one comment on that. At no time have I or my team-mates ever reported anything suspicious about each other, either to the ICC or to Sri Lankan cricket.
Q: What did the management report?
S: If anything had to be reported it would be done with the cricket board. The players are always told to report anything suspicious.
Q: Why have these reports appeared?
S: I don't know. I have no reason to suspect anything. The ICC has always encouraged players to report suspicious behaviour. Whether it is a direct approach, off-hand conversation, or a

photo with someone. The ICC should continue to encourage players. Media backlash or any other backlash should not [be] given much importance.

Sri Lankan officials did admit that a bookmaker had approached one of the players, Dilhara Fernando, in March 2009; this was immediately reported to the ICC, which investigated but has made no comment on the matter.

Dilshan, an aggressive opening batsman, and acclaimed for inventing the 'Dilshan scoop' in which he stretches down the wicket and lifts the ball back over his head, and the wicketkeeper's, has not responded to allegations that he was linked to bookmakers. Officials could find no evidence to support these accusations and there is no suggestion that he has done anything wrong.

Meanwhile cricket's rampant 'fixit' disease moved swiftly on to India, where all-rounder Irfan Pathan revealed that a 'stranger' had sent him gifts before a big match, and that the man was believed to be a bookmaker.

Why Pathan, who had been dropped by his country after injury and loss of form, decided to disclose the facts in September 2010, having received the gifts at least a year earlier, was a mystery in itself.

Even then, Pathan did not disclose what these gifts were, or when precisely he received them, and he gave no clue as to the country that India were playing against at the time, or where.

He limited his comments to: 'Expensive gifts were sent to my hotel room during a series, and I reported the matter to the team manager.

'I was in the team hotel when a stranger approached me. He sent three expensive gifts to my room. He later sent me two more expensive gifts, things that I couldn't afford.

'I thought it was wrong and I reported it to the team manager. I haven't seen the stranger since then.'

India's cricket officials took a different view and decided that such a serious issue should not be shrouded in mystery and secrecy.

M Baladitya, who was team manager at the time of the incident, said that it occurred during India's tour of Pakistan in 2006, and that the 'stranger' was suspected of being a match-fixer. Baladitya confirmed that Pathan reported that someone had left expensive gifts for him in his hotel room, and that he had no idea of the identity of this person.

After returning to India, the meticulous Baladitya included the Pathan incident in his tour report for the BCCI, and stated: 'Irfan told me that someone went to his room and left some expensive gifts for him. I told him to return them immediately. During the entire tour I kept telling our players not to accept gifts or contact anyone.'

CHAPTER FIVE

INDIAN GANGSTER APPROACHES AUSSIE STARS

Five leading Australian Test cricketers disclosed in 2010 that they had been approached by what they believed were illegal Asian bookmakers or undercover agents operating for illegal Asian bookmakers. Swashbuckling batsman Shane Watson revealed that a friendly Indian gentleman had approached him twice while he was staying at a leading west London hotel with the rest of the Australian tour party during the Ashes series in 2009.

Watson said his suspicions soared when the man suggested that they went in search of somewhere more private where they could share a drink and a chat. Convinced that he was being set up for a match-fixing bribe, Watson reported both incidents to members of the Australian management and provided a detailed description of the dubious gentleman.

Watson's information and description were rapidly relayed to the International Cricket Council's Anti-corruption Unit in Dubai, and a short time later he was told that the person who tried to befriend him was likely to be a gangster from Mumbai, who operated as an illegal bookmaker and with illegal bookmaking syndicates.

Wicketkeeper Brad Haddin and fast bowlers Mitchell Johnson and Brett Lee also reported to their management that an Indian gentleman had approached them in the five-star Royal Garden Hotel in west London around the same time as Watson was targeted there.

While recalling his weird experience, Watson said: 'It was an Indian fan – or that was what I thought he was – who knew a lot about me and what I was doing in the IPL and how I had been playing. He said that he enjoyed the way I played. It happened a couple of times when we were staying at the Royal Garden Hotel, and I just went through the right channels, and told [team manager] Steve Bernard.

'The first time was in the breakfast room while talking about cricket in general and then it got to "We'd like to take you out for a few drinks" and that sort of thing. Then the second time it wasn't so much about the cricket side of things but more about wanting to take us out and wanting to have some fun in London. I didn't think a great deal about it until I got more information, and [learned] that he was one of the illegal bookmakers trying to get involved.'

Haddin recalled that he was in his hotel room speaking to his wife in Australia on Skype when he heard a knock on his door. He said: 'I had just put my luggage outside the room as we prepared to move on to our next venue. About half an hour later I heard a knock on the door. It was someone asking if I would like to go across to his room for a drink, which I thought was a bit odd.

'I immediately rang Steve Bernard and John Rhodes [Anti-corruption Unit manager in Australia and New Zealand] and told them something weird had happened. You don't usually get a knock on your door by someone asking you to go across to a room for a drink, and then go to dinner with someone you don't know. I think they checked [hotel CCTV] footage of the person, and it was someone they were well aware of. I'd never seen the person [before], and never heard from him or saw him again.'

Watson was convinced that the man who tried to tap him up was the same person who knocked on Haddin's door, and said: 'I heard that Brad Haddin had a similar conversation with an Indian guy, and after talking to Brad, as well as describing the gentleman, it seemed like it was the same guy. We are very well educated on what we can and cannot do. We know exactly where the line is, and it's a very obvious line of what goes on.'

Watson has expressed serious concern at the lack of success from the Anti-corruption Unit, and believes that all investigations should be made public for the sake of transparency. Going straight to the heart of the matter, he claimed: 'I don't think the ICC want to get to the bottom of it because it could run so deep, but now that it is out with the public, now everyone knows about it, they must act, they can't cover it up. All the other stuff the Anti-corruption Unit had in their pipeline, they have to bring to the surface.'

Australian bowlers Brett Lee and Mitchell Johnson revealed that they were also approached by the suspect fixer when they stayed at the Royal Garden Hotel, and that they too turned down the man's offer to buy them drinks at the bar. Both Lee and Johnson were included in reports submitted by the Australian team management to the Anti-corruption Unit, and team manager Steve Bernard said: 'This gentleman was staying in the same hotel as us. Our guys were not approached about spot-fixing or anything like that. He was asking if he could buy them drinks. The players used their judgement, and reported it to me.'

Big-hitting opening batsman David Warner, an Australian specialist in One-day matches, was convinced that he was approached by an illegal bookmaker during the inaugural Champions League Twenty/20 in India in 2009. Warner reported his strange experience to the New South Wales team manager, Marshall Rosen, who said later: 'A group of guys approached David

Warner, and some other NSW players, at the bar while they were watching a Champions League match on television. He reported to me that the questions they asked, and their behaviour, wasn't like the practical Indian cricket fan.

'A seminar had been run before the tournament about gambling and match-fixing, and what to do should something arise. David did exactly what he was supposed to do. He reported it to me and I passed the information to the gentleman who was running the anti-gambling programme. I can confirm that a report was made by David Warner to me and that I passed all the details to the tournament officials in charge of that area.'

Talented Marlon Samuels was on the fringe of a huge future as a West Indian middle-order batsman when police in Nagpur reported that he had been caught speaking to Mukesh Kochchar, an Indian businessman who lived in Dubai. Police were also aware that Kochchar was an illegal bookmaker, and it was for this reason that they decided to tape-record telephone conversations that he was having with Samuels in Nagpur.

As a result of what they recorded on their tapes, the police alleged that Samuels had passed information to Mukesh Kochchar about a match in which the West Indies were taking part and that he had benefited by collecting money from him. Samuels accepted that he received the equivalent of $1,238 from the bookmaker, but insisted that it was nothing more than a small loan from a friend to pay an hotel bill because he had run low on funds.

Unfortunately for Samuels, the International Cricket Council rejected this explanation and banned him for two years – 'for receiving money, benefit, or other reward, which could bring him, or the game of cricket, into disrepute'.

In a particularly rare development, the Indian police released a verbatim transcript of a telephone conversation that they had tape-recorded when Kochchar rang Samuels around 24 hours before a

One-day International match between India and the West Indies in Nagpur.

Samuels was relaxing in room 206 at the city's top-rated Pride Hotel where the rest of the West Indies party had settled before the first of the four-match series that was due to start the next day. Indian police claimed that it was standard practice for known bookmakers to be monitored closely prior to matches at international venues, and that suspicions were aroused in Nagpur after Kochchar had made a number of telephone calls to room 206, and that four of these calls were recorded.

A verbatim transcript of some of the taped conversation between Kochchar and Samuels was released to the media, and began:

Bookie: Connect to 206.
Reception: 206, sir?
Bookie: Yes.
Reception: Hello, room number 206, Marlon.
Bookie: How are you Marlon?
206: [Not clear]
Bookie: Just relax, buddy.
206: Just relax…
Bookie: Hello my son, that's way [sic] I am here. Came for my some work and am held up.
206: Okay.
Bookie: Tomorrow night I am going back.
206: Okay.
Bookie: So how are things with you, and how is the preparation?
206: Preparation is good enough.
Bookie: Well, wish you all the best.
206: Thanks.
Bookie: You play well.
206: [Not clear] … talking to Robinson.
Bookie: Robinson… Yes.

206: Yes, our fielding well…
Bookie: Yes, good, that's a high-scoring game.
206: Early in the morning… Batting, move around the pitch.
Bookie: And in the evening, lower down.
206: Slow down.
Bookie: What do you think that…? Who will bat?
206: Well…
Bookie: Who? Who?
206: Dwayne [not clear]. He is making a debut tomorrow.
Bookie: New batsman, bowler…
206: All-rounder.
Bookie: He are [sic] a good player.
206: Making debut.
Bookie: Yah, I can understand that… Chris is in form.
206: [Not clear]
Bookie: And how is your batting going on?
206: My batting is good.
Bookie: Big… a… tall score tomorrow…
206: [Not clear]
Bookie: When do you get down to bowl?
206: [Not clear]
Bookie: Which over will you be bowling?
206: One down.
Bookie: Normally after 17th or 18th over…
206: By tomorrow [not clear]… I can bowl [not clear].
Bookie: He is seamer or spinner?
206: Seamer.
Bookie: He is a seamer who will start bowling tomorrow…
206: Dwayne.
Bookie: Dwayne.
206: Dwayne, 'Tail' [Taylor] and Bradshaw.
Bookie: 'Tail' and Bradshaw, they will open. You will be as third bowler…

206: Jerome Taylor... Chris Gayle will be fourth, and fifth bowling.

Bookie: You have a nice all-round team now.

Bookie: As a first match I want you to play well. Confident. And don't hurry up. Don't give the catches. Play well. Consolidate your position as well as possible, if even... if you want couple of balls, it doesn't matter. Don't get run out. Don't get excited. Have a strong position.

206: [Not clear]

Bookie: After this, you guys going to Cuttack, that's another place.

206: [Not clear]

Bookie: I am going back. We will be in touch with you.

206: Most welcome.

Bookie: Whenever you come back to Bombay... Most probably I will come there for one or two days.

206: I want to stay there for a couple of days.

Bookie: Yeah, after... [not clear].

206: Yeah...

Bookie: Let me know... I am flying back tomorrow.

206: Not yet.

Bookie: Yeah, my flight... [not clear] o'clock, and from there I will fly back to Bombay.

206: [Not clear]

Bookie: Thank you very much, chief.

206: [Not clear]

Bookie: All the best. After this I will have to work...

206: [Not clear]

Bookie: Okay. Good.

India beat the West Indies by 14 runs in the match that was played on the day after Kochchar and Samuels were tape-recorded, and they went on to win the series 3-1. Samuels conceded 53 runs in his allotted ten overs, and scored 40 runs off 60 deliveries in the West Indies run chase. Officials attached to the Anti-corruption Unit flew to Nagpur for detailed discussions with the police, and subsequently banned Samuels for two years.

A statement issued by the West Indies Cricket Board claimed that Samuels had 'received money, benefit, or other reward, which could bring him, or the game, into disrepute'. The ICC's acting Chief Executive, David Richardson, said: 'We hope the case serves as a reminder to players and officials to remain vigilant. It is never pleasant when a player is banned, but the process in arriving at this point has been an extremely thorough one.'

It later leaked into the public domain that the West Indies Cricket Committee was not happy with the ban and had recommended a suspended sentence, on account of Samuels' previous good behaviour. But the ICC contemptuously brushed aside this ambitious plea of leniency, and Richardson stressed: 'Corruption is a serious matter.' A second charge that Samuels had 'directly, or indirectly, engaged in conduct prejudicial to the interests of the game' was dismissed.

An Indian police commissioner later claimed that Samuels had specifically told Kochchar over the telephone at 11.30pm on 20 January that he would bowl first-change next day, and that this occurred just as he predicted. The police were also suspicious when Samuels chose to stay behind in Bombay (now called Mumbai) – ostensibly for a reality cricket match – after every other member of the West Indies tour party had flown home at the end of the series.

'Maybe they [Samuels and Kochchar] were in contact during that time,' pondered the police commissioner. Samuels fiercely protested against the allegations, and when told that the police had tape-recorded his conversations, he replied: 'I don't think he is a bookie. I usually talk about cricket, but I don't give out any such information. I don't do such things. I have done nothing wrong.'

Kochchar echoed the same 'I did nothing wrong' defence during a television interview, insisting that he was a friend of Samuels and a 'father figure to him', and that he was 'encouraging him to play better'.

Extensive police surveillance on suspected illegal bookmakers spread throughout Asia to try to identify and crack down on vast betting syndicates, who had dangerous underworld connections, the biggest of them believed to be operating in Dubai, Karachi, Mumbai and Delhi. Large gambling networks were also located in Nagpur and Bhopal, as well as in Lahore (Pakistan) and Kuala Lumpur (Malaysia).

India's top detective agency, the Central Bureau of Investigation (CBI), was tipped off that an infamous illegal bookmaker had let slip that he was paying a senior international umpire for important 'pitch' information to help him land bets.

Fixing the results of matches, and the huge increase of spot-fixing, had become so internationally widespread that CBI officers were not in the least surprised when a former leading Indian cricketer reported that a groundsman had demanded 50,000 rupees (£1,000) to ensure that the pitch for a crucial five-day Test was under-prepared, so that one side or the other would win the match. This would have eliminated the possibility of a draw, and the bookmaker accomplice would be able to gamble heavily on the result.

A ruthless team of tax officials carried out a coordinated raid on the homes of several top Indian cricketers and officials in July 2000, and called on former captain Mohammad Azharuddin, plus Ajay Jadeja, Navan Mongia, Nikhil Chopra and Kapil Dev, the national team coach. Around four months later Dev, a brilliant all-rounder in his playing days, resigned as coach while facing a government inquiry into corruption in cricket, and insisted that it should not be regarded as an admission of guilt.

The CBI reported that it had found no concrete evidence against Dev, but claimed that Azharuddin had confessed to fixing games with the help of colleagues, and he was later banned for life.

A total stranger telephoned Bangladesh all-rounder Shakib Al Hasan and offered to sponsor him in exchange for under-performing in a three-match series of One-day Tests against Ireland in March 2008. Shakib recalled: 'I didn't speak to him much because I had a team meeting to go to, so I told him "I'll talk to you later" and immediately reported what had happened to a member of the Bangladesh Cricket Board (BCB), and to someone from the ICC.

'I do not care about the money. I want to play for my country because that is a great honour for me. I want to continue to do well for my country. I am not concerned about the money.'

Bangladesh's cricket leaders were deeply concerned and promptly organised a tough 'awareness programme' for its national players with detailed advice on how to deal with suspected illegal bookmakers and gamblers.

BCB Media Committee Chairman Jahal Yunus was also worried about people who acted as agents for players, and had the right to telephone them whenever they wished, during the day or night. Jahal explained: 'Every player has an agent these days, and as we have no control over them we have asked for information [on the agents] so that we can examine their background and be more aware of the forces that influence our players.'

Two senior Test umpires, Rudi Koertzen and Cyril Mitchley, shocked the ICC when they revealed that substantial financial offers were made for them to influence the results of matches at different points in their careers. The two highly respected South Africans stressed that they rejected every offer that was dangled in front of them.

Koertzen stood in a record 108 Test matches and 206 One-day

Internationals. He was voted the world's top umpire in 2002, and walked through a guard of honour formed by the Australian and Pakistan players at Headingley in July 2010 – his last day of duty before slipping into retirement.

Koertzen was renowned for being honest and frank, and rarely ducked a question, no matter how difficult it might be. When asked for his opinion on Australia's ace pace bowler Glenn McGrath, there was typically no holding back, and Koertzen candidly said: 'He wasn't one of the happiest guys… He always moaned and whinged. If he wasn't getting wickets, and the batsmen were hitting him for a few fours, he got a bit personal and upset.'

After a short career as wicketkeeper for Transvaal, an ambitious Cyril Mitchley decided that he would rather be an umpire, and he was so good at it that he graduated from standing in domestic matches to officiating in 26 Tests and 61 One-day Internationals.

There was also some firm advice, and a gentle ticking off, for England's precocious young pace bowler Stuart Broad, who threw the ball back towards Pakistan batsman Zulqarnain Haider and struck him on the shoulder. Broad was fined 50 per cent of his match fee for being so stupidly reckless, and later wisely apologised to Haider. When asked to comment on the incident, Koertzen made it plain that he fully supported the punishment, saying: 'It is so unnecessary for a bowler to pick up the ball and throw it at a batsman. Broad is a good lad, but sometimes he gets a bit too emotional. When it happened I thought, here we go… He was reported, and that was a good thing. If he gets away with it one day, then the next day he is going to take advantage of players, and umpires, again.'

While he was head coach of South Africa in 2007, the highly respected Micky Arthur acquired a 'strong suspicion' that certain Pakistan players were involved in match-fixing in a One-day series against them. But Arthur decided not to make his huge concern public for up to three years – until he had quit as South Africa's national coach and moved on to Western Australia.

When he finally broke his silence, Arthur told a South African news website that his team suspected match-fixing when Pakistan collapsed dramatically to lose the final One-day Test in Lahore. He recalled: 'There was a strong suspicion of match-fixing; it took some of the gloss off us winning the series.'

Set 234 to win the match, Pakistan crashed from 129-2 to 209-6, and 219 all out. No official allegations were made against the Pakistan team or any individual player.

Arthur added: 'We had no proof, but when you've been involved in the game long enough, you know when something is not right. How else do you explain a batting side needing only 40 runs to win with seven wickets in hand, and then losing?'

CHAPTER SIX

BANNED FOR BLOWING WHISTLE ON CORRUPTION

Prolific batsman Qasim Omar, the only cricketer in the world brave enough to expose publicly the colossal corruption that is tarnishing the game, was banned for seven years by the Pakistan Cricket Board for having the audacity to stand alone and tell the truth. Omar was as fearless with his words as he was with his bat. Nothing and no one deterred him, whether it was the world's fastest bowler on the fastest pitch, or starchy officials at the International Cricket Council.

A devout Muslim, he decided to blow the whistle on international cricket's vast network of money-grabbing crooks because his troubled conscience would no longer let him stay silent. Suddenly the game was up. Omar's precise and colourful revelations sent shock waves through boardrooms and dressing rooms, where the anxious and guilty wondered whether they would be named and shamed in his explosive catalogue of crime.

As rival bowlers had often found, Omar was relentless and devastating in attack, hitting hard, showing no respect for icons or legends, and never worried about wild bouncers from those who resented his candid approach.

Omar confidently strode into the Anti-corruption and Security Unit (ACSU) offices in London and faced Paul Condon and his probing investigators in the same calm, composed way in which he walked to the wicket in Perth to meet the full ferocity of Australia's hostile pace attack.

I first met Omar in Durham City after I responded to his telephone call to my desk in *The People*'s investigations department in London. He invited me to meet him next day, and assured me that I would not be disappointed with what he had to tell me. His voice crackled with excitement, and my anticipation was high. He met me at the exit from Durham City railway station and immediately explained that he had married a local girl, Michelle, and lived there whenever he was not playing for the Pakistan national team, or playing club cricket in Karachi, where his mother lived.

We enjoyed a good lunch together and he talked about international cricket in general – like who was the fastest bowler he had faced, and the trickiest spinner – but it was pretty obvious that he was itching to get started on telling me why I had been invited there. Even then, he emphasised and repeated that what he was about to tell me was the truth, the whole truth, and nothing but the truth. He promised that he could produce documents, correspondence, photographs, and even film footage to verify what he said.

With relish, he declared: 'I want to tell everything because it's been on my conscience for so long. I took money for throwing my wicket away, and I'm ashamed of myself. I want all Pakistan's cricket scandals brought into the open so that the country's rulers can penalise cheats so heavily that young players will be too scared to get corrupted.'

Before meeting Omar that day I had checked his career record and found that he was born in Kenya, but his mother was a Pakistani, which qualified him to represent the country at cricket. He had played in 26 Test matches, and 31 One-day Internationals, and alongside such brilliant performers as Imran Khan, Wasim Akram, Salim Malik, Zaheer Abbas, Abdul Qadir, Sarfraz Nawaz and Javed Miandad, who later became the Pakistan team coach.

Literally putting his hands up, Omar shamefully began by confessing to using a jagged bottle-top to damage the ball to help Pakistan beat England in a Test match in Karachi in 1984. He further revealed that officials instructed staff at the ground to pour buckets of water onto the pitch after everyone had left in the evening, and to roll it into the turf so that it would dry overnight to help ace spinner Abdul Qadir to mesmerise the formidable England batting line-up next day.

Pace bowler Sarfraz Nawaz benefited most from having the ball scratched, and it swung so sharply that left-arm seamer Azim Hafeez was unable to control it and had to be removed from the attack. Omar's revelation of the immense illegal assistance that was given to the bowlers explained why Pakistan were able to triumph by three wickets, with Qadir bagging eight victims, and Sarfraz returning phenomenal figures of 4-42 in 25 overs, and 2-27 in 15 overs.

Wisden, world cricket's redoubtable bible, reported at the time: 'Gower excepted, England had little defence to [Qadir's] mixture of leg-breaks, top-spinners, and googlies…' And it continued: 'Sarfraz skilfully persuaded an ageing ball to swing…' Omar stressed that Sarfraz did not personally use a bottle-top at any time to achieve his remarkable figures.

England's stitched-up squad was Bob Willis (captain), David Gower, Ian Botham, Mike Gatting, Allan Lamb, Derek Randall, Graham Dilley, Norman Cowans, Graeme Fowler, Nick Cook, Vic Marks, Chris Smith, Neil Foster and Bob Taylor (wicketkeeper).

Zaheer Abbas, for many years Gloucestershire's registered overseas player, led Pakistan, who won the three-match series 1-0, with the two subsequent Tests ending in a draw. It was also Pakistan's first home series victory over England in 13 years. Gower took over as captain when Willis returned home early with a viral infection, and he was the only England batsman to score a century in the series, with Lamb suffering most with a depressing average of just 15.60 runs.

Omar slowly and carefully recalled how the astonishing plot to cheat England in Karachi was first discussed during a drinks break in Brisbane a few months earlier while Pakistan were locked in battle with Australia. He said: 'We had about three months to prepare, and four senior players discussed how England could be beaten if we did the job properly. They said that at least one player would have to use a metal bottle-top to scratch the ball to make it swing more than it normally did.

'We started to use bottle-tops against Australia, but the pitches were usually flat and hard down there, so we couldn't take advantage of what we were doing. Schoolboys as young as 12 get to know how to use a bottle-top in Pakistan, and they've come to think that it's all part of the game.

'England had never won a Test in Karachi, and that's how we wanted it to stay. Metal bottle-tops were left on our dressing-room table, and I was told to put one of them in my pocket and to use it whenever I got the chance. I had seen other players doing it, so I agreed to cooperate and to do my best.

'England batted first, and I used the bottle-top from the first over, and it worked brilliantly for us. Then, when I went back from my hotel to collect my squash racket from our dressing room later in the evening, I saw people pouring buckets of water onto the pitch, and someone was going up and down with the roller.

'They had waited until everyone had left the ground, and I straight away realised that they were doctoring the pitch for our spinner Abdul Qadir. I was disgusted, and I rushed out to the groundsman, and said, "Why are you doing this to the pitch? It's against the laws."

'He said that he had been told to do it, and that he was sorry, but he had a wife and children to feed, and that if he didn't do it, he would lose his job. He even advised me to keep my nose out of it, as it was a very old practice. In any case, what they did to the pitch almost backfired on us because when it dried out England's spinner Nick Cook looked like winning the game for them with his slow left-armers. Both teams struggled on a very difficult pitch, but we scraped home by three wickets after all had seemed lost for us.

'It was a very hot day with no clouds. They were poor conditions to get the ball to swing, but it went all over the place. Sarfraz Nawaz, who had nothing to do with the bottle-top business, did brilliantly in both innings.'

England were shot out for 182 in their first innings, and for only 159 when they batted for the second time. David Gower struck 58 and 57, but no other England batsman reached 30. Spinners Abdul Qadir with 5-74 and 3-59, and Nick Cook 6-56 and 5-18, found conditions ideal for them, as did Pakistan off-spinner Tauseef Ahmed, who also picked up four wickets. The two drawn Tests were played at Faisalabad and Lahore.

Omar recalled that Botham was always complaining that Pakistan cricketers were like old women, and he agreed. 'We were worse than old women!' he snapped. 'All we did was bicker and argue among ourselves. While I was in the team, we couldn't have a conversation about cricket without bringing up different ways to cheat. I was in the team when we cheated against Australia, New Zealand and India. Bottle-tops have been part of our club cricket, and even school cricket, for a very long time.'

At this point I recalled standing on the boundary at a Thames Valley League match on a Saturday afternoon in Slough when their young, wicket-taking Pakistan pace bowler shuffled up to me at the end of his over and whispered: 'Do me a favour, mate, look after this for me. I think the umpire might have seen it…' And he rapidly slipped a metal bottle-top into my hand.

'You rotten cheat,' I thought, and I later warned him that if I ever had reason to think that he was using that bottle-top again, or anything else to damage the cricket ball, he would be reported to his club, and to the League, and would inevitably be banned for a long time.

Omar admitted to having lots of differences with his captain, Imran Khan, and even refused to tour India with him because of their bitter rows, but he still regarded him as the most positive leader he had ever played under. Omar said: 'Though he later admitted to tampering with the ball in matches, I never heard him tell players to cheat. Some of our players tried to con umpires into thinking that batsmen had been caught by a close-in fielder when they knew for sure that the ball had gone nowhere near the bat. One of our guys was really bad, and would jump up and down shouting "Howzat! Howzat!" and he tried to get us all to do the same as him. There was no limit to what some of our players would do to win matches.'

According to Omar, the biggest earner was a batsman who deliberately gave his wicket away in return for a large cash bung from an illegal bookmaker or gambler. He said: 'Players have made big money from telling bookies and punters how they would be dismissed. Deliberately giving their wicket away without scoring has always been the best earner. Being bowled or run out also pays well.

'Corrupt captains have pocketed up to the equivalent of £1,500 just for saying whether he would bat, or bowl, if he won the toss. I've done it myself. I've given my wicket away for money, and now I'm disgusted with myself. One bookie tried to bribe me after I'd scored 210 in a Test match against Sri Lanka in Faisalabad. He came to my mother's house in Karachi and said that, as my place in the team was safe, I could earn £1,000 in rupees if I got myself out for nought in the next Test. He said everyone was doing it, and that some of our big names were earning up to £5,000 in Pakistan currency. It was very tempting, but I turned him down.'

Omar produced from his black briefcase a sheet of paper with a list of fees for players who cooperated with bookmakers. It had been converted from rupees into pounds sterling to give a clear idea of what was on offer:

BATSMEN
- £5,000 run out first over.
- £3,000 bowled first over.
- £2,000 stumped in match.
- £1,000 run out in match.
- £500 caught or lbw first over.

BOWLERS
- £1,000 concede boundary in first over.
- £500 to bowl a wide or no-ball in first over.

CAPTAINS
- £1,500 for decision on winning the toss.
- £500 for naming opening bowler.
- £500 for stating which end of the ground first over would be bowled.

FIELDERS
- £1,000 to drop a catch.

Omar made it clear that distance was no problem for Pakistan bookmakers, who flew to be with players while they were on tour in England, Australia, India, Sir Lanka, the West Indies, and even as far as New Zealand. With a mischievous chuckle, he talked about the brazen bookmakers who, totally ignoring Pakistan's strict no-gambling laws, opened shops in the main streets and filled their windows with sports goods, furniture or lace items, while up to ten people would be crammed in a back room taking bets direct from cricket grounds all over the world.

Omar laughed when he revealed that bookmakers even had a room at the back of a Karachi hospital: 'It was a big gambling den. A film producer ran it at first. Then his son took over. I went there a few times, and I even had a lift in an ambulance when I was late for a flight.'

Pakistan umpires who officiated in club matches were also deeply involved and on the take, according to Omar, who said: 'I remember the day when the ball brushed my pads, and the wicketkeeper put out a massive appeal for a catch, which the umpire turned down, and I went on to make a big score.

'Later that evening the umpire rang me up, and said: "Congratulations on your score... but that was a big appeal early on, wasn't it?" I realised immediately what he was implying. He went on to say that he needed a couple of new umpiring shirts, so I went straight out and bought them for him because I had enough sense to know that he could do me a lot of harm if I didn't look after him.

'Another umpire asked me to bring a particular gift back from Sri Lanka for him on my first tour of that lovely country, but when I handed it to him, all beautifully wrapped up in pretty paper, and told him how much he owed me for it, he smiled and said: "Go home and relax... When you next bat in front of me, you'll be all right."

'I was in a room once when I heard a Pakistan umpire tell a bowler, who was standing next to me, that if he struck this particular batsman on the pads in a match that was coming up, and appealed for lbw in a big way, he would give him out, because he didn't like him.

'They'd had a big fall-out in a recent match, and he wanted to show him who was the boss. I knew the batsman well, but there was nothing I could do to help him. And if the umpire had got to hear that I had tipped the batsman off, he would definitely give me a dodgy decision when I next played in front of him.

'During the match, the ball did strike this batsman's pads, though it was well wide of the stumps, but the bowler appealed, as he had been advised to do, and the umpire's finger shot up without a moment's thought. The batsman understood what had happened, and he later took a nice gift to the umpire, and their rift was healed, and they became good friends after that.'

Indian umpire Uday Vasant Pimple was just 20 years old when he died from serious head wounds after a wicketkeeper went wild and attacked him with a stump because he turned down an appeal for a catch during a club match in Nagpur.

Omar believed Pakistan's international wicketkeeper Salim Yousef often went too far with his appealing, and recalled an unpleasant incident involving England's beefy all-rounder Ian Botham. Still livid about it, Omar protested: 'We all could see that the ball had hit the ground before Yousef caught it, but he kept running around claiming it was a fair catch. I was disgusted with him.

'Viv Richards also threatened to beat him up after he'd spent all afternoon appealing for catches. Viv was furious, and screamed at him: "If you appeal once more, I'll give you such a hiding you'll never play cricket again." I don't think Viv really meant it, but I stepped in and cooled him down, just in case. I actually went further than Viv, and I did beat him up in his hotel room in Lahore.

'Yousef had tried to disturb my concentration all through my innings, and I told him that if he didn't stop nattering I'd sort him out later. So I went to his room, dragged him from his bed, and gave him a pasting that he'll never forget. Two of our players heard the noise, and had to burst in and drag me off him.

'But he wasn't so lucky when he upset batsman Sajid Abbasi, who pulled a stump from the ground, and cracked him across the head with it. Blood gushed everywhere, and Yousef had to be rushed to hospital for lots of stitches.'

Even groundsmen who prepared pitches at Pakistan club grounds were able to boost their earnings by taking bribes. Omar recalled being the captain of a side that arrived to compete against a team that included the brilliant Abdul Qadir, a legend among Pakistan spin bowlers. Omar remembered it well: 'We immediately noticed that two pitches had been prepared for the match. One was a proper batting strip, and the other was very rough. Perfect for a spinner.

'The groundsman came up, and chatted about them, and when we refused to pay him he said the match would be played on the rough one. Abdul Qadir ran straight through us. He was unplayable. We were hammered for refusing to be part of a bribe.

'It's common practice in Pakistan to find groundsmen asking for money or gifts to prepare a pitch to suit a particular team, and they can end up with a smart new shirt, or a pair of shoes, or something useful for their home.'

Omar was well known in cricket circles as a powerful match-fixing broker who could summon up a bookmaker with a click of his fingers. If a player needed cash, Omar was the man to contact. Bookmakers did exactly the same with him when they wanted to take a player on board for a major bet.

There is no doubt that the biggest and most audacious request Omar ever received to organise a crooked deal came from a wealthy Karachi bookmaker shortly before the Pakistan tour party set off for a Test series in Australia. Omar was handed 2,000 American dollars in advance as a deposit for bribing Australia's star batsman Greg Chappell to throw his wicket away in as many matches as he would agree to.

Vividly recalling the moment the bookmaker approached him, Omar said: 'He came to me after big bets had been placed on Chappell to score lots of runs in the series. Pakistan had several good bowlers missing, and it was a poor attack, so the way was open for Chappell to fill his boots. Some of our players were expecting him to hit at least three centuries against us.

'The bookie asked me to talk Chappell into accepting $25,000 to get himself out for less than 30 runs, and that he'd be paid a further $25,000 if he did it again. It would be $25,000 every time he did it.

'Before we reached Australia our team had a night's stopover in Singapore where I spent $1,000 of what I'd been given on duty-free goods. The bookie rang me at our hotel on the evening before our first match to wish me luck with my approach to Chappell, and he was one of the first players I saw practising in the nets next morning.

'I had always looked up to Chappell as a great batsman, and he was something of a hero to me. Until then I had only been able to dream of watching him play, but now I had to approach him and offer him money to play badly, and I had already spent $1,000 dollars of my fee, so I had to find the courage from somewhere. But I panicked, and couldn't go through with it, so I now had the problem of finding the $1,000 dollars that I had already spent to pay the bookie back.

'He kept trying to reach me on the phone at my hotel, but I didn't take his calls, and I thought I'd heard the last of it until we reached Perth, and he turned up from nowhere and said that he had booked dinner for the two of us at the Sheraton Hotel. While we dined and chatted he handed me an envelope with 3,000 dollars in it, and said that massive bets had been placed in Pakistan and India on Chappell scoring lots of runs in the Test matches.

'I told him I didn't have the courage to speak to Chappell, and I wanted him to take his money back, but he said: "Don't worry. Keep it as a gift. There'll be other times." He was right. There were other times, many of them, and he was always generous.'

Omar provided film footage to a leading Australian television company of him twice deliberately throwing his wicket away, and in the second incident, a perceptive commentator was right on the mark when he observed: 'That certainly looked like a premeditated shot!'

Fortunately not all international cricketers are greedy and corrupt, and Omar named several who had rejected his lucrative offers from bookmakers to take bribes. Among them were Indian all-rounders Ravi Shastri, who also played for Glamorgan in the English championship, and Sandip Patil, as well as West Indian off-spinner Clyde Butts.

Omar recalled asking Shastri to get himself out for a low score in a Test match at Lahore, but he hit back sharply with: 'You'd better find someone else. I'm not into that type of thing.' Patil was asked to give his wicket away for fewer than ten runs in a Test match at Faisalabad, but he brushed Omar aside and scored a century.

Omar approached Butts before a Test match in Karachi and told him that a bookmaker would pay him big money if he guaranteed conceding a boundary in his first over. With a shrug, Omar recalled: 'I told him that it was only one bad ball in a lifetime and that he could pick up a lot of money for doing it, but he turned me down. He took several wickets in our innings, including mine when I popped a catch to silly mid-on.'

One of the most brazen attempts at cheating took place in an important Pakistan club match when a furious captain took all his players off the field and refused to finish the game. Omar smiled, as he recalled: 'The match ball was struck over the boundary and no one knew exactly where it had ended up. Then the batting side's 12th man suddenly ran onto the field holding up a ball, saying that he had found it near the pavilion, and he threw it to the umpire.

'But the fielding side's captain protested that this was not the match ball that had gone missing, pointing out that it was far too worn to be the match ball, and he took his players off the field. Several weeks later the Pakistan Cricket Board banned him for six months and fined the team manager 1,000 rupees.'

Pakistan officials seemed to have a problem in deciding how to deal with downright cheats, and in many cases preferred to penalise the people who stood up for justice and fair play, and incredibly allowed the charlatans and crooks to escape without question or reprimand.

Omar then lifted the lid on what was yet another common ruse: 'Captains would often pick up the coin from the ground before a match and say "heads" when it was "tails" because he wanted to lose the toss to please a bookmaker who would have taken bets on it. I've done it myself.

'Aqeel was the first bookie I worked for. He owned a supermarket in Karachi, and several factories. He was very rich. One of my best bookies was Shafiq Ahmed, a good guy who had a top job in a national bank in charge of sports events. I did lots of fixing for him, especially in big club matches. Most of his clients were wealthy businessmen who had accounts at his bank, and they would bet on cricket in rupees up to the equivalent of £20,000.'

Omar said that he often warned Shafiq to be careful that the bank didn't find out about his betting, but he got caught and was sacked. He was very angry with his bosses because he thought he was safe, especially as a number of the bank officials knew what he was doing and had let him carry on.

There were times when Omar felt that Shafiq was passing his very good 'inside' information on to certain people high up in the bank, and it was probably for that reason that they hadn't stopped him, and feared that something must have gone badly wrong for them to fire him, as he was a great source of private income for them.

Tariq Qamar was another big bookie who did a lot of business with Omar, and the high-scoring batsman recalled an occasion when Tariq wanted to bet that Omar wouldn't score his third double century of the season in a club game, and Omar passed a message to him during the lunch break that he could take as many bets as he liked because he would definitely get himself out before he reached this milestone.

Omar remembered it well, and said: 'When I reached 179 it

seemed a good time to go, so I hit the ball high in the air, and straight down the ground, and was caught at long-off. Two days later, Tariq came to see me and paid me £600 in rupees.'

Qaurruddin was another wealthy bookie who went all over the world with the Pakistan team and he handed Omar large sums of money to share among players who agreed to do various things in matches for him.

Omar insisted that the scale of corruption was huge and that it went far deeper than the people in authority could ever imagine, and he added: 'Pakistan officials have always known that players take money from bookies. An official found out about me and said that I could carry on, but to make sure that I never got caught. One Mr Big was based in Sharjah, and he masterminded many great betting coups from there.

'The truth is, bookies have run Pakistan cricket at all levels for years and years, and they are still running it. Betting is huge. No one will stop it. Just about everyone who plays the game in, and for, Pakistan see cheating as part of the game.

'I saw it, did nothing about it, and joined in. I took bribes and deliberately got myself out for bookmakers. I've been an agent for bookmakers. I've introduced them to players so that they can do deals to cheat for money.'

Now full of remorse, Omar confessed that he was delighted when he eventually came to his senses and realised what a 'greedy, horrible fool' he had been, and stopped.

He went on: 'I admitted that I had done lots of wrong things in cricket, and that I could no longer continue to be a hypocrite. It was the best decision I ever made in my life.'

Qasim Ali Omar was born in Nairobi, Kenya, on 9 February 1957. A flamboyant right-handed batsman, he played in 26 Test matches and 31 One-day Internationals for Pakistan between 1983 and 1987. He scored two double centuries, one century, and five 50s.

His highest score was 210 against India at Faisalabad in 1984/85. It was also a record individual Test score at Faisalabad, shared with Tasleem Arif, and part of a record second-wicket partnership of 250 with Mudassar Nazar.

Omar later scored 206 against Sri Lanka, also at Faisalabad, in 1985/86. He scored 642 runs in One-day Internationals, which included four half centuries, including his highest score of 69. Omar also played as a professional for Burnhope Cricket Club in the North Durham League in England when not involved in the Pakistan domestic season.

In addition to Omar, the rapidly developing cricket nation of Kenya proudly spawned Maurice Odumbe, a flamboyant captain who, at his peak, owned three top-of-the-range BMWs and a Mercedes, rented a mansion, was flushed with money, and enjoyed a lifestyle observers felt could not be sustained by the earnings of a professional cricketer, even if he was the best in the country.

It was such an imbalanced financial situation that tongues wagged with deep suspicion about how he could possibly manage to fund it all while also spending lavishly on his wife and two children, and two stunning girlfriends.

So it came as no surprise when news broke that Odumbe was under investigation by the International Cricket Council for alleged links with bookmakers, and a dossier of overwhelming evidence was produced at an ICC tribunal in Nairobi in August 2004 when the fallen star faced 12 charges of fixing matches and associating with bookmakers.

Justice Ahmed Ebrahim, a former Zimbabwean Supreme Court Judge, who presided at the four-day hearing, concluded that Odumbe had had 'inappropriate contact' with a known Indian bookmaker, and he banned him for five years for bringing the game into disrepute, a decision that was fully backed by the ICC and the Kenyan Cricket Association.

Problems escalated for Odumbe when his former wife, Katherine, told the hearing that she had collected thousands of United States dollars on his behalf, and alleged that six other Kenyan players had also each received 5,000 dollars from the bookmaker who had paid her husband.

Katherine, a schoolteacher, was summoned to attend as a witness, and testified that a bookmaker's agent had approached Odumbe to throw a match, and that six of the team were invited to be involved because he couldn't do it alone.

It was the close relationship between Odumbe and the bookmaker that Katherine claimed had destroyed their two-year marriage, and she revealed: 'I was very unhappy about their relationship because Maurice had said that this bookmaker was a gangster, and I did not want any friendship with that person because I disapproved of the match-fixing business.'

Katherine recalled one occasion when Odumbe sent her to collect 10,000 United States dollars from the bookmaker at a Nairobi hotel, and she told the hearing: 'He handed me a roll of American dollars. I was uncomfortable, and I expressed concern about all this money.

'I was worried that I was participating in something I did not know, but he said the money was for a pharmaceutical business. This is no business I am aware of. The only pharmaceutical was medicine for Maurice's mother, who was ill with hypertension.'

One of the main allegations against Odumbe was that he accepted 5,000 United States dollars to fix a match against Zimbabwe.

During his summing up, Justice Ebrahim said: 'Mr Odumbe has shown himself to be dishonest and devious in relation to the game of cricket. He has been callous and greedy.

'There is no suggestion that he was in dire need of money. The evidence, if anything, shows him living a lifestyle of pleasure and irresponsibility. Far from taking the dire warnings of the consequences of such behaviour, Mr Odumbe chose to thumb his nose at [the ICC] and continued his dishonest ways. He has exhibited no remorse. He has not indicated any intention to mend his ways. Indeed, he has chosen to cast doubts on the honesty and integrity of people who have despised his behaviour.'

Malcolm Speed, who was then Chief Executive of the ICC, accepted the Ebrahim Report with extreme concern, and said: 'It highlights that the risk of corruption remains very real, and everyone must be alert to the dangers.'

Odumbe was found guilty on 12 charges:

- associating with a known bookmaker
- admitting to receiving 5,000 United States dollars for fixing a match in Zimbabwe
- receiving 10,000 United States dollars in cash from a known bookmaker in June 2002
- receiving 8,000 United States dollars in cash from a known bookmaker on an unspecified date in 2002/03
- accepting that he received 5,000 United States dollars to fix a match
- accepting 6000 rupees (approximately 130 United States dollars) during a stay in an Indian hotel in May 2002
- accepting 317 rupees (approximately 7 United States dollars) when checking out of an hotel in November 2003
- accepting hotel accommodation in India in January 2002 from a known bookmaker and/or his associates
- accepting hotel accommodation in India in May 2002 from a known bookmaker and/or his associates
- accepting accommodation at the Sun-n-Sand Hotel in India in October 2002 from a known bookmaker and/or his associates
- accepting hotel accommodation in India in October 2002 from a known bookmaker and/or his associates
- accepting hotel accommodation in India in November 2002 from a known bookmaker and/or his associates.

Odumbe was a right-hand batsman and off-spin bowler who played in 63 One-day Internationals, struck a career best 207 against the Leeward Islands, and was Man of the Match in three consecutive World Cup tournaments.

When the five-year ban was imposed, Odumbe was 35 years old, so the suspension effectively ended his international career, and he promptly sold his three cars, left his mansion, and moved into a flat. Despite the vast volume of evidence, he argued that the verdict was 'ridiculous and unfair'.

CHAPTER SEVEN

RICHARDS AND BOTHAM
GO TO POT...

When I took a telephone call from a high-ranking official at Somerset County Cricket Club in September 1986, little did I imagine that I would soon be confronting West Indian batting genius Viv Richards with allegations of taking drugs before and after matches.

Neither did I expect that this desperate call would lead me to tawdry tales of sex and booze by the errant Richards and his prodigious Somerset team-mate Ian Botham, hailed by millions as the greatest all-rounder ever to pull on an England sweater. Both of them were genuine sporting icons and role models across the world, which made it all the more regrettable that they should be linked to sleaze and drug-taking.

The call came while I was a news and sports investigator on *The Sunday People*, a popular tabloid that lived up to its garish boast of being 'frank and fearless'. My caller said that he wanted me to meet him at his home in Taunton 'as soon as possible' to talk about a serious matter within Somerset Cricket Club that could not be discussed on the telephone.

We met within the next 24 hours, and he wasted no time in telling me that he wanted the public to know all about Richards and Botham, and that he had lined up an attractive young woman who was willing to tell all about her intimate times with both players.

I was told that everything was in place for me to get started on the story, and all I had to do was call at the River Island clothes shop in Taunton town centre and ask to speak to Bobby Thompson, a sales assistant there. 'She'll be expecting you,' the club official assured me. 'Take her to lunch, and let her talk. She has plenty to say. You'll be fascinated…'

It was exceptionally rare for a story of this size to drop in my lap, and be made so easy for me. I welcomed it and looked forward to meeting up with Bobby Thompson, who turned out to be an absolutely charming young lady, and solid as a rock.

We met for lunch at a top Taunton hotel where Bobby slowly, almost teasingly, opened her can of sleazy worms, and when we ran out of time – she had to be back in the shop at 2pm – she promised to complete her recollections in a longer meeting later in the week. She also offered to make important telephone calls to corroborate her allegations, and to provide photographs and written evidence to back up everything that she would tell me next time.

Bobby began by revealing that she and Richards were lovers for about two years and that she stuck with him even though he dropped her many times while having a fling with the latest groupie who came on the scene and was invited back to his apartment.

There was a lot of general chat about nightlife in sleepy Taunton at first, before Bobby moved into top gear and opened up to her torrid times with the giant West Indian cricketer. Bobby was a bright lady and had carefully prepared what she wanted to disclose. She calmly rested her cutlery at the edge of her plate and said: 'I'm going to start by telling you why Viv and I split up, and then I'll go into detail about the two years we were together…

'It was like this. A number of Somerset cricketers had gone to the

Gardner Arms one evening after a match here in Taunton, and I drove there in my Avenger, which was once used by the police. Viv was already there, and when I walked in and caught his eye, I expected a smile and a bit of a welcome, but he totally ignored me, and I was not happy. We were close friends, and he was out of order.

'And it didn't get any better as the evening drifted on, so I got drunk on vodka and orange juice, and went up to him in the bar, and I was very rude to him. He didn't like what I said to him, which was the truth. He got up and left and was angry with me. So I went out to my car and drove to the house that he shared with Ian Botham, and banged on the door, and shouted that I wanted a joint [cannabis].

'Viv came straight out, and handed me a joint, but he didn't say a word. He just closed the door behind him and went straight back inside where his latest one-night stand was waiting for him.'

Bobby was now in such a foul mood that she lost all control of her senses – and her car – and reversed into a lamppost with such force that she forgot all about the joint Viv had given her.

She recalled staggering back to Viv's front door, and telling him that she'd been in an accident, and she collapsed right in front of him. When she came round, she could see that the police had arrived, and that they were waiting to take a statement from her.

Digging deep into her memory, Bobby said: 'One of the officers asked Viv straight up if he knew who I was, and he amazingly replied: "I've never seen her before." I thought "You bastard!" I felt devastated. This guy had been my best friend for a long time, and here he was telling the police that he'd never seen me before. We had shared the same bed more times than I could remember, and now he didn't want to know me.'

A police officer searched through Bobby's car and soon found the joint under the front passenger seat, and asked her where it had come from. She recalled: 'I didn't want to tell them that it had come from Viv, so I covered up for him.

'I ended up in court and was fined for being drunk in charge of my car, and for possessing cannabis. I was a very innocent person caught up in a lot of unsavoury things. Other women were doing exactly the same in Taunton, and they were married, but I was not.'

Bobby was a clerical officer in the Motor Tax Department in Taunton when she first met Richards, who asked her if she could register his bright yellow Ford Capri with the personalised number plate 666S. Richards was apparently highly impressed by what he had seen in Bobby, and he asked his best friend, the local 'Mr Fixit', to ring her and say that Viv would like to take her out for a drink. She politely replied: 'If Viv wants to take me out, then he'd better ask me himself!'

Later that day Viv rang Bobby and said that he would be playing at Taunton the following weekend, and if she went to the ground, and said that she was meeting him there, she would be allowed to go in without having to pay.

Looking back at their early times together, Bobby said: 'What I soon noticed about Viv was that he didn't drink alcohol in public very often. He usually drank orange juice at the bar, though he did like an occasional glass of wine at home. After a few drinks, we usually went back to his flat, had a Chinese meal, and ended up in bed together.

'One night Viv and I were in bed when one of his old flames burst in. She could see we weren't having tea and biscuits, but she wouldn't budge. She had very long fingernails, and I got a bit scared that she might set on me and rip me apart. Viv hopped out of bed and took her into a room for a chat, and got rid of her. She eventually ended up marrying a well-known England cricketer.

'It was like a game of Monopoly with Viv. Some nights another girl would nip in before me, and I had to wait my turn.'

As well as their nights of passion in Richards' apartment, Bobby recalled the wild parties in rooms above the souvenir shop at the Taunton cricket ground. She said: 'There were three or four rooms that had beds or mattresses, and there were always plenty of girls around. They were great parties. There was lots of cannabis, and little blue pills were passed around, but I never touched them, and never found out what they were.

'One of Ian Botham's friends would come up from Yeovil and prance around in the nude. We called him Chopper. Viv would always leave early because he preferred his sex in private at home.'

Bobby was keen to stress that Richards was not married at the time, and that he took full advantage to waltz off with any girl willing to spend time in private with him, and frequently went into matches completely shattered after a night of non-stop sex.

Because cannabis was so readily available, Bobby was sure that Richards managed to stay alert during a whole day of playing cricket thanks to a 'fix' that he took first thing in the morning. She said: 'Viv smoked pot almost every time we were together. He didn't roll his own, but they were always perfectly rolled when he brought them out. Some mornings he would smoke pot when we got up after a hard night, and before he went off to play cricket.

'He never ate breakfast in all the time I knew him. All he had before he left home was a cup of coffee, and maybe a joint. I was convinced it acted as a stimulant, and that it kept him awake and made everything seem sharper to him.

'When Viv smoked cannabis it left him with a glassy look. His eyes went bright and his pupils got bigger. When I smoked it with Viv, it left me high as a kite, like being drunk, only it didn't cause me to stagger around. I felt in control of everything, and my senses were sharper. I imagine it did the same for Viv.'

Bobby also clearly remembered Viv's best mate Botham being at the sex-and-pot parties, and the Somerset club official who brought in the girls. Botham was banned for a number of months after testing positive for cannabis, and Richards was hauled in front of the Test and County Cricket Board's disciplinary committee to explain why he refused a random drug test after a match between

Somerset and Gloucestershire. He explained that it was because he wasn't satisfied that it was random, and the case was dropped.

Bobby Thompson also alleged that some Somerset officials knew of Richards' drug-taking, but the club's Chief Executive, Tony Brown, denied any cover-up, and countered: 'You can say we've been loyal and supportive.' And of the drug test that Viv refused, Brown added: 'We thought he should have taken it, but we decided to stand by him.'

Bobby admitted that she was fascinated by Richards' impressive physique, and that he too was proud of it, and extremely vain. She said: 'Viv was obsessed with his body. He took a special protein to help him stay in shape, and he spent hours in the bathroom, splashing on his favourite after-shave.

'Viv was not easy to get to know. I could never really understand what he was thinking, feeling, or even saying at times. But when it came to sex, everything was much clearer. You couldn't say it was making love, it was more of a physical encounter. I was the one who did all the leaping around, and he called me his "Livewire".

'Viv would drop me off in the morning and go straight to the cricket ground, having had no sleep worth talking about. I was shattered. I wouldn't have had enough energy for 30 minutes of cricket, let alone be on the field all day like Viv had to be. It amazed me how he kept going.'

My next duty, after being given all these highly personal details by Bobby, was to find Richards so that he could have the chance to respond, and I caught up with him at the National Stadium in Karachi on the last day of a Test match against Pakistan.

As my editor thought nothing of sending me half-way round the world to question him, a British Airways ticket was reserved at Heathrow, and I was in the air in 24 hours. There was no time to collect Pakistan currency, or for the usual protective medical injections, so, determined not to eat or drink anything to risk infection, I squeezed five Mars bars and six cans of Coca Cola into a shoulder bag and took off. Though I stayed at a top European hotel, only the Mars bars and the Coca Cola passed my lips.

Immediately play had ended for the day, I hurriedly followed the players to the pavilion, where I knocked on the West Indian dressing-room door. Tour manager Jackie Hendricks, a former West Indies wicketkeeper, came out and when I told him that I was a journalist from London, who had flown out to talk to Viv Richards regarding a serious personal matter, he replied: 'I don't care if you've flown from the moon, there's no way you'll be speaking to Mr Richards!'

He turned sharply, and was about to slam the door behind him, when I managed to blurt out: 'Well, do me a favour, Mr Hendricks, just tell Mr Richards that a London journalist is outside who would like to talk to him about his relationship with Bobby Thompson, who has spoken to him about it. I think he should know that...' Hendricks returned in record time, sprinting faster than Linford Christie, and politely opened the door and said: 'You can come in. Mr Richards will talk to you...'

Richards greeted me with a smile and a solid handshake and led me through the West Indies dressing room to a quiet area close to where the players were heading for their after-match shower.

'Right,' he said, 'what's this all about?'

I related all that Bobby Thompson had said about their lives together, particularly about their sex and cannabis, and the wild parties above the souvenir shop. I left nothing out. And I tape-recorded every word.

He was totally relaxed at first and confirmed that he and Bobby had had a steamy affair during his bachelor days, and with a chuckle in his voice said: 'I did all the things a normal bloke would do. But I believe anyone who takes drugs to compete is evil. I am always clean when I play. There are evil forces out there. I can see them. I can see them in my sleep sometimes.

'Players and committee men. I'm going to come right out and

expose the whole scene. I couldn't care two f***s. I've given my heart. Given my all. People used to say "Hip, hip, hooray, it's Viv Richards," but now I'm supposed to be the worst person in the world.

'When I get time, I'm going to look into some things. Players are jealous. It's sick. I'm going to get nasty with a few people soon. One thing I've learned is to have respect for human beings, but if human beings don't have respect for me, I'm going to do the same.'

We chatted for around 50 minutes, and when I walked away I noticed that every other West Indian player had showered and changed, and was sitting in the team coach waiting for Viv to join them, but he was still in his match whites and showing no sign of speeding up in a totally deserted dressing room. Richards later admitted 'experimenting' with smoking marijuana, saying that no one ever forced him to try it, and that he did it of his own free will. He is now happily married to Miriam, and they have two children. He also fathered a daughter in a brief affair with an Indian actress.

The Somerset official who steered me to Bobby Thompson was delighted to see the back of Richards and Botham.

Richards' ten years with club ended when he and fellow West Indian, Joel Garner, were told that their contracts would not be renewed, and Botham promptly resigned as a gesture of support for his two team-mates.

Brian Langford, the club's cricket chairman, a former captain and a Somerset player for 21 years, said: 'Botham is not as popular in Somerset as he is nationwide. All talk of people loving him down here is a myth.' Langford had no compunction in branding Botham a bully, and continued: 'He's not a club man. He's interested in one person only – Ian Botham!

'He and Richards should have been lifting our spirits, encouraging our young players, giving them the benefit of their experience, building up team spirit. But they're not a bit of good in that respect. We have young players who have been offered contracts for next season, but they won't sign until they know whether Richards and Botham will still be here. Both of them are fine strikers of the ball, but the club doesn't win anything. We've become a laughing stock with our results.

'Richards is a changed person. He's hostile to the young players. He's no help to them at all. He keeps blaming the young players. He tells them that they are no good, and that they shouldn't be playing first-class cricket. Our youngsters are delighted to see the back of them, especially Botham.'

One Somerset committeeman recalled an incident when a young bowler was trying his hardest in a match, and Botham shouted to Richards: 'Have you ever seen such rubbish as this?' Still seething, the committeeman fumed: 'And Botham was captain! It was said loudly enough so that all the players could hear it, and people all around the ground could hear it.

'There was another time when a 17-year-old lad was batting in the nets and every ball Botham bowled at him was up around his ears. Then when the lad went on to bowl, Botham took an almighty slog at every ball, trying desperately hard to hit him out of sight. Botham was a bully.

'The committee has taken a lot of stick [over Richards and Botham leaving the club] and it's time we spoke up. Botham conned the Australians in 1985. He bowled long-hop after long-hop, and the Australians kept playing stupid shots, and got themselves out.'

Having completed a sustained blast against Botham, the committeeman then switched to a full-blooded attack on Richards, and concluded: 'It seems captaining the West Indies has gone to his head. And he's got at our young players by saying: "I know 25 who are better than you back in Antigua." That's a terrible thing to say to young players…'

Maybe it was appropriate that Bobby Thompson should have the last word on the Somerset crisis, and holding nothing back, she insisted: 'It's the best decision ever made by a cricket club. Now that he [Richards] has left, Somerset will have a cricket team, not a circus.'

Richards disclosed in detail in his autobiography *Hitting Across the Line* the pain and disappointment he felt when some Somerset officials turned against him. He said: 'In the later years my concentration did suffer a bit. But certain people were openly accusing me of cricketing apathy, and that was like a red rag to a bull to me.

'There were many awful, and totally unjustifiable, things said… I could feel a certain undercurrent of tension without fully understanding what it meant. Because I was concentrating on my cricket, I never really saw some of the things that were going on, the scheming of the people who wanted Viv Richards out of the club.

'There were hints. People would sneak bits of information out of committee meetings, which seemed to signify that the end was in sight for me, and for Joel [Garner], but I did not take too much notice. There was a lot of talk about Viv Richards and Joel Garner being arrogant personalities and a disruptive influence on the team. Someone put the notion around that I was a bad influence on Ian Botham. How ridiculous!

'As far as I can understand it, the club committee thought we were attracting the wrong sort of media coverage. Joel and I were seen as the big bad men. Some of the committee thought that by getting rid of Joel and me they would purify the club. Then there was the repeated whisper that I was not trying. That was below the belt.

'The sacking was sudden… After 11 years' service I was told I was not wanted. To be kicked out in that way was deeply hurtful. One good thing that came out of the whole affair was the support of Ian Botham, who rang me and said: "Viv, I'm going to resign."'

Richards spent a year with Rushton in the Lancashire League after being fired by Somerset, and returned to county cricket with Glamorgan, helping them to win the AXA Sunday League. Several years later Somerset Cricket Club named a set of entrance gates and a grandstand after Richards, so someone, somewhere in the West Country had plainly forgiven him.

Famous players from at least three countries have consumed drugs that were smuggled across international borders, and into cricket grounds, incredibly concealed in a star's batting gloves. England, Pakistan and West Indian cricketers whom the public admired and loved to see perform were secretly involved in a cannabis craze in the late Eighties and Nineties. Ample supplies were cleverly hidden in the 'sausage' fingers of the doctored gloves.

Pakistan batsman Qasim Omar admitted to carrying the gloves after a senior international player 'exploited his youthful innocence' and promised him rewards.

Omar said he was approached in his hotel room in Melbourne where the Pakistan team was staying while in Australia for a series of matches involving four countries.

He was specially chosen because he was far less known than the large number of stars playing in the tournament, so he stood less chance of being searched at airports and checkpoints.

As time went on, the naïve Omar gradually lost his nerve and feared that he would be caught and convicted as an international drugs courier, so he handed the gloves back. Omar eventually named this player to the Pakistan Cricket Board, as well as naming other players who went to his room for their 'fix'.

When I caught up with Omar and asked him about this astonishing ruse, he said: 'At first I thought I was dreaming. He pulled the gloves from a bag and put them on a table in my room. They were green and white. The sausage type... He showed me where the stitching had been undone and the padding taken out to make room for cannabis, and how the fingers had been taped up again to make everything look normal. This player, a very big name, said he smoked cannabis quite a lot, but only for pleasure and for sex. He thought it improved his stamina.'

Omar recalled the evening when he smoked his first joint in his hotel room with this star player, and said: 'He had started to laugh very loudly at nothing at all. Then he pulled himself together and asked me if I'd ever smoked the stuff. I said that I hadn't and that I was afraid of becoming hooked, but he kept on at me, and I took a few drags but didn't feel any different, and I gave it back to him.

'After a while he wasn't speaking properly and I found it hard to understand what he was saying because he'd become very slow and slurred. One minute he was talking about cricket, then it was girls, which was a favourite subject with him, then it was business. Everything was jumbled up.'

Omar continued to carry the drugs loyally and provided the cannabis as instructed until he started to twitch at the thought of being apprehended and ending up with a criminal record. He said: 'I became scared. He hinted one day that he could say the gloves were not his if someone found out what we were doing, and this frightened me, because he was a very big name and I was new on the scene, so people in authority would more likely believe him than believe me, so I handed them back to him.'

Very soon afterwards Omar was propositioned by one of the world's greatest batsmen to carry consignments of heroin to contacts in America and Europe. Omar named this player, and said: 'He tried to get me involved with talk of how much money I could earn, and how easy it would be.

'When I said it was risky, he said there was always a risk in big business. He said that I'd become very rich if I delivered heroin for him, but I turned him down. I'd worried enough carrying the cannabis, and I wanted to wash my hands altogether of being involved in drugs.'

To support his explosive allegations, Omar wrote to Zulfiqar

Ahmed, then secretary of the Pakistan Cricket Board, and named the drug-taking players. Ahmed said he was 'shocked' by the names and launched an internal investigation, but the players were huge in world cricket, so it was probably no surprise that the inquiry petered out and no action was taken.

Incredibly, many big names in Test cricket have hoodwinked specially trained Revenue and Customs sniffer dogs with their colossal skills at smuggling drugs. Large quantities of cocaine, heroin and cannabis have passed through Britain's major airports literally under the noses of the world's sharpest canine experts that would normally identify drugs in less than a minute.

In most cases the drugs were ingeniously concealed in cricket balls and bat handles, and meticulously assembled in a small factory in a village near Peshawar in Northern Pakistan. Customs officials were suspicious that vast importations were entering the UK, and carried out covert operations to track down the smugglers, but found it impossible to pick out the drug-filled bats and balls because the assemblers, quite frankly, were too smart for them.

One highly successful Pakistan cricketer admitted that he had been propositioned to carry drugs through Heathrow and Gatwick, and that similar requests had been made for him to smuggle them into Australia, New Zealand and South Africa.

This popular international batsman explained that cricket balls were being sliced open at the scam, and that the little cork ball that nestled in the middle was being taken out and replaced by a packet of cocaine, heroin or cannabis. Superglue was then used to stick the ball together again, with the assemblers carefully ensuring that there was not the slightest scratch to arouse suspicion. This lucrative trick brought a whole new meaning to ball tampering!

Concealing drugs in cricket bats was just as effective. Channels were delicately cut below the rubber strips in the handle – commonly known as the 'spring' – so that the handle was cleverly adapted to carry the drugs. Customs officers conceded that their brilliant sniffer dogs stood no chance against either of these master strokes.

A senior Customs officer admitted: 'Millions of articles arrive at Heathrow and Gatwick, and we can't destroy every importation. It's a bit hit-and-miss unless we have something specific to work on. Having names makes our job so much easier.'

Cricket's drug smugglers were shocked and terrified when news broke that a bag of heroin had burst inside a young club player on a mission to Bombay, and that he was fighting for his life in a Karachi hospital. The incident was so horrific that the authorities decided on a total news blackout; the player was never named and no details were ever released about whether he pulled through or died from an accidental overdose.

Lord Condon revealed in a comprehensive report on investigations carried out by his Anti-corruption Unit that allegations had been made in various parts of the cricket world that players past and present had used unlawful drugs to enhance their performance, and for recreational purposes. The ACU had also received allegations of baggage and equipment being used to move drugs by international teams on tours.

CHAPTER EIGHT

SWEATY ATHERTON HAS DUST ON HIS HANDS

E ngland captain Michael Atherton was seen taking dirt from his pocket during a Test match and was fined £2,000. A sharp-eyed television cameraman caught him in the act during the First Test between England and South Africa at Lord's in 1994, and film footage was available for match officials to study as evidence. There was instant suspicion that Atherton had foolishly resorted to tampering with the ball for his bowlers to gain an advantage, a curse that was bedevilling international cricket at that time.

To change the condition of the ball, Atherton would have needed to rub the dirt on one side in order to rough it up, while also ensuring that the opposite side remained shiny. Bowlers and fielders usually achieved a bright shine by rubbing the ball up and down their thighs, often leaving a bright red line down their sparkling white trousers. All pace bowlers dearly hope that once the ball is in this acutely balanced state of being 'rough and shiny' it will swing sharply – and cause big problems for perplexed batsmen.

On this particular remarkable occasion, Atherton had one of the world's best exponents of swing bowling right there at his disposal in Darren Gough, and the cynics immediately suspected that the ball was being surreptitiously worked on for the exuberant Yorkshireman to gain an unfair advantage.

Atherton had been captain for just 12 months, and several commentators initially felt that he had been naïve, rather than having succumbed to a moment of blatant cheating. Highly regarded English umpire Dickie Bird and Australian Steve Randell were on duty that day, and they checked the ball at the end of virtually every over to be sure that there was no skulduggery taking place behind their backs that was too subtle for them to spot.

Atherton was tipped off a few overs before tea that a ball-tampering issue was being discussed at the highest level, and that he had to go straight to the dressing room once he had left the field. England's coach Keith Fletcher, along with chairman of selectors Ray Illingworth, were already there, and Atherton was given the disturbing news that television cameras had picked up on him taking dirt from his trouser pocket.

Atherton left the room seemingly satisfied that Fletcher and Illingworth had accepted his explanation that he had broken no rules, and that the matter was closed, so he was understandably shocked on returning to the pavilion at the end of the day's play to be told that match referee Peter Burge, a formidable Australian, wanted to speak to him and to Fletcher.

As it was obvious why he was being called in again, Atherton took his match trousers with him, hardly regarding it as incriminating evidence. Bird and Randell were also present, as well as Mervyn Kitchen, the third umpire, and Alan Curtis, the public-address announcer who operated the video.

Burge, who played in 72 Tests for Australia as a brutal middle-order batsman, ran the television footage and asked Bird and Randell whether the condition of the ball had changed. They both said 'no' and were told that they were no longer needed.

Sometime later Atherton revealed that Burge had asked him three direct questions: Did he have an explanation for what he did? Did he have resin in his pocket? Did he have any other artificial substance in his pocket? According to Atherton, in answer to Burge's first question he said that he was 'drying my sweaty hands', and to the second and third questions, he replied 'no'.

It never became clear whether 'dust' was considered an artificial substance, or whether the word was ever used in this private meeting with Burge. As for resin, it was well known that certain countries had used it in the quarter seam of a cricket ball to make one side heavier, which was yet another illegal means of helping to make it swing.

Atherton was then asked to leave the room for a short time before Burge recalled him and told him that no further action would be taken. But this was far from being the end of the matter – or the Burge/Atherton 'dust-up' – and word spread fast around Lord's next morning that Burge was livid and had stated that he would have banned Atherton for two matches if he had known about the dust when they met. Burge, it seemed, had not been informed of Atherton's 'economy with the truth' until late the previous evening.

Atherton was now effectively being accused of lying to Burge, or at least deliberately deceiving him, when he replied 'no' when asked if he had anything in his pockets, but Atherton hit back by claiming that he believed Burge was referring to substances like resin or lip salve.

Any length of suspension would almost certainly have cost Atherton the captaincy, yet he still had to provide a feasible explanation in a statement that Burge would accept before he was entirely off the hook, which he did.

Atherton referred to his statement in his autobiography, although he carefully did not reveal all that he said in it, and limited it to: '… A statement is found which is finally acceptable to him [the match referee] on the grounds that I get a heavy fine. I find some of the statement objectionable, especially the apology to South Africa.'

Atherton was subsequently fined £2,000 after Illingworth stepped in and, according to Atherton, imposed the penalty on two counts of improper conduct – lying to Burge, and for 'actions with the ball' – although Illingworth, apparently, still thought that his captain had done nothing wrong.

Atherton's fine followed a dreadful performance by England, who lost the match with a day to spare. Set 456 to win, England were dismissed for a paltry 99, their lowest score at Lord's for a century, and it was also their worst defeat to South Africa in 106 years of Test cricket between the countries.

There was general surprise that Atherton survived as skipper, especially as the media had set about him like a pack of hungry greyhounds tearing at a dummy hare. All through a torrid press conference he gave the impression of dodging bullets, as his head swung wildly from side to side, as a fusillade of hostile questions flew in from every direction.

Confronting the media was never high on Atherton's list of favourite duties, and he came close to being sued for defamation after he insulted a journalist when he snapped: 'Can someone get this buffoon out of here?'

Atherton captained England a record 52 times, although he won only 13 Tests and suffered 19 defeats, and beating New Zealand 2-0 was his only overseas success. His disappointing reign was rather humanely ended after England were trounced 3-1 by the West Indies, a series remembered mainly for Brian Lara's world record 375 in Antigua.

For all his captaincy calamities – not least referring to sections of the media as the 'gutter press' – Atherton was a supremely determined and disciplined opening batsman who could infuriate fast bowlers by disdainfully shrugging his shoulders as he watched the ball fly past his face at speeds of up to 90 miles an hour.

To his enormous credit, Atherton also scored stacks of runs and spent many hours at the crease when crippled with a chronic degenerative back condition that ended his career after the 2001 Ashes.

England's two precocious quick bowlers, James Anderson and Stuart Broad, were accused of tampering with the ball on the third day of the Third Test against South Africa in Cape Town in January 2010. Television cameras had zoomed in and appeared to show Anderson picking at the rough side of the ball, and Broad standing on it and rubbing it in the ground with his spikes.

South Africa's management believed that both incidents could be a deliberate attempt to damage the ball to make it 'reverse' swing, which England's talented pace duo excelled at when conditions were right for them.

As soon as play ended for the day, South Africa 'made their concerns known' to match referee Roshan Mahanama, and a spokesman confirmed: 'We have raised our concerns with the match referee over the condition of the ball, and we have left it to him to decide whether action is necessary. We will not be saying anything more about this because of International Cricket Council regulations.'

The scoreboard showed South Africa at 312-2, already a massive 330 ahead of England with two days still left to play. Hard-hitting captain Graeme Smith was 162 not out. Broad insisted that he was just being lazy because of the heat: it was 40 degrees Celsius.

England team manager Andy Flower stressed that he had seen nothing sinister in what Broad and Anderson had done, and claimed to be puzzled that no one from the South African management had made him aware of the allegations, or anyone else in his dressing room or on his support staff.

Flower said: 'Over the years we have seen a lot of tall fast bowlers stop the ball with their boot. I don't see anything sinister in this at all. It will be up to the officials to decide whether we have a case to answer.'

Flower then quite facetiously added: 'This amazing amount of reverse swing gained by Stuart Broad standing on the ball obviously hasn't worked very well. As far as I'm concerned, our bowlers have gone about their business very honestly today. They have toiled hard in the heat while South Africa's batsmen have played extremely well.' Match referee Mahanama confirmed that he had received an 'unofficial approach from South Africa, but nothing formal'.

Former England captain Nasser Hussain, who became a forthright television commentator after he retired from the game, said: 'Stuart Broad and James Anderson were wrong to behave in the manner they did, and I've no doubt that if a player from another country did the same thing we'd have said they were cheating.' Hussain did not divulge whether he had 'another' specific country in mind.

South Africa thought hard before deciding not to bring charges against Broad or Anderson, and the International Cricket Council later confirmed that the deadline had passed, and that the matter was closed.

International cricket has been awash with every imaginable scam since the late 1980s, and South Africa can fairly boast that it tried to use what was probably the most creative of them all when captain Hansie Cronje brazenly walked onto the field in a World Cup contest against India wearing an ear-piece to take instructions from coach Bob Woolmer. India complained to the umpires immediately they spotted the tiny contraption, and match referee Talat Ali ordered Cronje to remove it without delay.

The ICC was outraged and fired a brusque message to those in charge of cricket in South Africa: 'The World Cup is not the event to experiment with new devices without first seeking permission from the ICC.'

Anxious Woolmer responded swiftly to diffuse the row, and said: 'If I have upset anyone, I apologise. I was just trying to be innovative. We probably should have asked permission from the ICC, and I suppose it was a little naïve of me not to do that. It is nothing more than a two-way radio which allows me to talk to the players. All we're trying to do is give the players advice and help them more quickly, rather than send on someone with gloves, or whatever, to pass on the same information.'

South Africa won the match by four wickets, though it was impossible to know whether Woolmer's gadget had played any worthwhile part in the victory. And as far as cricket at large was concerned, that was the last anyone saw of this tiny piece of enterprise, although it would be foolish to assume that it has gone from the game for ever, as gimmicks and strokes have become more and more prevalent while cheating and corruption have become more and more sophisticated.

One of the most bizarre on-field 'tampering' incidents featured Pakistan's controversial stand-in captain Shahid Afridi, who was twice caught biting the ball to readjust the seam. Film footage proved beyond doubt that Afridi's sharp teeth had sunk into the seam during a match against Australia in Perth during a One-day series, which Australia went on to win 5-0.

Once the attention of both umpires was drawn to Afridi's extraordinary appetite, they inspected the ball and noted that there was clear evidence to show that it had been illegally altered, and promptly replaced it. Afridi, who was deputising as captain for Mohammad Yousuf, pathetically tried to claim that he was attempting to smell the ball, but this absurd excuse was brushed aside and he was banned for two Twenty/20 international matches.

On-field umpires Asoka de Silva and Paul Reiffel, plus third umpire Rod Tucker and fourth official Mick Martell, brought the charge against Afridi. Match referee Ranjan Madugalle imposed the maximum punishment allowed under the code, explaining that he reminded Afridi of his 'responsibilities as a national captain, which is to ensure that the match is played according to the laws of the game, and in the spirit in which it is intended to be played'.

Afridi apologised to Madugalle, saying that he 'regretted his actions'. In a subsequent public statement, Afridi admitted that he had tampered with the ball, adding: 'I shouldn't have done it, but it just happened. I was trying to help my bowlers, and win a match. There is no team in the world that doesn't tamper with the ball, but my method was wrong, and I'm embarrassed.'

The International Cricket Council confirmed that Afridi had received two suspension points for an offence that related to 'changing the condition of the ball in breach of law 42.3 of the Laws of Cricket'.

Two suspension points can cause a player to be banned for either one Test match or two One-day Internationals, or two Twenty/20 internationals. Pakistan's coach Intikhab Alam called the incident 'unacceptable' and stressed that 'a captain should be above everything'.

With so much cheating sweeping through modern-day international cricket, many officials and supporters are not particularly surprised when certain players are caught trying to gain an illegal advantage. 'Oh, it's him... Not surprised, are you?' comes the casual reaction.

But there was no such indifferent shrug of the shoulders when India's phenomenal superstar Sachin Tendulkar – probably the greatest batsman the world has ever seen – was banned and fined for ball-tampering. Again it was the all-seeing television camera that caught Tendulkar appearing to use his fingernails to interfere with the seam of the ball during a Test match against South Africa in Port Elizabeth in November 2001.

Match referee Mike Denness issued Tendulkar with a suspended one Test ban and fined him 75 per cent of his match fee. When later pressed by a determined and glamorous television interviewer to explain why he did it, Tendulkar shuffled nervously in his seat and desperately tried to avoid answering the question.

But the tenacious young woman showed scant regard for his universal fame, refusing to back off and continuing to press him on the question. In his great career, Tendulkar had tamed every bowler in the world, but he was now suddenly in a spin and finding it difficult to cope. His grim expression told it all, as he desperately tried a verbal straight bat: 'It's not something I want to talk about…'

The taunting interviewer calmly went straight back at him with yet another tricky top-spinner question. Pressure on Tendulkar was enormous, but to his admirable credit he never once became aggressive, flippant, rude or arrogant. He was dazzled in the headlights all right, and he finally gave up the fight, and the interviewer's persistence paid off.

She captured what so many of the world's best bowlers had longed to achieve – the wicket of the great Tendulkar, who meekly padded up in the end, and she bowled him over with a wry smile and a cute nod…

She began by asking him: 'You were also embroiled in a scandal where referee Mike Denness accused you of ball-tampering. How did you personally deal with it?

Tendulkar: 'I think I'll just leave that…'

Interviewer: 'You won't answer that?'

Tendulkar: 'No. I don't think so. I don't need to get into all those controversial things.'

Interviewer: 'Even if the viewers are going to want to know your thoughts on it, and how you dealt with it?'

Tendulkar: 'Well, I mean, all those things were a bit unfortunate, but it happens all over the world. It's not that it's only happening in today's cricket. It happened earlier. There were plenty of controversies earlier, as well, but now there is much more media attention.'

Having succeeded in getting Tendulkar to open up, the skilful interviewer then allowed him to relax and talk casually about his career achievements, which he greatly welcomed and recalled them with relish.

Tendulkar made no attempt during the grilling to deny that he had tampered with the ball, even though the ICC had wheeled out its well-oiled damage-limitation machine and claimed that: 'Tendulkar had not been found guilty of tampering with the ball, but had been punished for removing grass from the ball, and not telling the umpires.'

In truth, it seemed nothing more than a pathetic attempt to placate the Board of Control for Cricket in India, especially as the match referee had not confirmed what was now being claimed, and there was no sign of the ball as supportive evidence.

Swashbuckling Virender Sehwag, who ironically opened the batting with Tendulkar for India, was also banned for one match during the same Test for 'excessive appealing', a common tactic used by close-in fielders to try to deceive umpires into thinking that a catch has been legally taken when the player knows full well that it has not struck the bat at all.

Yet another top Indian batsman and vice-captain, Rahul Dravid, was in trouble when television film footage appeared to show him intentionally applying a lozenge to the shiny side of a white ball during a 24-run victory over Zimbabwe in a One-day Test. West Indian giant Clive Lloyd, a prolific run-scorer in a momentous playing career in the Seventies, was on duty as the International Cricket Council's match referee, and he fined Dravid 50 per cent of his fee for ball-tampering.

Dravid, who had earlier top scored with 84 in India's total of

255-6, protested that he had done nothing wrong, and he was fully supported by his captain, Sourav Ganguly, and coach John Wright, the former high-scoring New Zealand opening batsman. Both argued that Dravid had been the victim of a complete misunderstanding and that the sweet had merely fallen from his mouth onto the ball in a straightforward accident.

But Lloyd refused to budge, which was completely reminiscent of his stubborn batting days, and he countered: 'It couldn't have been accidental because he's been fined. It was shown that he was applying a substance to the ball. I looked at the film, and it was conclusive. The rules are there. You can only [legally] apply saliva and sweat to the ball. India can say that it was accidental, but the point is, the footage shows that something has been applied to the ball, and the rules state you are not allowed to do it. Once the charge is brought you have to show the evidence. Something was being applied to the ball quite obviously, and he must have known it. It's quite conclusive on film.'

Wright continued to claim that it was an innocent mistake, and eagerly tried to explain that the players had eaten energy sweets during the drinks break, and that Dravid was shining the ball with saliva at the same time as he was eating a sweet. In full cry, Wright protested: 'He didn't realise there was a problem until he looked down and saw a yellow stain on the ball, and he tried to wipe it off. I've worked with Rahul Dravid for four years, and he's what cricket's all about. He's a credit to the game. We're not into that sort of thing. He is upset about it because he's a man of integrity. He respects the sport and its laws.'

A senior unnamed Indian cricket official agreed with Wright, and said: 'He wasn't trying to change the condition of the ball with a jelly baby. It's a sweet...' Lloyd would not be placated, and again responded: 'We could have fined him 50 per cent or 100 per cent of his match fees, a Test, or two One-day Internationals, but we took into account his past [unblemished] record.'

Even Australia's normally non-controversial captain Ricky Ponting joined in, saying: 'It's an ICC issue which has been dealt with by the match referee. It's a different one, a strange one. It's certainly something we are very aware of. A lot of these issues have come up over the past couple of years. Different players from different countries have been suspended, and fined, and things… I don't think you'll see us doing anything like that.'

Pakistan's exceptional all-rounder Imran Khan, who played in the English championship for Sussex, finally admitted in the comfort of retirement – when he faced no threat of punishment – that he had scratched the ball and lifted the seam on numerous occasions during matches. He confessed that when he failed to persuade the ball to swing in a match against Hampshire, he asked the 12th man to bring a metal bottle-top onto the field, and the ball swung instantly. Sussex won the match, and the umpires saw nothing.

After Pakistan had routed New Zealand with sharp reverse swing in their first two Tests in 1990, little-known seam bowler Chris Pringle decided to take things into his own hands literally – and illegally! On the first morning of the Final Test in Faisalabad he set about doing what he had learned while experimenting in the nets. He cut an old bottle-top into quarters and covered the serrated edge with tape, making certain to leave a sharp point exposed.

During the first drinks interval, the umpires decided that they did not want to examine the ball and, with Pakistan making smooth progress, Pringle covertly began to scratch the ball with his masked bottle-top. Pakistan crashed from 32-0 to 102 all out, and Pringle finished with his best Test figures of 7-52 and an impressive match analysis of 11-52. As he left the stadium after the first day's play, a local dignitary apparently tapped him on the shoulder and whispered: 'It's fair now. Both teams are cheating!' Pakistan won by 65 runs to complete a 3-0 series whitewash.

Pringle represented New Zealand in 14 Tests and 64 One-day

Internationals. He played in the Bradford League in England for a short time, and also in Holland before his career was cut short by an ankle injury.

Both Pakistan pace bowlers Waqar Younis and Azhar Mahmood were reprimanded by match referee John Reid for altering the condition of the ball against South Africa in the Singer Triangular Series. Younis was banned for one match and fined 50 per cent of his match fee, while Mahmood was fined 30 per cent of his match fee. In addition, Moin Khan was severely reprimanded for 'allowing the spirit of the game to be impaired'.

John Reid regarded the incident as 'very serious', especially as he had personally warned Younis and the Pakistan team management after 'problems' during a previous match in the series, which explained why Younis was punished more severely. Reid turned his attention to the damaged ball after television cameras focused on both bowlers just after it had been changed in the 35th over, and Younis could be seen clearly scratching its surface.

In Pakistan's previous match against Sri Lanka, umpires Steve Bucknor and Peter Manuel had shown John Reid the ball after the television producer had provided similar film footage. On that occasion, Younis not only scratched the ball but lifted the quarter seam as well. Both Younis and Wasim Akram subsequently obtained considerable reverse swing, though it was to no avail, as Sri Lanka's star batsmen Marvan Atapattu and Sanath Jayasuriya powered to a record-breaking opening partnership.

With its tight-lipped secrecy, profound intrigue and incomparable subterfuge, the One-day Test at Lord's in August 1992 would have attracted critical acclaim as a riveting whodunnit on the West End stage. Dramatic plots and subplots behind closed doors in the world famous pavilion surpassed all that took place out in the middle.

England were leading Pakistan 3-0 in the series, and rain had caused the fourth match to continue into the second morning.

Having been set 205 to win, England were precariously placed at 140-5 at lunch, and a short time later umpires Ken Palmer and John Hampshire – after consulting with the third umpire, Don Oslear – ordered that the ball should be changed under Law 42, which dealt with the condition of a cricket ball during a match.

Suddenly, with their fingers wrapped around the replacement ball, Pakistan's lethal pace duo of Waqar Younis and Wasim Akram quickly ripped through England's middle and lower order, with their last four wickets crashing for just ten runs, and Pakistan joyfully won the match with four runs to spare.

Then followed the most intriguing inquiry that produced more twist and turns, and ludicrous red herrings, than an Agatha Christie novel. The genesis of the 'plot' is spelt out in an account by Oslear: 'The umpires entered the umpires' dressing room at Lord's, and showed me the ball with its badly gouged surface. They asked me to fetch the international referee, Deryck Murray.

'To begin with, Murray agreed that the cover of the ball appeared to have been split, possibly with a thumbnail, possibly with some instrument. Intikhab Alam, the Pakistan team manager, was summoned, and he made no objection when the umpires told him they were going to change the ball. I next showed it to Alan Smith, the TCCB's Chief Executive, who expressed horror at its state.' The TCCB (Test and County Cricket Board) was the governing body at the time before it was renamed the England and Wales Cricket Board (ECB).

Oslear's account continued: 'Gradually the ramifications of the incident began to dawn on the officials and the first step in the attempt to disguise the truth came when it was suggested that the media should be informed that the ball had been changed because it had gone out of shape. I made it clear, on behalf of my colleagues, who by this time had returned to the middle, that I could not accept that, and said it would be better in the long run if the truth were told.

'By now, I was aware that a lot of pressure was being exerted on the top officials. I believed some of it was at the highest diplomatic level, since to say that Pakistan had broken the rules would undoubtedly lead to their being called cheats in the press, and no one wanted to contemplate what the consequences might be.'

For whatever reason, the TCCB decided to admit that the ball had, indeed, been changed – but not to disclose why! Such a strange decision predictably exacerbated an already confused and suspicious situation, and precipitated inevitable backlash from an incredulous media.

Curiosity and concern grew even greater when no one from the England camp attended the post-match press conference, and neither the TCCB nor the ICC wished to be represented. When challenged, Waqar snapped: 'I don't care what anyone thinks… the new ball swung more, anyway. Every time we win, people start to say these things. We won fair and square.'

Pakistan's tour manager Khalid Mahmood made the sole official statement and claimed: 'An impression has been created in certain sections of the press that the change of ball was due to tampering by the fielding side. It is clarified that such insinuations are a distortion of the facts, and are totally unfounded, and speculative in nature. Such press stories represent a false and scurrilous attack on the integrity, conduct and reputation of the Pakistan cricket team, which is unjustifiable.'

Mahmood even claimed later that Pakistan had twice asked for the ball to be replaced before lunch, as it had gone out of shape. Oslear wrote a detailed report of the entire incident and submitted it to the appropriate authorities. Sir Colin Cowdrey, the then esteemed Chairman of the ICC, telephoned Oslear a few days later and reminded him that his terms of contract totally prevented him from disclosing what had taken place.

Oslear finally stated: 'The guardians of the game should stand for honesty of purpose and truth on and off the field, but given the unwillingness to tackle openly the many problems cricket faces, one can only question the probity of some of those paid servants whose only answer seems to be to sweep it all under the carpet.'

Lieutenant-Colonel John Stephenson, who was at the ICC, claimed two years later that certain members of the Pakistan management team had put him under immense pressure not to say a word about what had gone on. Right up to today, the TCCB, and subsequently the ECB, have firmly refused to allow anyone to see the contemporaneous umpires' reports, or the controversial ball, which continues to be hidden away under lock and key.

It is right and proper that the spotlight on cheating and chicanery is principally, and continually, focused on the international scene, although I was reminded in October 2010 that in the murky shadows of Test match scandals lurks the inventive club cricketer desperately seeking ways of gaining an illegal advantage.

Jittendra Patil, a left-arm fast bowler from Maharashtra, was charged with ball-tampering in an Indian under-22 C K Nayundu Trophy match against Uttar Pradesh. Patil was caught applying cream on the ball four deliveries into Maharashtra's 39th over on the third day of the match. Once this was noticed, the umpires ordered the ball to be changed and later awarded five penalty runs to Pradesh. Evidence, indeed, that there is absolutely no limit to where, or when, cheating will take place. As those honest, unimpeachable gentlemen would say: 'It's just not cricket!'

CHAPTER NINE

THE MYSTERIOUS LIFE AND DEATH OF HANSIE CRONJE

There can be no doubt that the late Hansie Cronje – who died in a plane crash in 2002 – was the biggest conman ever to play international cricket. Worst of all he was a liar. South Africa's disgraced captain was tape-recorded doing deals over the telephone with an Indian bookmaker. Even then, he brazenly tried to deny his involvement, only later to change his mind, having realised that a distinctive voice like his was far too difficult to imitate.

Cronje professed to be a devout Christian and proudly wore a wristband with the letters WWJD (What Would Jesus Do?). South African sports fans hailed him as a national hero. He was born Wessel Johannes (Hansie) Cronje in Bloemfontein on 25 September 1969. He graduated at the University of Orange Free State with a Bachelor of Commerce degree, and played cricket for Free State from 1987 to 2000.

He played for South Africa from 1994 to 2000, and his captaincy was praised as inventive and inspirational. He was the absolute paragon of virtue... or so everyone thought until he was exposed as a wilful, skilful, gluttonous fraudster.

Prominent businessmen excitedly entertained him at dinners. On the face of it, he could be trusted with the key to the vaults that held your life savings. In truth, he couldn't be trusted with your last fiver! Slippery Cronje was deftly leading two incredibly different lives and brilliantly covering his tracks to conceal his duplicity.

But as so frequently happens with arrogant crooks, his luck ran out, and with his head bowed in shame he was forced to confess to taking stacks of money from any number of bookmakers for match-fixing and under-performing. After an official inquiry in 2000, Cronje was banned for life from playing and coaching cricket anywhere in the world. He had persistently lied to his wife and family, and disgraced his sport, his country, and his religion. His life was wrecked at just 31.

Practically in tears, he reflected on the first time that a bookmaker approached him in a Pakistan hotel with a bribe to throw a match, and he said: 'I wish I could say today that I told him to get lost, but my reply was: "Let me think about it. Call me later..." I was sucked in, and that was no one's fault but my own. Greed, stupidity, and the lure of easy money got me into this mess. That's the beginning and end of it.'

Investigators found that Cronje possessed 72 bank accounts, many of them offshore and in the Cayman Islands, plus an account with NatWest bank in England, an investment portfolio with Merrill Lynch, various trust funds, and a substantial property portfolio.

Cronje admitted to receiving £150,000 for a cricket bat sponsorship; £100,000 for clothing and footwear endorsements; £100,000 from a restaurant deal; £280,000 from a Benefit Year fund; and up to £5,000 for every speaking engagement. On top of this was a large sum for his role as captain of the South African cricket team, match bonuses, and countless other financial perks.

It is impossible to estimate what he was truly worth, although we can be sure he was a millionaire many times over. But even then he wasn't satisfied. As alcoholics crave for drink, Cronje was addicted to cash. At one point he even consulted a psychiatrist to disentangle his confused life. The psychiatrist later disclosed that he found his patient to be suffering from a 'depressive disorder'.

Shortly after his phoney life had been stripped apart, Cronje admitted to being 'annoyed' for turning down £200,000 to lose a One-day International match, and confessed: 'I probably should have taken it.'

It was on 7 April 2000, while he basked in sublime national adulation and masqueraded as the perfect human being, that Cronje suddenly felt the first frightening tremor that grew into a roaring earthquake. It ripped through his false integrity, destroyed his career, and unmasked him as a deceitful charlatan, obsessed with money and stained with corruption.

Delhi police had acquired a tape-recording of a telephone conversation of Cronje discussing the possibility of fixing cricket matches with Indian betting agent Sanjay Chawla. Three other prominent South African players – Herschelle Gibbs, Nicky Boje and Pieter Strydom – were also heavily implicated in the same match-fixing allegations.

Once the Delhi police had referred the matter to the United Cricket Board of South Africa (UCB), its officials went straight to Cronje, who snapped back at them: 'These allegations are completely without substance.' Probably based on Cronje's categorical denial, and his reputation for truth and honesty, the UCB vigorously denied that its players had done anything as dastardly as fixing matches or under-performing.

But Cronje, the ultimate conman, was living on borrowed time, and his fatuous pleas of innocence were quickly dropped when he learned that the police had tape-recordings of his betting conversations. He went straight to Ali Bacher, managing director of the UCB, and admitted that he had not been 'entirely honest', which was a pathetic euphemism for 'I've lied through my teeth'.

Cronje was instantly dropped from a Test series that was coming up against Australia, and Bacher explained: 'Hansie phoned me, and Percy Sonn [President of the UCB], at three o'clock on Tuesday morning and told us that he had not been entirely honest with us regarding his involvement [in match-fixing]. We immediately decided it would be in everyone's best interests if he stood down from the series.' Bacher added that Cronje had decided not to elaborate on his statement.

Cronje was subsequently faced with the transcripts of taped telephone conversations with the Indian bookmaker in which he had discussed payment for himself and others in return for throwing a match in the series that India won 3-2.

Bob Woolmer (who died several years later in mysterious circumstances while coach of Pakistan) was the South Africa coach at the time, and he said: 'It would devastate cricket in South Africa if the accusations are true. It would be the end of Hansie's career, and a real kick in the teeth for South African cricket.' Shaun Pollock, who was South Africa's vice-captain, stepped up to replace the suspended Cronje.

Leaders of the South African church, which the two-faced Cronje faithfully attended, reported that he had sent them a nine-page letter in which he admitted that he had not been completely honest with the UCB on match-fixing allegations, and that he 'wanted to get it off his chest, and off his conscience, and to say that he had done wrong, and made a terrible mistake'.

Cronje promptly admitted to accepting between $10,000 and $15,000 from a London-based bookmaker, later identified as Sanjay Chawla, for forecasting results during a One-day Test series in India. Gibbs then claimed that Cronje had offered him $15,000 to score fewer than 20 runs in the fifth One-day International at Nagpur, and Henry Williams said Cronje offered him $15,000 to concede more than 50 runs in the same match.

Gibbs responded by hammering 74 runs off 53 deliveries, and

Williams injured his shoulder so badly that he could not complete his second over, so neither of them received the cash that was on offer. Even off-spinner Derek Crookes was surprised when asked to open the bowling in that Nagpur match and there was no obvious reason or explanation for it.

When Cronje finally came clean he was compelled to release a statement in which he purportedly revealed *all* his contacts with bookmakers, and now suddenly recalled pocketing $30,000 from India's biggest bookmaker, Mukesh Gupta, to persuade his team to lose wickets on the last day of the Third Test in Kanpur, and to lose the match.

South Africa had reached 127-5 in their bid to score 460. Cronje was already out, and he insisted in his statement that he didn't speak to any other member of the team, but he did admit to receiving $50,000 in total from Mukesh Gupta for team information during the tour.

All of a sudden the full extent of Cronje's mammoth cheating cascaded from his own lips, as he also recalled that Marlon Aronstam, a South African sports betting agent, offered him 500,000 rand for the charity of his choice, plus a personal gift – later revealed as a leather coat – to influence the result of the Fifth Test match against England at Centurion Park in Pretoria in January 2000.

South Africa were precariously poised on 155-6 at the close of play on the first day; rain then badly affected the second, third and fourth days; and only 45 overs had been possible when the fifth and final day arrived. Of course, it was not known at that time that Aronstam had secretly contacted Cronje and had urged him to 'make a game of it', which prompted a thrilling mixture of drama and pantomime on the final day.

Millions of cricket fans all over the world were baffled by what followed, until Cronje agreed to pull back the curtains and revealed all the disgraceful skulduggery that had gone on behind the scenes.

To pocket Aronstam's wad of dirty money, Cronje had to act fast, and he decided that South Africa would continue to bat and that he would declare the innings at a particular point, and that both teams would then forfeit an innings, which would leave England with a run chase for victory. By doing it this way, Cronje was cunningly setting up the match for a positive result for one side or the other to win, and to eliminate a draw.

Gamblers and bookmakers would have looked at the match on that final day, and, on seeing that South Africa had an innings and a half still to bat – and England had both innings ahead of them – only a draw could be considered a realistic possibility and any other result appeared completely out of the question. But they were about to be stunned, as Aronstam and Cronje had brilliantly fixed the 'impossible' result, and had set the bookies up for a massive sting.

Cronje declared the South Africa innings on 248-8. Both teams then forfeited an innings, just as Cronje and Aronstam had corruptly planned, which meant that England's strong batting line-up had to score 249 in 70 overs for victory. In Test match terms, a run-scoring rate of less than four an over was extremely generous, and England hit the winning runs with two wickets and five balls to spare. It also ended South Africa's brilliant run of 14 Tests without defeat.

Though no details ever emerged about how much Aronstam pocketed from using Cronje's vital 'inside' information on this fixed result, it would certainly have been an exceptionally large amount. It was a masterful sting by any standard.

Aronstam slipped 50,000 rand into Cronje's grubby hands straight after the match, as well as a leather coat, plus a further 50,000 rand as 'advance' payment for future cooperation with information on 'pitch reports'. Cronje insisted that the massive 500,000 rand that Aronstam had promised him at the outset never reached him, and he recalled receiving several calls from 'Sanjay' asking him to fix a match, and he gave the names of Gibbs, Strydom and Boje 'to try to get rid of him'. Gibbs and Williams were fined and banned for six months from international cricket, but Strydom was not punished in any way.

In 2000, along with several other prominent South African cricketers, Cronje was summoned to give evidence to the King Commission, an independent public inquiry prompted by the UCB and chaired by Judge Ewin King to scrutinise the match-fixing scandal. A series of crucial testimonies were given in a microscopic quest to establish the truth, and these included:

- 7 June: Former South African bowler Pat Symcox testified that he was approached by Cronje about throwing a match against Pakistan during the 1994/95 season. He also claimed that during a team meeting in Mumbai in 1996, Cronje had conveyed an offer of $250,000 to lose a One-day match.
- 10 June: Cronje is offered immunity from criminal prosecution in South Africa if he makes a full disclosure about his role in match-fixing.
- 13 June: Jacques Kallis, world-class all-rounder, corroborated evidence by wicketkeeper Mark Boucher and big-hitter Lance Klusener that Cronje had made an offer to the three players in an hotel room before the Second Test against India in Bangalore in March 2000.
- 15 June: Cronje confessed to taking about $100,000 in bribes from gamblers since 1996, but claimed that he had never thrown or fixed a match. He also announced his retirement from cricket. Cronje told the King Commission that former Indian captain Mohammad Azharuddin had introduced him to a bookmaker, who offered him money to throw a Test match during South Africa's tour of India in 1996. Azharuddin later dismissed Cronje's claim as 'rubbish'.
- 23 June: Cronje was led away in tears after his three-day

examination ended. He gave his evidence clearly and precisely, admitted that he accepted money from bookmakers, and said that his 'great passion for the game, and for my team-mates' was matched by an 'unfortunate lure of money'.

Cronje had played his last cricket match on 31 March 2000, blasting 79 runs from 73 balls for South Africa against Pakistan in the Sharjah Cup final. On 11 October the disgraced Cronje was banned for life from playing and coaching cricket anywhere in the world, and his subsequent appeal that the ban was too severe was swiftly dismissed.

Cronje led South Africa to 27 Test victories and 99 One-day International successes, scored 1,301 runs for Leicestershire in his one summer in England, and played one season for Ireland.

All through his career, Cronje was respected as a placid and thoughtful captain, so it was very much out of character when he threw a stump through the umpires' dressing-room door after Australian batsman Mark Waugh had been given not out during a five-day Test and had stayed at the crease for 400 minutes to save the match.

Cronje slipped away from all forms of cricket after his life ban, but he remained strong in himself and soon seized opportunities to make money in various other ways, which included penning an autobiography and expanding his programme of speaking engagements.

For specialist advice on new business ideas, Cronje contacted Max Clifford, the skilful London-based public relations consultant, who stoutly defended his new client by insisting that he was 'not a child molester or a murderer. All he did was rip off crooked bookmakers.'

Cronje's spiritual adviser Ray McCauley pleaded with him not to make money on the back of his match-fixing scandal and urged him to reconsider his plans to secure lucrative deals for books and films.

With cricket no longer on his mind, Cronje turned his attention to improving his golf swing at a private course near to where he lived, and where the resident professional said: 'Hansie is a fine golfer and very competitive. It's a private club, and he'll come here and have a chat while chipping and putting.'

As much as Cronje enjoyed playing golf and mixing with his fawning friends, who incredibly saw nothing wrong in what he had done, it was not enough for someone who had always relished a stiff challenge, so he accepted the position of financial manager of Bell Equipment, an international company that specialised in manufacturing earth-moving machinery. It also meant that he could use his Masters degree in business leadership. Bell Equipment bosses believed he was the right man to be put in charge of finances and were not concerned that his tarnished reputation would harm the company's image.

They were so proud to employ him that they even hung a portrait of him on the boardroom wall with the glowing inscription 'Our Hero', and they grabbed every opportunity to boast that they took at least ten telephone calls a day congratulating them on giving him a second chance. Bell bosses described him as 'a gentleman like we have never met before'.

Little was seen or heard of Cronje in public life as he knuckled down to doing a job that captivated his attention and provided a stimulating fresh focus. Then on 1 June 2002 came the shocking news that Cronje had been killed in a plane crash. It was such appalling news that even some of his strongest critics were overcome with emotion at seeing his life cut short at just 32 years of age. A whole nation united in sympathy for his wife Bertha, brother Fran, and sister Esther.

When it emerged that Cronje had boarded the plane in an emergency after his scheduled flight had been grounded by bad weather, conspiracy theorists pounced on the circumstances and formed the view that he had been murdered to ensure that he never blew the whistle on all that he knew about corruption in world cricket.

Bell Equipment had employed Cronje for just five months, and he called at their offices close to the city that fateful afternoon after a business conference in Swaziland. It had been a busy Friday for Cronje, who had been trapped in traffic in the outskirts of Johannesburg while on his way to the airport to board the scheduled flight back to his luxury home on the Francourt Golf Estate at George in the Western Cape.

Cronje's secretary vividly remembered the last moment she saw him before he left the offices to board his emergency flight, and she said: 'It was late in the afternoon, and most of the staff had gone home. It was freezing cold, and Hansie asked if anyone wanted coffee… he seemed anxious, and a little uneasy.' Although this edginess was most likely due to his missing his booked flight, conspiracy theorists saw it differently and believed that he was seriously worried about something sinister.

Cronje commuted weekly from his home in George, and he had established an arrangement with a small airline called AirQuarius, which allowed him to travel as a sole passenger on its cargo planes. Although Bell Equipment was happy to pay for Cronje's return flight, he often opted to travel free with AirQuarius, as he knew most of its pilots; they had stayed with him and his wife in a wing in their house, and played golf with him on the course next door.

Gavin Branson, Chief Executive of AirQuarius, confirmed the private arrangement and said: 'Our crew lodged at his house. We rented it from him. The pilots played golf with Hansie a lot. He didn't pay to fly with us.'

After Cronje had failed to board his scheduled flight at Johannesburg airport, he succeeded in hitching an emergency ride as the only passenger on a Hawker Siddeley HS 748 turboprop cargo aircraft for the journey to George, which is situated around 430 kilometres east of Cape Town and at the heart of the Western

Cape's Garden Route, a fashionable holiday destination and home to many of South Africa's most affluent residents.

As the plane approached George airport and prepared to land in atrocious weather conditions, it crashed into Cradock Peak on the Outeniqua Mountains, killing Cronje and its two pilots. Wreckage was scattered across the frozen mountainside, but Cronje was reportedly still strapped in his seat when a search party eventually arrived on the scene.

At first it was assumed that the pilots were unable to land because low cloud had badly restricted their visibility, that the plane had 'unusable' navigational equipment, and that they were circling when they struck the mountains.

Branson, who admitted to being puzzled by the crash, commented afterwards: 'There are a lot of unknowns about what happened. I think it will be a long time before the official report comes out. I have a million questions. We had flown that route daily, and in far worse weather conditions, without ever a hint of trouble.'

Conspiracy theorists were fuelled by further speculation that George airport's ground-landing system had been tampered with, and they linked this assumption to the prospect of ruthless people having enough money in the illegal betting world to have the right contacts to cause the crash to keep Cronje's mouth closed once and for all.

They even backed up this conjecture by insisting that enough people knew about Cronje's arrangement with AirQuarius, and claimed that a number of police investigators close to the case had privately admitted that they believed he was murdered, and that at least one investigator had been threatened on the telephone. But all these intriguing theories appeared to be blown to shreds at the inquest into the crash when Judge Siraj Desau concluded that the aircrew had not followed the correct procedures on their second attempt to land at George airport.

Openly critical and decisive, the judge said: 'The complacency of the pilot in command was surprising… the co-pilot failed in the circumstances to do what a reasonable pilot would have done. It is the court's view that the death of Wessel Johannes (Hansie) Cronje was brought about by an act, or omission prima facia, amounting to an offence on the part of the pilots.'

During the inquest it emerged that the pilots believed they were flying over the sea, and that they ignored as many as 13 ground-proximity warnings given by the aircraft's navigation equipment.

These official findings should have been more than enough to silence the conspiracy theorists, but that was far from the case, and they continued to cling tenaciously to rumours that investigators had found evidence of sabotage. They have remained convinced that Cronje was murdered, and that the final chapter of his extraordinary life is still to be revealed.

CHAPTER TEN

BRAVE HAIR BRUSHES ASIDE OVAL WALKOUT CHAOS

Darrell Hair is a tall, broad, imposing Australian. He gives the impression of being someone who is mentally strong, authoritative, and defiant when put under pressure unfairly. These are all essential qualities – along with fair play and common sense – that form the basis of a reliable, trustworthy, conscientious arbiter. Having the ability to remain calm to assess a volatile situation with a clear mind is a further imperative requirement.

As a world-class Test umpire, Hair had emerged exonerated, though sometimes mentally bruised, from controversial on-field examinations, but none of them as demanding and explosive as the rumpus that erupted at The Oval cricket ground in south London on 20 August 2006.

It was late afternoon on the fourth day of the Fourth Test between England and Pakistan, with a transfixed crowd filling the vast ground and millions more watching on television. Pakistan had already registered a substantial 504 in their first innings. England had replied with just 173 in 53 overs and were now anxiously following on, and at 218-3 in 51.5 overs.

The sun shone brilliantly, the spectators were in good humour, and the cricket was attractive and meaningful. It was an idyllic Sunday afternoon of consummate relaxation, with the game itself providing the perfect backdrop. Then bang! Suddenly all hell broke loose. There are no other words that can describe adequately the chaos, tension and bitter controversy that swept through this stunned sporting arena.

Pakistan's strapping paceman Umar Gul produced an absolutely unplayable swinging Yorker that struck England's left-handed opener Alastair Cook painfully on the toes, smack in front of the stumps, for a certain lbw. It was exceptional reverse swing even for Gul, who had an envious reputation for getting the ball to deviate sharply and late. At the end of the over, umpire Hair asked to see the ball to check on its condition.

Obviously satisfied that it was not damaged in any way, Hair returned the ball to the Pakistan fielders, and it was safe to assume that Gul's extra swing had come from a combination of skill and legitimate shine on one side of the ball, which can enhance a sudden swerve. Paul Collingwood then went to the middle to join Kevin Pietersen. Only 11 runs came in the next four dull overs, with Pietersen breaking the tedium, striking a boundary off leg-spinner Danish Kaneria, though even then the ball just crept over the rope at deep cover.

Collingwood collected three to get off the mark, followed by a single, and Pietersen stroked two and a single as the watchful pair realised the need to consolidate with the minimum of risk. At the end of over 55, Hair again asked to see the ball. This time there was obvious concern about its condition, which left everyone wondering how it could possibly have deteriorated so badly in just 20 minutes to cause such a fuss. After all, apart from Pietersen's boundary blow, not a shot had been played in anger!

Should the ball be damaged in any way then it surely could not have come from being battered against the boundary boards; so was there something more sinister at work? It certainly seemed that way. Cynics and second-guessers would have concluded that a Pakistan player, or a number of them, had covertly used fingernails to dig into the ball's surface on one side to scratch and even gouge it, while continuing to polish the other side vigorously.

For reasons known to those with expert knowledge of aerodynamics, a ball bowled over 22 yards in this condition would be far more likely to swing fast and late than one that had not been 'worked' on. Hair, and his genial West Indian umpiring colleague Billy Doctrove, inspected the ball carefully, turning it over and over, holding it up high, and looking particularly at its quarter seam. Players and spectators watched incredulously.

There was obvious concern, which left Hair and Doctrove with a tricky dilemma. They could ignore any damage to the ball and hope that it would not deteriorate further, or change it within the laws of the game. The umpires also had to consider whether it was possible – even probable – that the ball had been deliberately tampered with in order to acquire an unfair advantage.

Such a momentous decision could be made only if they were satisfied beyond doubt that the damage was so severe that it could not have been caused by any other means. Essentially, both umpires had to agree on whatever decision was to be made. There is no such thing as a 'senior' or 'junior' umpire, with one having more power than the other. Hair could not lead Doctrove, or the other way round.

They decided, jointly and firmly, that the ball *had* been tampered with, although they did not know by whom or how the damage had been achieved. That was an issue that would be investigated at the highest level some time in the future. Complying with cricket's strict legal procedures, the umpires then changed the ball immediately, informed both batsmen of what was happening, awarded five penalty runs to England, and told the Pakistan captain, Inzamam-ul-Haq, what was occurring and why.

A small box of used balls was then taken to the middle where Collingwood was allowed to select the replacement. This caused Inzamam great displeasure, but the International Cricket Council's 'Playing Conditions', which override the Laws of Cricket, categorically state that when a ball is deemed damaged unfairly, the opposition batsmen have the right to choose its replacement.

Still not content, Inzamam asked to see the damaged ball. The game's fourth umpire, Trevor Jesty, a former popular England all-rounder and a highly respected international umpire for many years, readily took it from his pocket and showed it to the Pakistan captain, who calmed down and instructed his team to continue playing.

It was crucially important that Inzamam was told precisely why the ball had been changed, and that five penalty runs were being awarded to England, because both umpires had decided that the ball had been deliberately damaged to obtain an unfair advantage.

Both umpires would need to ensure that the Pakistan captain, above all others, would know every detail of what had taken place so that he could not justifiably protest later that he had told his team to continue playing when he had not been given all the relevant facts. However, Inzamam did complain later that he was not properly informed, inevitably shifting the blame to Hair and Doctrove for allegedly not telling him. But what else could all the on-field discussions – with Inzamam fully part of them – have been about?

But back to the match. Play eventually resumed after a delay of around four minutes and continued for a further 15 overs until 3.45pm, when increased cloud cover caused the light to fade, and Pietersen and Ian Bell, who was now at the wicket, accepted the umpires' option to leave the field because of bad light. By now England had progressed to 298-4. As the stoppage came within 30 minutes of the scheduled tea break, the interval was taken immediately, with play scheduled to resume at 4.05pm.

No one, not even the laudable Mystic Meg (who used to foretell

National Lottery numbers on UK television), could have predicted the unprecedented Test match scenes of drama and fury that were about to explode. Umpires Hair and Doctrove, who were pleasantly refreshed after a pot of tea and sandwiches, emerged punctually at 4.05pm to test whether the light had improved sufficiently for the match to re-start, and after a further 20-minute delay, they agreed that it could resume at 4.40pm.

Fourth umpire Trevor Jesty was asked to advise both teams of what had been decided. Loud applause greeted Hair and Doctrove as they walked onto the ground at 4.36pm and placed the bails on the stumps for the match to resume. It is normal for the fielding side to follow the umpires fairly quickly onto the ground, and then the two not-out batsmen.

But there was no sign of the Pakistan players, and their dressing-room door was firmly closed. Hair and Doctrove waited patiently for four minutes, and at 4.41pm discussed the situation earnestly, as it was becoming more and more likely that Pakistan had no intention of returning to play.

With this in mind, the umpires had to follow cricket's precise laws for such an unusual situation. Although it was acceptable for just one umpire to consider whether Pakistan had refused to play, the laws required that both umpires had to obtain the reason for this refusal, and they jointly had to inform Inzamam, the Pakistan captain, of what was being considered. Inzamam would also have been advised that if Pakistan continued to refuse to play, then cricket's laws would give the umpires no option but to award the match to England.

It is known that Hair and Doctrove arrived at the Pakistan dressing-room door at exactly 4.46pm, where they were met by team manager Zaheer Abbas, who was soon joined by Inzamam and team coach Bob Woolmer. Above all else, it was plain to see that Hair and Doctrove were standing solidly together on everything under discussion, which included the condition of the ball, Pakistan's refusal to play, and every procedure needed to be taken within the laws of the game in such extraordinary circumstances.

At no stage did Hair and Doctrove enter the Pakistan dressing room, but an animated conversation was seen to be taking place near the doorway, with Inzamam having a great deal to say. There was no suggestion that Pakistan had changed their minds about wanting to play as Hair and Doctrove made their way to the England dressing room where the two not-out batsmen were padded up and ready to resume.

The umpires then returned to their private room to pick up their hats and counters, and walked straight onto the ground. It was now 4.54pm. Both England's not-out batsmen followed them, but there was still no sign of the Pakistan team. Ironically, the only Pakistan player in view was wicketkeeper Kamran Akmal, who was calmly reading a newspaper on a seat outside the dressing room. He was not wearing his pads or gloves, and he seemed to be sending a clear message that he, at least, was going nowhere.

Around two minutes went by while Hair and Doctrove discussed the next move and, as it became known later, both agreed that, as Pakistan had rejected three requests to come out and play, they had effectively forfeited the match. Doctrove removed the bails first, Hair then did the same, and England had won. It was now 4.58pm – exactly 18 minutes after the umpires had decided that the light was good enough for play to resume.

On leaving the field, the umpires reported to match referee Mike Proctor that Pakistan had forfeited the Test, and that England had won. Proctor then left his room to inform the Pakistan team and management what had been decided, although it was never confirmed that he arrived.

What can be safely assumed is that international cricket's high-powered administrators were frantically, even hysterically, trying to resolve the problem behind the scenes to head off potential political repercussions and all sorts of allegations from the super-sensitive Pakistani contingent.

Everyone in authority must have known that there was no scope for manoeuvre. Both umpires had ruled that the Test was over. There was no logical, or legitimate, way of altering what had been done in compliance with the laws. David Morgan, the ECB Chairman, and David Collier, the ECB Chief Executive, were soon on the scene, desperately hoping Hair and Doctrove would change their minds, as the Pakistan players were now, apparently, willing to play. Morgan and Collier could offer nothing that would enable the Test to enter its fifth day.

Shaharyar Khan, then Chairman of the Pakistan Cricket Board, was interviewed on BBC radio at 5.42pm and said: 'We feel that there is no evidence whatsoever of deliberate scuffing of the ball. Once you accuse a team of deliberately tampering with the ball, it becomes a very big deal. We felt we should make a protest, but we simply said that we would stay inside for a few minutes and go out when the protest had been registered. We are still hopeful that the match can start again.'

Khan did not define precisely what he meant by 'a few minutes', and it did not seem to reconcile with the separate requests from the umpires spread over a fairly considerable period. Some people might reasonably argue that it is understandable for high-ranking officials of governing bodies to preach the gospel of 'the game must go on at all costs'. But it would surely be seriously wrong for any organisation to be prepared to turn a blind eye to cheating, and ignore fair and lawful decisions by the world's best umpires in order to allow a game to continue.

Finally, at 10.35pm, a joint statement from the ICC, ECB and PCB was released confirming that they had officially agreed that Pakistan had forfeited the Test match, and that there would be no play on the fifth day. It clearly stated: 'After lengthy negotiations which resulted in agreement between the teams, the ICC match referee, and both the England and Wales Cricket Board (ECB) and Pakistan Cricket Board (PCB), it was concluded with regret that there will be no play on the fifth day.

'The 4th npower Test match between England and Pakistan has, therefore, been forfeited, with the match being awarded to England. In accordance with the Laws of Cricket it was noted that the umpires had correctly deemed that Pakistan had forfeited the match, and awarded the Test to England.

'At a meeting between the captains, ECB, PCB and ICC match referee, the players, ICC match referee and Boards indicated that they would offer to resume play if at all possible on day five. The umpires, having awarded the match to England, and having consulted with the Pakistan captain, reconfirmed their decision to award the match to England.

'The Pakistan team was aggrieved by the award of five penalty runs to England. The award of those penalty runs for alleged interference with the ball is under review by the ICC match referee Mike Proctor, whose report will be considered in due course. The ICC will be issuing a separate report concerning action which may be taken in relation to the forfeiture of the match by Pakistan.'

It came as no surprise to learn that no other Test match over a period covering more than 1,000 games had ended in such a controversial manner. Officials at the ICC, so often castigated for their weak handling of disciplinary cases in order to protect the game's image, again might have hoped that this embarrassing incident would fade rapidly and be forgotten.

But no such luck. This time they took on the formidable Darrell Hair, an honourable man with a reputation for relishing a fight, should it mean defending integrity, whether it happened to be his or in any way related to cricket. He later took the covers off the astonishing affair, and revealed in great detail what had taken place behind those closed doors at The Oval, and candidly suggested where he believed unnecessary problems had arisen, and who were to blame.

Hair angrily disclosed that senior officials from the ECB, along with their counterparts from the PCB, all became involved in a veritable circus, and that politics took over to such an extent that any hope of reconciliation for the match to continue was eliminated.

Fearing no one, Hair recalled: 'We played on until tea, so I suppose you could say that by playing on, the players accepted what happened. It wasn't until they arrived back in the dressing room that politics took over. Too many people from Pakistan and the ECB got involved.

'I will name them all one day, probably when I write my book. There is no doubt that they got involved when they shouldn't have done, which further inflamed the situation. The PCB thought they had some allies who would assist them. The Pakistan team had accepted the ruling until they got back to the dressing room.'

Many people high up in international cricket, as well as media commentators renowned for their sound thinking, surprisingly assumed that Hair had acted alone in the decision to change the ball, and that he never consulted his colleague Billy Doctrove. Hair was determined to put the record straight and stressed: 'He [Doctrove] played an equal part. I'd like to see any tape of my frogmarching Billy around. There was no coercion. I'm an easy target because [my] strength of character can be mistaken for arrogance or obstinacy. But if Billy had said "I don't think the condition of the ball had changed," we would have carried on.'

The ECB refunded fourth-day spectators 40 per cent of their ticket price, and gave an automatic 100 per cent refund to those with tickets for the fifth day. But the PCB flatly refused an ECB request to pay £800,000 towards the lost income, although they did agree to a Twenty/20 international in England, for which their players would waive all fees.

Hair has had no personal contact with Doctrove since that unfortunate incident, although nothing has been said, or even publicly hinted, about anything in particular that has kept them apart, but with one living in Australia and the other in the Caribbean, it seems nothing more than a logistical situation. The ICC, ECB and PCB all later agreed that cricket's laws had made it right for England to be awarded the match.

Several former prominent Test cricketers who had retired to a comfortable career in a television commentary box seized the chance to pontificate about the dispute, and the people involved. Former England captain Michael Atherton criticised Hair for not continuing the game, but completely overlooked the fact that Doctrove was an equal part of the decision.

Atherton might have found it a trifle difficult to comment on such a controversial issue, bearing in mind his 'dust-in-the-pocket' clash with Peter Burge, another powerful Australian umpire, in a Test match against South Africa at Lord's in 1994. Nasser Hussain, another former England captain, sided with Inzamam, saying he would have done precisely the same as the Pakistan captain.

Former Australian skipper Steve Waugh was in no doubt that umpires Hair and Doctrove had acted correctly, saying: 'No one is bigger than the game. The laws are there for that reason.' Michael Holding, the former West Indian bowling legend, thought the umpires had over-reacted by applying the five-run penalty, and believed every law had room for flexibility.

It was a strange remark, coming from one of cricket's most clear-thinking commentators. To suggest that Hair and Doctrove should have meddled with the regulations that were there for them to enforce would have amounted to law-tampering, which would have been far worse than the actual ball-tampering, which they dealt with admirably.

Former Pakistan heroes Imran Khan and Wasim Akram both fiercely attacked Hair, again forgetting that Doctrove played an equal part in every on-field decision. ICC officials later announced that Hair had offered to resign from the Elite Umpires Panel, and then leaked into the public domain a confidential e-mail that Hair had allegedly sent to Doug Cowie, the ICC's umpire manager.

The ICC claimed the e-mail was entitled 'The Way Forward', and that Hair had offered to resign in return for a non-negotiable one-off payment of $500,000, to be paid directly into his bank account. It transpired a few days later that Hair had specifically asked that his offer should be kept confidential to both sides, so it was quite shameful of the ICC to do exactly the opposite by disclosing it to the world.

Hair was contracted to the ICC until March 2008, so there were virtually two years still to run on their time together. And it was with this in mind that he had quite reasonably calculated that any closure payment would compensate for loss of future earnings and retainer fees. To make it simple for everyone, Hair later withdrew his $500,000 offer, although he still maintained that it represented compensation for the four or more years that he would have gone on to umpire at the highest level if The Oval ball-tampering controversy had not come about. Hair believed that the years he expected to lose 'would be the best he had to offer to international umpiring'.

Using all his tenacity, Hair hit back at the ICC and stated publicly that the game's governing body had actually been in negotiations with him before he had sent that controversial e-mail. Hair stressed: 'During an extended conversation with Mr Cowie, I was invited to make a written offer. The figure in the e-mail correspondence was in line with those canvassed with the ICC.' The ICC countered Hair's recollections by insisting that Cowie had not invited such a claim, and then Hair insisted yet again that he had never considered retirement.

Pakistan captain Inzamam-ul-Haq was banned for four One-day matches at an ICC hearing for 'bringing the game into disrepute', but totally cleared of being involved in any alleged ball-tampering in The Oval incident. Ranjan Madugalle, who chaired the hearing, said in his report: 'Having regard to the seriousness of the allegation of ball-tampering, I am not satisfied, on the balance of probabilities, that there is sufficiently cogent evidence that the fielding team had taken action likely to interfere with the condition of the ball.'

It was a strange conclusion, bearing in mind that every ICC-appointed match official on duty at The Oval – who were Trevor Jesty, Mike Proctor, Peter Hartley, Doug Cowie, Darrell Hair and Billy Doctrove – had all agreed that markings on the ball indicated tampering.

Former England batting legend Geoff Boycott, well known for his penchant for disagreeing with popular opinion, thought it was a 'good ball, not just a playable ball'. Ex-Middlesex seam bowler Simon Hughes believed that Hair – again no mention of Doctrove – had 'guessed', and that the ball was in a 'pretty good condition' when he examined it.

Of course, both Boycott and Hughes had no experience of elite-level umpiring, or of any other serious umpiring for that matter, so the intricate laws of the game, and how and when to enforce them, were not really their strongest points, so it might have been better for their credibility if they had stayed silent on this occasion. Without the essential experience, and knowledge, their comments were worthless, and impartial observers must have wondered why the ICC had considered them worthy to testify as witnesses.

Pakistan Cricket Board's Chairman Shaharyar Khan seized on Madugalle's muted verdict, and announced that his Board had not ruled out charging Hair – yet again no mention of Doctrove – with bringing the sport into disrepute. It was a hasty and crazy remark, and one that so easily could have ignited further international problems for Hair, and even possibly put him and his family in physical danger.

Why, oh why was Hair being singled out? Why didn't the ICC, the whimpering mouse that it can be, not stand up on this highly sensitive occasion and defend its employee? Why did it not remind those with their heads stuck in the soil that there were *two* umpires on duty in that match? And in every match!

Hair and Doctrove had applied the rules correctly. They had performed their onerous duties honestly and bravely. So it was absurd – some may say outrageous – that Hair should be pilloried personally for upholding the laws of the game. Having built the bonfire and doused it with petrol, the ICC was then forced to admit that Hair was, indeed, at risk, and announced that for 'security reasons' he would not be umpiring at the 2006 ICC Champions Trophy.

Malcolm Speed, Chairman of the ICC, disclosed that its decision to exclude Hair for security reasons was taken after listening to 'independent advisers' – although he noticeably did not identify those 'advisers', or reveal whether specific threats had been made to harm Hair should he be allowed to officiate.

Four weeks later, on 4 November, the ICC announced that it was banning Hair from umpiring in all international matches. In a terse statement made in Mumbai, ICC President Percy Sonn said: 'He [Darrell Hair] shall not be allowed to officiate in any future international games until the end of this contract [which was due to conclude in March 2008].' Both Speed and Sonn added that, despite banning Hair, there was 'no issue' with the result of The Oval Test, which Pakistan had forfeited. Doctrove was unaffected by the ban on Hair, but again the ICC gave no explanation why he had been left off the hook.

As expected, the decision to ban Hair was greeted with jubilation by the Pakistan Cricket Board, which had earlier demanded that Hair should be sacked. Intrigue then mounted when a strong rumour took off that a 'reliable source' had leaked Hair's sacking to an Indian television station 24 hours before the official ICC announcement.

This unnamed source had apparently claimed that ten Test-playing nations had voted on whether Hair should stay or go, and that India, Pakistan, Sri Lanka, Zimbabwe, South Africa, Bangladesh and the West Indies (home of umpire Doctrove) had all voted for him to be removed, while England, Australia and New Zealand had fully supported him.

Former Pakistan batting icon Javed Miandad, many times at the centre of on-field controversies, said the ICC had set an example which meant that 'all other umpires will be under pressure to make the right decisions'. It was a masterpiece of Miandad muddled-thinking, when taking into account that the ICC had already accepted that the ultimate result was the correct one, and the entire band of elite ICC umpires on duty at The Oval had unanimously agreed that the ball showed signs of tampering.

Former Sri Lankan captain Arjuna Ranatunga also welcomed the ban. He claimed that Hair had a 'prejudice against Asian teams' and that he was 'happy that he is finally out' and that the decision 'will do good to [sic] future cricket'. Many might contend that Ranatunga's comments were reckless. At the very least they were distasteful, insulting and wholly out of place for a former captain of any national cricket team.

Cricket Australia understandably emphasised its full support for Hair (who was born in New South Wales in September 1952) and demanded to know from the ICC why the ban had been imposed. Its Chief Executive, James Sutherland, said: 'Umpires need to have confidence in the system, and that they are supported by best-practice administration and processes.' One incensed Australian journalist complained bitterly: 'Having seen how brutally Hair was abandoned after his tough call, only a brave or foolish umpire would be courageous enough to throw himself into the lion's den.' There is no official record of the ICC ever responding to Cricket Australia's request to know why Hair was fired.

In total contradiction to what the ICC had thought of Hair, a poll conducted by the Wisden *Cricketer* magazine in the aftermath of The Oval incident had hailed him as Umpire of the Season, having polled more than a third of the votes. Even more embarrassingly for those who had condemned Hair, a leaked ICC report showed that immediately before The Oval rumpus he was rated the second-best umpire in the world overall, and world number one for decision-making.

After thinking long and hard about all the discrediting comments made against him, Hair felt impelled to take legal action, and in February 2007 he confirmed that he was suing the ICC and the Pakistan Cricket Board for racial discrimination. Hair believed he had been made a scapegoat for The Oval debacle, especially as he was banned while colleague Doctrove escaped punishment entirely.

Leaving no one in doubt, Hair said: 'I can confirm that I have instructed my lawyers, Finers Stephens Innocent, of Portland Street, London, to issue an application to the London Central Employment Tribunal alleging racial discrimination from the International Cricket Council and the Pakistan Cricket Board. Therefore it is inappropriate for me to make further comment, as this matter is yet to be determined by the Tribunal.'

He also poignantly added: 'I have not spoken to anyone about this. I hope you understand that I have not released any information about this. Someone else obviously has. I have no idea who [did this] but I value confidentiality. Unfortunately I have discovered that other people do not.'

Dr Naseem Ashraf, Chairman of the PCB, responded to news that a writ was on its way, saying: 'Mr Hair was removed from the ICC panel of umpires because of his bad umpiring and poor judgement. It is crass for him to say a black West Indian was let off [whereas] he was a white man and, therefore, he was charged. Mr Hair was the senior umpire, and he literally took over that Oval cricket match. I was there. There was only one man that evening who did not want cricket to be played. [It was] a black spot [an unfortunate choice of words] on the history of cricket, thanks to Mr Hair.'

Lots of speculation followed that the PCB, and the ICC in particular, would not wish to fight a legal battle, and that some type of compromise would be engineered to placate Hair, and persuade him to drop what seemed a strong case. So it came as no surprise when Hair withdrew his writ in October 2007, and the ICC revealed that he would be undergoing a six-month development programme aimed at placing him back in top-level matches. There was an apparent huge sigh of relief from the ICC and PCB that Hair had been pacified.

During those six months, it was decided that Hair would also be allowed to officiate in second-tier ICC associate matches, and the ICC went further in March 2008, restoring him to the Elite Umpires Panel. This was total vindication for Hair, who had battled with dignity and determination and refused to capitulate to the power brigade and slip away to a quiet life in the country.

Just three months later, on 22 August, Hair handed in his resignation to the ICC in order to take up a coaching position, ending a 16-year career as an international umpire. He stood in 78 Test matches and 135 One-day Internationals. Since breaking contractual ties with the ICC, a non-forgiving Hair has called for its current President, David Morgan, to resign over its handling of The Oval Test (thereby pitting a South Walian against a New South Walian).

His demand coincided with the ICC astonishingly changing its mind over The Oval Test result, stating that the match should now be officially recorded as a draw, and not an England victory, as previously decided in line with the laws.

With customary forthrightness, Hair responded: 'All the board members who were involved in the earlier decision should resign now. This should also include the present ICC President David Morgan. First to go should be David Richardson [ICC general manager, cricket] and Doug Cowie [ICC manager for umpires].

'I felt the gun was loaded by the ICC Board, and Richardson and Malcolm Speed [then Chief Executive] were only too happy to pull the trigger. They tried to destroy my life. People like me pay for standing up for what is right. I had a lot of support around the world, but unfortunately no one who worked at the ICC was among them.'

Hair's passion for cricket began as a powerful right-arm fast-medium bowler for Mosman in the competitive Sydney Grade League. He later graduated through club cricket as a high-quality, no-nonsense umpire, and made his Test debut at Adelaide in January 1992 in the match between Australia and India, which Australia won by 38 runs.

In the only match that Hair officiated between Australia and Sri Lanka, in Melbourne in December 1995, he no-balled leg-spinner Muttiah Muralitharan seven times in three overs for an unlawful action. He genuinely believed that Muralitharan was throwing the ball, a breach of cricket laws that could get him banned from the game.

Shocked by Hair's bold calls, and concerned about possible political repercussions, the ICC ordered an immediate biochemical investigation into Muralitharan's unusual action, which concluded that a congenital elbow deformity was partly responsible, and this cleared him to continue playing… and to go on to become a record-breaking superstar.

But apparently not totally satisfied with this biochemical appraisal, the ICC brought in a so-called panel of 'experts' to conduct a further review, and subsequently raised the elbow extension limit to 15 degrees for all bowlers. This ostensibly brought Muralitharan well inside the game's strict law and effectively slammed the door on umpires like Hair who would be brave enough to no-ball perpetrators, and by doing so endanger political unrest between cricketing nations and the ICC.

Hair is now enjoying a stress-free life as Executive Officer for the New South Wales Cricket Umpires and Scorers Association, and on his return from a recent presentation address to the Victorian Government Traffic Accident Commission in Melbourne on integrity and resilience, he e-mailed to remind me that it was 'something very close to my heart'.

Above all else, Darrell Hair possessed unshakeable principles during his admirable umpiring career. He continually made it plain that no matter how iconic a batsman or bowler a person might be, no one should be bigger than the game itself.

Hair has encapsulated all his fine principles in his formidable autobiography *In the Best Interests of the Game – The Darrell Hair Story*.

CHAPTER ELEVEN

ENGLAND STAR TURNS COCAINE SMUGGLER

E ngland's disgraced all-rounder Chris Lewis was sentenced to 13 years in prison in May 2009 for smuggling cocaine from the Caribbean after a charismatic and highly controversial playing career. Lewis was born in Georgetown, Guyana, on 14 February 1968, and represented England in 32 Test matches and 53 One-day Internationals as an aggressive lower-order batsman and fast-medium bowler. But it was for his explosive off-field performances, rather than his on-field achievements, that Lewis will be best remembered.

Notoriety and Lewis first became linked when he reported that an Indian businessman had offered him £300,000 in cash to persuade at least two team-mates to under-perform in the Third Test between England and New Zealand at Old Trafford in August 1999. Lewis further claimed that he had been assured that every England player who took the bribe would each pocket £100,000.

In particular, he had been asked to try to coax wicketkeeper/batsman Alec Stewart and left-arm fast bowler Alan Mullally on board as a starting point, with a view to doing more business in the future. Lewis claimed that Aushim Kheterpal, an Indian sports promoter, had put the sensational offer to him after he had made contact with him through 'other Indian sources' in England.

But instead of rushing off to proposition the players as Kheterpal had requested, Lewis drove straight to the England and Wales Cricket Board offices in St John's Wood in north London, where he shocked the game's top brass with details of the alarming offer. Within minutes of Lewis walking into their building, the ECB hierarchy dispatched a senior member of staff to accompany Lewis direct to a police station in central London to report the match-fixing approach.

In a statement to the police, Lewis claimed that Kheterpal, who had substantial business connections in the UK, had invited him to a small room above a newsagent's shop in Harlesden, north London, where the £300,000 offer was made. The Serious Crimes Group at New Scotland Yard launched an immediate international investigation, and their interest soared when it was found that Kheterpal was a close associate of Sanjay Chawla, the alleged paymaster to match-fixer Hansie Cronje, the infamous South African captain who died in a plane crash (see Chapter Nine).

Cronje had publicly confessed that he had received £6,000 from Chawla for favours in a Test match against England in Pretoria in January 2000. The highly dubious Chawla ran a clothing business in Hendon, north London, and detectives swooped on his home, and grilled him on suspicion of conspiracy to commit deception.

Police simultaneously interviewed Kheterpal in Delhi, where he had landed after leaving London in a hurry once Lewis had reported the clandestine match-fixing meeting to the ECB. Kheterpal ran Radiant Sports Management, a company that had featured in business deals with the World Professional Billiards and Snooker Association, which was based in Bristol.

When Kheterpal was questioned about his meeting with Lewis,

he said that he was in England to organise a benefit match to be played in India, and that he had spoken to Lewis about him writing a newspaper column, as well as the possibility of sports sponsorship and a cricket bat deal.

Around the same time, New Zealand captain Stephen Fleming reported to his team's management that Kheterpal had also spoken to him. Fleming told Scotland Yard detectives that Kheterpal had originally approached him with a view to writing a newspaper column before making suggestions about 'tanking games', a term for match-fixing. A senior investigating officer said at the time: 'Fleming realised where the conversation was going, and basically told Kheterpal to get lost.'

Detectives interviewed every member of the England team who played in the suspect Old Trafford Test, and were satisfied that Stewart and Mullally had not taken bribes, had not considered taking a bribe, and were never under investigation. The match ended in a draw.

Officers of the Serious Crime Group were also interested in speaking to Cronje in the hope that he could produce valuable information, and a police spokesman said: 'From a witness point of view, Hansie Cronje could be very helpful to our inquiries, and we would readily fly out to meet him. We believe we've just scratched the surface. There's a lot more to uncover yet.'

For whatever reason, Cronje was never officially approached, but detectives did fly to Trinidad to interview West Indian legend Brian Lara, stressing that he was only a witness helping with their inquiries. On their return to the UK, a senior investigating officer said: 'We were aware that Brian Lara had a meeting with Kheterpal at Heathrow airport, and we were keen to know what they spoke about. Lara said that Kheterpal had wanted him to arrange a cricket benefit match in India, which we understand was never played. We are aware that Kheterpal has arranged a number of cricket benefit matches in India in the past.'

Scotland Yard was eager to emphasise that its investigation was not part of the International Cricket Council's probe into allegations of worldwide match-fixing that was being headed by Sir Paul Condon and his London-based Anti-corruption Unit.

As the Lewis tip-off inquiries spread to include Interpol, officers at Scotland Yard discovered that Kheterpal had close links with the World Professional Billiards and Snooker Association, as well as major televised tournaments all over India, and a list of players and officials they wished to interview was drawn up.

Kheterpal was also being investigated about reports of possible fixed matches in snooker and tennis, including a Wimbledon final, but he was never apprehended on any of these inquiries.

Scotland Yard presented its dossier of evidential documents about the alleged Old Trafford match-fix plot to the Crown Prosecution Service in January 2001. Statements taken from every member of the 1999 England squad were included in the bundle, and the large file was handed to lawyers at the CPS offices around the same time that Chawla was being re-bailed at a London police station.

A high-ranking Scotland Yard officer said: 'Though the CPS has been kept up to date about our investigations, this is the first time for them to see documents and statements. It's a starter for ten. We have a lot more to follow.'

The elusive Kheterpal remained at home in Delhi, and made sure he was well away from the pivotal areas of the inquiry, and detectives were confident that he would be in no hurry to return to the UK. Scotland Yard officers, however, were determined not to let distance come between them and Kheterpal, and they worked closely with the Indian police, both in London and in Delhi, to maintain pressure on him.

At one point, Scotland Yard were poised to apply to the Home Office for permission to bring Kheterpal back to the UK for a full-blown grilling, but decided in the end that such extreme action would be taken only if their inquiries reached a stage where it became absolutely necessary.

A helpful Scotland Yard officer admitted: 'As it stands we would not be able to get Kheterpal back to interview him. We would need to provide letters of request through the Home Office.'

Then, in June 2001, a Scotland Yard spokesman, who sounded deeply disappointed, telephoned me and groaned: 'Lawyers for the CPS have come back and said that they believe there is insufficient evidence to get a realistic chance of a conviction [against Chawla or Kheterpal].

'We have spoken to Chris Lewis and informed him of this decision, and told him that he won't be required any more. We thanked him for his excellent cooperation, and made clear to him that this decision does not reflect on him in any way. He could not have been more helpful.'

Quite undaunted, Scotland Yard detectives decided that the information it had gathered on Chawla about the alleged attempt to fix the Old Trafford match might be made available to the Indian police – on condition that it went through all the official channels, with approval from the Home Office.

The spokesman added: 'We will assist the Indian police wherever we can. We will deal through Interpol, and the Home Office. If the Indians want him back they would have to obtain an extradition warrant. As for ourselves, if there is something else out there that could open a new line of inquiry, we would take it up. The case is closed for the time-being, but any fresh evidence would be reviewed.'

No fresh evidence was ever produced from any source to warrant re-opening the case, so Chawla and Kheterpal remained free from further questioning, although it might be foolish to assume that the police in England and India didn't keep them under close surveillance, and may still be doing so today.

Chris Lewis was a member of the Leicestershire playing staff during the match-fixing investigations, later moving to Nottinghamshire, who unexpectedly released him in July 1995 with three years of his six-year contract still left to run. The Lewis family home was in Wembley, north London – just a decent free-kick from the famous football stadium – and he desperately wanted to join a championship cricket club in London, and hoped that Middlesex or Surrey would sign him.

I interviewed him at that time for a national newspaper to learn about his plans for the future, and I found him surprisingly anxious and emotional; he came across as someone who, despite his immense talent, was deeply insecure, confused, and badly lacking in confidence.

Many good cricket judges had predicted that he would mature and develop into England's next Ian Botham, but while speaking to him in private that afternoon I formed the view that there was something so seriously lacking in his character that it would be a major surprise if he grew into a world-class player.

While we peered into his crystal ball he suddenly said that should Middlesex and Surrey not sign him, he always had the pulpit as a primary alternative. He proudly explained that his father, Philip, was a popular minister, who had done most of his preaching in America.

'My dad has always maintained that I would follow in his footsteps,' Lewis boasted, and his smile and manner convinced me that he regarded it as a realistic option should everything else fail. It took me by surprise! Could I really imagine this swashbuckling hitter, and hostile bowler, calming down sufficiently to stand in front of 100 people or more in a church on Sundays, and deliver a sermon of meaning and purpose? No! Definitely not! And I told him so.

He grinned, and hit back… 'Look, I've never ruled it out. I'm articulate, clean-living, and a religious person. I admire what my dad's doing, and I know what's required. And I don't drink, smoke or gamble. I'm just relieved that the Nottingham problem has been sorted out in a satisfactory way. It was never anything personal with the people there. I just found it hard to settle in Nottingham because I wanted to be close to my family and friends in London.'

Lewis had regretted signing a contract that committed him to Nottinghamshire for six years, and believed that two years would have been enough. His prayers were very much answered when Surrey signed him for the 1996/97 season, and the following summer he returned to Leicestershire where he remained until 2000, when he decided to leave professional cricket altogether after his form had plunged because of a persistent hip problem.

Brief spells of club cricket with Clifton, in the Central Lancashire League, and Stockton, in the Newcastle and District Cricket Association, were all that he could muster, until Surrey incredibly popped up again in summer 2008 and signed him as a specialist all-rounder for their One-day matches.

However, it was a brief and disastrous comeback. He played in just one Friends Provident Trophy match, in which he conceded 51 runs in six overs, and in one Twenty/20 fixture, and took no wickets in either of them. Cricket's curtain had finally fallen on a player who promised so much more than he ever delivered. So where next for the man who was still desperately seeking his elusive destiny? The pulpit? Not likely…

When Lewis landed at Gatwick airport on a flight from St Lucia on 8 December 2008, two officers from HM Revenue and Customs led him away and opened up his luggage in a thorough search. Among his personal belongings were several cans of fruit and vegetable juice that seemed ordinary and harmless, but when closely analysed they were found to contain dissolved cocaine with a street value of more than £140,000.

Former London Towers basketball star Chad Kirnon, who like

Lewis lived in north London, was also stopped as he stepped off the same flight. The following May both were found guilty at Croydon Crown Court of smuggling a liquid form of cocaine into Britain, and they were each gaoled for 13 years, although they both strongly denied smuggling Class A drugs.

While giving evidence at the trial, Lewis claimed that he did not know that cocaine could be converted into a liquid form, and insisted that he had no idea that drugs were in his cricket bag until he was stopped at Gatwick. He repeatedly claimed that he thought he was carrying fruit juice, and insisted that he had been in St Lucia on holiday.

Members of the jury were told that five tins of juice found in Lewis's Puma cricket bag contained a brown liquid that smelt of chemicals, and turned out to be dissolved cocaine. Traces of cannabis resin were also found on a silver grinder in his luggage, and on cigarette papers tucked into a paperback book. Lewis told the jury that he had travelled alone, and that only he had packed his luggage.

Three tins of dissolved cocaine were found in Kirnon's baggage when he was stopped ten minutes after Lewis. He also had 'no idea' that the tins contained drugs, and he insisted that the juice was a gift for his mother. It was alleged that Lewis and Kirnon had acted together to import the 'very valuable consignment' in a 'joint enterprise'. When Lewis's luggage was inspected, his Puma cricket bag was labelled with Kirnon's name.

Judge Nicholas Ainley told Lewis and Kirnon that greed had motivated them, and scathingly stressed: 'In a cowardly attempt to evade justice, you each sought to blame the other for a crime you obviously jointly committed. Drug smugglers would not entrust a valuable cargo like this to an innocent traveller.'

Addressing Lewis, the judge added: 'You made it to the top of your profession. This was greed, and I am sure that you ran the risk that you did because you deduced that the risk was worth it because the rewards were substantial. You were knowingly, and willingly, engaged in major organised crime.'

Lawyers for the prosecution said it was the 'first of a number of links between these two defendants' and evidence 'of what they were, together, up to'. During the eight-day trial, Lewis and Kirnon continued to protest their innocence and cast suspicion on each other.

After they were sentenced, Peter Avery, Assistant Director of HM Revenue and Customs Criminal Investigations, said: 'Sportsmen and women who are regularly in the public eye have a responsibility to act as role models and ambassadors for their sport. It is, therefore, even more disappointing when such role models get involved in the criminality of attempting to smuggle Class A drugs into the UK.'

For those who had supported and admired Lewis from his junior days as a young cricketer full of talent and ambition, seeing him driven away in a prison van was a distressing moment, and it was difficult to understand how he could have ended up in such disgrace.

It brought back many memories to those who had known him well, including the day uproar broke out around Lewis's home in Wembley after former England stars Geoff Boycott, Bob Willis and David Gower had slated him from their commentary box during a Test match in the West Indies. The illustrious trio were working for Sky TV and had broadcast that, in their opinion, Lewis lacked aggression, had lost heart, and appeared not to care much about playing for his country.

Officials at Wembley Cricket Club, where Lewis was idolised, were incensed by what had been said about him, and Chairman Tony Smith, a Department of Transport officer, raged that it was a witch hunt, saying: 'We are appalled by these comments that Chris doesn't try. We are sick to the back teeth of it. He has been a club member since he was 14, and has always given us 100 per cent.

'He broke a leg badly once when he tripped while fielding, and though the leg was in plaster he kept turning up to watch our matches. On one occasion we were a player short, and when Chris learned that it was a bowler, he cut the plaster off, and hobbled out and opened our attack.

'Then next morning he went back to the hospital and had the plaster put on again. That took huge courage, and that's the true Chris Lewis. And that's how much a game of cricket meant to him. So let's get the record straight. Let's stop using him as a scapegoat whenever England are struggling.'

Mr Smith also offered a piece of 'friendly' advice to England's captain Mike Atherton, and team manager Keith Fletcher, on how to get the best out of their unpredictable all-rounder, saying: 'Chris is a shy guy and a tremendously nice guy. He enjoys the simple things of life. There is no "side" to him. If he lacks anything, it is self-belief. He needs to be encouraged. That's what Atherton and Fletcher should be concentrating on – giving him confidence. People should be telling him how good he is, not finding fault with him.

'These commentators should be doing the same. Some of the things they've said about Chris have made us boil. People like Boycott, Willis and Gower should know better. We've been champing at the bit to hit back at them because what they've been saying is so unkind and untrue.'

Smith, who clearly held Lewis in high admiration, continued: 'Chris is being maligned by people who don't understand him. I've known him since he joined the club as a 14-year-old. I was his coach. Because he's a shy guy, he doesn't push himself, and it is this, perhaps, which works against him. So our message to England is keep boosting his confidence, stick with him, and you'll find you've got a match-winner.'

These were stirring words from a loyal friend who believed that Lewis was being greatly misunderstood. By the time he came up in front of Judge Nicholas Ainley many years later, the lad who promised so much was being dismissed with the stinging words: 'You were knowingly, and willingly, engaged in major crime…'

It brought a sad end to a cricket career for someone who was one of the most enigmatic players ever to wear an England shirt, and all those fans and friends at Wembley Cricket Club who had praised him as their prodigy had every right to feel profoundly let down.

CHAPTER TWELVE

TOP BOOKIE NAMES HIS DRESSING-ROOM CONTACTS

Repeated claims that India's top cricketers were involved in bribery and corruption with bookmakers and gambling gangs disturbed the country's leading politicians so much in the early Eighties that the Ministry of Sport instructed the Central Bureau of Investigation (CBI) to start a thorough and extensive inquiry.

Government sources admitted that illegal betting on cricket was getting out of control, and it feared that the maximum punishment of six months in prison for a first offence under the Public Gambling Act was not severe enough to deter the increasing number of crooks and cheats.

Officers at the CBI confirmed that the lure of easy money had attracted the most dangerous underworld gambling gangs, and that there was a real threat of them taking direct control, which could put the country's cricket – and even its national security –at risk. Leaving no stone unturned as they searched for incriminating evidence, the CBI officers collated information about Indian Test players, former players, officials, umpires, bookmakers, punters, and the middlemen – those slippery individuals who often brokered the corrupt deals.

Many of the names that the CBI officers came across had already appeared in the media, but by using specially designed computer software, a great deal of new incriminating evidence was uncovered, particularly from printouts of private landline telephone accounts and mobile phone accounts.

The property and business connections of the people under suspicion were also scrutinised, as well as details of telephone calls made by players from hotel rooms during matches, and voice recordings provided by a senior Pakistan player. One extremely wealthy Mumbai businessman admitted that he had installed a special telephone exchange with 112 private lines exclusively for bookmakers and gamblers to bet on cricket, and that the lines remained open right through every match, no matter where in the world it was being played.

All calls to players were protected by strict codes, and one major bookmaker admitted that his bets would usually be on predicting the individual score of a particular player, and on team scores. He confessed to running a huge gambling operation, and that he worked with bookmakers in Dubai.

Another Indian businessman admitted being in touch with bookmakers and gamblers in Bombay, Madras, Delhi, England, France, Belgium, Germany, Switzerland, Hong Kong, Singapore, Thailand, and even as far as Australia. There was no limit to his enormous network.

CBI officers hit the jackpot when they uncovered printouts of mobile phone calls made by bookmakers to players, many of them timed while matches were taking place, or just before play began. Every member of the public who had information about match-fixing was urged to speak to a CBI officer in the strictest confidence.

Once the CBI had completed its inquiry, it confronted a large number of players, past and present, as well as bookmakers and officials, and took statements from them. So that no one was left in any doubt about the purpose of the inquiry, the CBI disclosed its match-fixing terminology, which was broken down into five categories:

1. A player, or group of players, who received money to under-perform.
2. A player who placed bets in matches in which he played that would naturally undermine his performance.
3. Players who passed information to a betting syndicate about team composition, probable result, pitch condition, etc.
4. Groundsmen who were paid to prepare a pitch to suit a betting syndicate.
5. Present and past players who helped bookmakers to gain access to Indian and foreign players to influence their performance for money.

When it presented its detailed in-depth report, the CBI stressed that the cricketing fraternity had generally maintained a 'conspiracy of silence' and rarely offered specific information that was relevant to the inquiry. Not a single player, past or present, or any official – other than those who had made vague and general allegations in the media – volunteered any additional information.

Despite the stonewalling resistance from players and 'ignorance feigned by former players and officials', the CBI still succeeded in collecting crucial evidence through its exceptional diligence and determination. A number of players and 'others' even broke down when challenged, and when the evidence was slid under their noses they were forced to admit to being involved.

In a particularly fascinating disclosure, the CBI referred directly to Mukesh Kumar Gupta, a prominent Delhi bookmaker who had worked as a bank clerk for seven years before taking over a jewellery showroom with his father, a former government employee. He was also known as 'MK' and 'John'.

Gupta had told the CBI that he became interested in cricket when he noticed people betting in small stakes in the streets at the time India won the 1983 World Cup, so he decided to join in with them while returning home from his job at the bank. As all small-time gamblers knew very little about the nuances of cricket, Gupta started to read about the game in newspapers and books, and listened to BBC radio commentaries. It was a clever and professional way of gathering vital information that would put him ahead of other people who bet on cricket.

Armed with this knowledge he placed intelligent bets and won so much money that he moved his burgeoning gambling activities to bigger bookmakers, and he was introduced to a customer at the bank who was a keen gambler who also bet on tennis, football and hockey.

Gupta boasted to the CBI that he became successful quickly, and that he was able to move up and bet among the biggest bookmakers in Bombay. He also recalled a special moment in 1988 when he saw Indian Test star Ajay Sharma score lots of runs in a club match in Delhi.

In a highly revealing statement, Gupta admitted that he was so impressed with Sharma's performance that he handed him a sum of money, and said that should he ever have a problem in life to contact him, and he wrote down his telephone number for him. Gupta told the CBI that he regarded it as an investment, and hoped that he would reap the benefits from it. The CBI report stated: 'After about 15 days, Ajay Sharma got in touch with him [Gupta], and a relationship began which was to prove beneficial to both of them.'

From this point, the CBI report refers in detail to several leading international cricketers, and their alleged links to Gupta, the shrewd and ubiquitous bookmaker.

The report added: 'India were touring New Zealand in 1990 and Ajay Sharma and Manoj Prabhakar were in the team. MK [Gupta] requested Ajay Sharma over the telephone from India to introduce him to Manoj Prabhakar, and they spoke on the telephone.

'During the tour, he [Gupta] regularly rang up Ajay Sharma to gather information about the weather, pitch, team composition, etc. Based on that information, he [Gupta] operated his business, and made a good amount of money. He does not remember if he had paid money to Ajay Sharma for this, but said he might have given him some gifts.'

India were scheduled to visit England after their New Zealand tour, but Ajay Sharma was dropped, and this prompted Gupta to ask Sharma to introduce him personally to Prabhakar. The CBI report stated: 'Ajay Sharma duly did, and Prabhakar was paid to help MK during the England tour. MK also promised to pay him money equivalent to a Maruti Gypsy [SUV vehicle], which Manoj Prabhakar wanted to purchase, if he could provide him with useful information.

'According to MK, Manoj Prabhakar gave him information about all aspects of the Indian team, and he also under-performed in one of the Test matches, which ended in a draw. After the tour, when the team returned to India, MK fulfilled his promise and paid money to Manoj Prabhakar to buy a Maruti Gypsy with wide tyres. Somewhere around that time, MK also visited Manoj Prabhakar's house in Ghaziabad and had dinner with him. Manoj Prabhakar promised to introduce him to other international players.'

Gupta told the CBI that West Indian batsman Gus Logie was contacted over the telephone, but he refused to cooperate. While making his explosive statement to the CBI, whistle-blower Gupta also alleged that when Sri Lanka visited India, Manoj Prabhakar had introduced him to Aravinda de Silva 'for a price'.

On this matter, the CBI reported: 'MK established a good rapport with Arvinda de Silva, and later MK contacted de Silva for an introduction to Martin Crowe [New Zealand star batsman] and de Silva called Martin Crowe over the telephone and told him about MK. Accordingly, MK met Martin Crowe in New Zealand in 1991 and also had lunch in his house. MK added that Martin's wife, Simone, was also present during the meeting. MK has stated that he paid a sum of $20,000 to Martin Crowe in exchange for information about the pitch, weather, team composition, etc, whenever the New Zealand team played. MK stated that Martin Crowe refused to fix any matches for him.'

Gupta then referred to a match in Delhi between the Indian winners of the Wills Cup against the Pakistan winners of their Wills Cup tournament. The CIB reported: 'He [Gupta] does not remember the name of the Pakistan team, but he does remember that it was captained by Javed Miandad [a brilliant Test batsman].

'MK requested Prabhakar to introduce him to Salim Malik [another leading Pakistan batsman], which he did. He thereafter met Salim Malik at Hotel Maurya Sheraton, and struck a deal with him to fix that match without the knowledge of Javed Miandad. Pakistan lost the match in a close finish, and he paid Salim Malik, and MK earned roughly the same amount. He does not know the players Salim Malik roped in to fix this match.'

Gupta was so convinced of the importance of having information about how the cricket pitch would help bowlers and batsmen, weather conditions, and other related factors for betting purposes, that he trained a young lad on how to acquire this intelligence and sent him to England to gather it from newspapers and television broadcasts, and to relay it to him in India, which proved successful in his gambling business.

With his network of contacts expanding almost daily, Gupta recalled telephoning Manoj Prabhakar in Sri Lanka, where he was playing in an international cricket festival, and asking him if he could find an Australian player to speak to. Prabhakar is alleged to have rung Gupta with the news that every team in the tournament was staying at the Hotel Taj Samudra in Colombo, and that he could introduce him to Australia's prolific batsman Dean Jones.

Gupta told the CBI that he flew to Colombo immediately and paid Prabhakar for his information.

According to Gupta, the busy Prabhakar, who seemed to be using more energy off the field than on it, also introduced him to West Indian superstar Brian Lara and Sri Lanka's captain Arjuna Ranatunga, 'but they were not paid any money'. There is no record of Lara or Ranatunga providing information of any kind to Gupta.

Bookmaker Gupta continued to build his impressive betting empire, and he boasted that he had struck a deal with Manoj Prabhakar to arrange that a number of matches involving India in Australia (prior to the 1992 World Cup) would be fixed. Gupta recalled making 'good money' in two One-day matches involving India and Australia thanks to information from Prabhakar, but also admitted that he had lost a huge amount during the World Cup because nothing had worked according to his plans.

Australia's star batsman Mark Waugh was the next name on Gupta's list, and he alleged that Prabhakar had brought them together during a six-a-side tournament in Hong Kong, and that Waugh had accepted $20,000 in exchange for providing information on Australian team morale, team meetings, and chances of winning or losing. He also alleged that Prabhakar had been paid for making the introduction.

England and Surrey batsman/wicketkeeper Alec Stewart was Gupta's target on England's tour of India in 1993, and Prabhakar was again allegedly paid for introducing them. According to Gupta, he handed Stewart £5,000 for information about 'weather, wicket, team composition, etc whenever the English team played...' It must be emphasised that Stewart was completely exonerated from any allegation of wrongdoing.

Meanwhile, the extremely active Prabhakar had admitted that he had fixed two One-day matches that were played at Gwalior, and that he had informed Gupta of what was happening, but his information turned out to be wrong; India won both games and

Gupta lost heavily. Gupta claimed that he quickly recovered some of his losses in a One-day match at Bangalore, thanks to information from Prabhakar.

Not satisfied with the information he was receiving from complying players, Gupta spread his net to pull in umpires, and allegedly recruited Piloo Reporter, who 'assured him that he would give his assessment of matches'. Reporter was allegedly 'paid a small amount of money' after his advice about the First Test match in Calcutta turned out to be correct. India won comfortably by eight wickets.

Reporter also officiated in the dramatic fifth One-day Test at Gwalior when England's last seven wickets fell for only ten runs, and India won by three wickets with two overs to spare. During a tense encounter, Alec Stewart was hit on the head and slightly hurt by a piece of concrete thrown from the crowd.

Gupta further alleged that Sri Lanka's batting stars Ajunda Ranatunga and Aravinda de Silva both agreed to under-perform in the First Test at Lucknow on their Indian tour in 1994. It was Gupta's view that as Ranatunga was captain, and de Silva the vice-captain, no other Sri Lankan player needed to be involved. Sri Lanka lost the match, and Gupta claimed that he 'made a good deal of money' out of it, and that he paid de Silva the sum of $15,000.

The Gupta-Prabhakar partnership failed to stay the course, and was inevitably doomed when Gupta became suspicious that some matches were being fixed behind his back through Prabhakar, who had cut him out entirely. Gupta seemed sure that Prabhakar, the 'very money-minded' medium-fast bowler who also played for Durham in the English championship, had become involved with bookmakers from Delhi and Bombay, and with big punters.

There was a further blow for Gupta when he flew to Sharjah for a series of matches that involved Australia, Sri Lanka and Pakistan: Australian batsman Mark Waugh and Pakistan captain Salim Malik both refused to provide him with 'inside' information.

Undaunted by the setbacks, Gupta pursued Malik to Sri Lanka, where the host country – along with Pakistan, India and Australia – was competing in the prestigious international Singer Cup. Gupta alleged that he contacted Malik on the telephone, and that the Pakistan captain assured him that his team would lose a particular match against Australia. They did, and it 'earned him good money'.

By the end of 1994, Gupta was no longer a bookmaker, having switched to being a high-rolling gambler. He claimed that in this role as a punter he met West Indian legend Brian Lara during the 1994 West Indies tour of India, and that Lara 'offered to under-perform in two One-day matches', and that he 'made some money by betting on those matches'. Gupta told the CBI inquiry that he paid Lara $40,000 (£26,000) for the information. Lara was later cleared.

To make it absolutely plain, the CBI stated that most of the report's conclusions, especially those concerning foreign international cricketers, were based on the evidence of a number of bookmakers, particularly Mukesh Gupta. It further stressed that the report did not provide conclusive proof of wrongdoing, and emphasised that the CBI had not conducted an in-depth inquiry into connections between overseas players with Indian bookmakers and punters, and that foreign players had not been examined to verify the evidence that came from Indian bookmakers and punters.

Several players, including England's batting ace Alec Stewart, vigorously denied any involvement with Gupta or any other bookmaker. Prabhakar, however, confirmed that Ajay Sharma had introduced him to Gupta, whom he had met several times, he had spoken to him on the telephone, and seen him in countries outside India.

Prabhakar said that he knew Gupta as 'John' and had received money from him for providing information about cricket matches, but he claimed that Gupta paid him only when his introduction to foreign players resulted in a profitable relationship. The Indian Cricket Board banned Prabhakar for five years for his links with Gupta, and for being involved in betting.

Both Mark Waugh and Martin Crowe were cleared of any wrongdoing. The Australian Cricket Board decided that there was no evidence to support Gupta's claims that Waugh had been involved in match-fixing. A former High Court judge and a lawyer produced a 60-page report that stated that Crowe was 'truthful' and that there was no evidence to corroborate Gupta's allegations.

Lord MacLaurin, who was then Chairman of the England and Wales Cricket Board, said: 'Lord Condon's Anti-corruption Unit has undertaken a very thorough investigation into the allegations against Alec Stewart, and has concluded that no substantive evidence exists to justify proceedings against Alec in relation to this matter, which is, therefore, closed.'

Lord MacLaurin's statement followed earlier comments by Gerard Elias QC, Chairman of the Disciplinary Standing Committee at the ECB, who had disclosed that Mukesh Gupta had declined to make a statement to the ACSU, or to assist in any inquiry, or appear at a disciplinary hearing to substantiate his claim.

Elias said: 'No independent evidence confirming, supporting, or corroborating the allegation has been found by the Anti-corruption Unit that could be brought forward to any disciplinary hearing.' He went on to state that Stewart had categorically denied receiving money as alleged by Gupta, and had made his financial records available.

Elias continued: 'In these circumstances, the assertion of the Indian bookmaker, untested, and unable to be tested, being the only source of allegation against him, it follows that there exists no substantive evidence to justify proceedings against Alec Stewart in relation to this matter.'

Lawyer Desmond Fernando was appointed by the Sri Lankan Cricket Board to investigate the serious allegations against

Ranatunga and de Silva, and he stated in an 11-page report to the governing body that he was 'unable to question or cross-examine Gupta and was, therefore, forced to accept the testimonies of the players'. To support his conclusion, Fernando added: 'His [Gupta's] statement lacked precision,' and he added that Gupta had not said where the conversations took place, where the money was allegedly handed over, or whether it was in cash or otherwise.

Ranatunga led Sri Lanka to their 1996 World Cup triumph, and de Silva was the country's most prolific run-maker in Test matches. Both denied Gupta's allegations that they had received $15,000 from him to throw a Test match against India at the K D Singh Babu Stadium in Lucknow in January 1994, and further denied that they ever agreed to under-perform, or had accepted money for doing so. Ranatunga blamed poor umpiring for him and de Silva jointly scoring only 33 runs in four innings in the match.

India batted first, amassing 511, then bowled Sri Lanka out for 218, routed them again for just 174 when they followed on, and won the match by an innings and 119 runs. Ranatunga scored 9 and 0, and de Silva 13 and 11.

India repeated the hammering in the Second Test at the M Chinnaswanny Stadium in Bangalore later in January, when they declared at 541-6 and bowled Sri Lanka out for 231 and 215, to win by an innings and 95 runs. On this occasion, Ranatunga scored 26 and 28, and de Silva 17 and 8.

It was all very much the same in the Third Test at the Gujarat Stadium in Ahmedabad, where India delivered another trouncing, this time by an innings and 17 runs. Sri Lanka could muster only 119 when they batted first; India replied with 358 all out, and Sri Lanka were then dismissed for 222 in their second innings. Ranatunga scored 15 and 29, and de Silva 7 and 14.

It was a depressing three-match series for Ranatunga, who averaged slightly over 17, but it was even worse for de Silva whose 70 runs in six innings left him with an average of less than 12.

Fernando's report claimed that the denials by Ranatunga and de Silva under questioning had a higher 'evidentiary value' than the 'mere statement' by Gupta to the Indian police. It did emerge, however, that de Silva had admitted that he had established a relationship with Gupta, and identified him in a photograph that was produced during an interview. Ranatunga was less sure, and said that he 'might have' met Gupta.

Embarrassed and baffled by their disastrous tour, the Sri Lankan Cricket Board launched an internal inquiry that ended with a forthright report that criticised Ranatunga's captaincy and de Silva's attitude to other team members. The report also stated: 'There is evidence that a bookmaker of Indian origin has attempted to make his presence felt in the national cricket team.'

CHAPTER THIRTEEN

SANTA STANFORD GETS THE SACK – AND PRISON

It was around two o'clock on 11 June 2008 that Sir Allen Stanford landed like some mid-summer Santa Claus in a black helicopter on the lush, manicured outfield at Lord's cricket ground in north London with a proverbial sack bulging with $147.5 million to give away for the good of the game.

He touched down in glorious sunshine to broad smiles and generous applause from cricket legends that included the three Sirs – Richards, Botham and Sobers – and with several leaders of the England and Wales Cricket Board (ECB) excitedly lining up to see him like bedazzled 6-year-olds on Christmas morning.

Out in front were the ECB's elated top two: David Collier, the Chief Executive, and Giles Clarke, the Chairman. Stanford stepped elegantly from the helicopter, and waved in presidential style to no one in particular. As the bumptious Texan strutted and swaggered towards the nearby Nursery Pavilion, his entourage craned forward to catch every twanged word. Fawning had reached a new, and laughable, level.

Yet no one dared snigger or whisper a word of disdain – for this apparently was the game's great new saviour. 'Mr Moneybags' had flown in to donate umpteen millions to an impoverished sport, and maybe pick up some useful worldwide publicity for himself at the same time. Frankly, no one really cared a toss about him seeking some personal publicity, all they desperately wanted was to see the colour of his money – and to count it bundle by bundle, if that could be arranged.

Even then, at this very early stage, amid all the pomp and promise, it sounded far too good to be true. Yet two years of irreverent Allen Stanford hysteria slipped by before this colossal dream turned into a tawdry nightmare, when he was arrested as a fraudster, shamefully put in prison, and twice savagely beaten while locked in the cells.

A large logo proclaiming 'Twenty/20 for 20' was draped impressively at the back of the Nursery Pavilion on that unforgettable visit to Lord's in the summer of 2008, which ended with Botham, Richards, Clarke and Collier standing proudly alongside Stanford, and directly behind a black box with a glass top which purportedly contained $20 million in bundles of crisp notes for the phalanx of photographers to snap for next day's newspapers – and that in just 20 months would be available to remind them all of Act One of the Stanford Horror Show.

For several weeks, Stanford, the ECB and the Professional Cricketers' Association had worked tirelessly to reach an agreement on how the money should be distributed, and it was eventually decided that all England players on central contracts who had not been involved in limited-over matches would be left out entirely.

So it was finally agreed that Stanford would promote an annual Twenty/20 series of matches between England and the Stanford Superstars (a team of West Indian players) for a winner-takes-all $20 million every time. From this enormous pool of money, a massive $11 million would be shared between the players of the winning team, plus $1 million among squad players who did not take part in the match, and a further $1 million to its management personnel. The remaining $7 million would be divided between the ECB and the West Indies Cricket Board.

An enormous amount of media and television coverage greeted the first match at the Stanford Cricket Ground near the financier's home in Antigua, where he strolled around the boundary edge smiling profusely for the cameras, stopping frequently to chat to spectators who rushed up to shake him by the hand and ask for his autograph.

Stanford left no one in doubt that he was deeply in love with himself. At one point he mingled among the wives and girlfriends of the England players, who were out on the field at the time. The players were furious with him when they turned round and saw him trying to persuade the 'WAGs' to sit on his knee.

Troubles had mounted before this match, as Digicel, sponsors of the West Indies cricket team, had expressed concerns about the way in which the event was being promoted, but the bitter row happily blew over, and the Stanford Superstars humiliated England in a thumping ten-wicket win.

England's dejected squad went home with not a penny to show for their efforts, although they still looked forward to returning the following year to fill their pockets – except there would be no second attempt, as by then Stanford would be facing fraud charges.

Cynics and many highly respected media commentators had condemned the ECB deal as 'tacky' from the start, and some even wondered whether Stanford genuinely possessed all the money that he was giving away so generously. The ECB quickly reassured the niggling doubters that he had been thoroughly checked out, so it became a frustrating question of 'let us wait and see...'

In a totally separate proposal, Stanford had offered to unload a further $47 million for an annual four-nation Stanford Challenge at Lord's between England, the West Indies, and probably New Zealand and Sri Lanka, which thankfully never materialised because his mythical empire had crashed before the deal was completed.

Stanford's enthusiasm for the annual Superstars v England

contest automatically followed from the Stanford Twenty/20 tournament that he had created and funded in the West Indies. The first, played in Antigua during July and August 2006, was remarkably low key for the flamboyant so-called philanthropist, but a lot more glitz and glamour had been generated for the second tournament in February 2008, which attracted a global television audience of 300 million, and was won by Trinidad and Tobago.

This was the ideal precursor for a showdown between the Caribbean Twenty/20 kings and their counterparts in England, which turned out to be Middlesex. In a thrilling match under floodlights, Trinidad and Tobago were crowned winners of the Super Series, and walked away with $280 million.

Stanford, who often boasted that it was 'fun being a millionaire', arrived in the Caribbean in the 1980s, settling down on the small British colony of Montserrat, where he started the highly controversial Guardian International Bank. Faced with having his licence revoked for dubious dealings, which he vehemently denied, he renamed it the Stanford International Bank and moved its operations to Antigua and Barbuda, the next island along, best known for its active volcano.

During those halcyon days, Stanford held dual citizenship, being resident in Antigua and Barbuda and the United States, and in 2006 he became the first American to be knighted by Antigua and Barbuda for his 'services to the community and economic development', and Stanford proudly used the title 'Sir Allen'.

The tall, imposing Texan gave many good reasons to be accepted as a trusted and genuine self-made millionaire, a conclusion that was practically endorsed by *Forbes* magazine when it named him the 605th richest person in the world. Yet all those millions of people who had blindly pinned their faith in him woke up on 17 February 2009 and gasped in shock when they opened their newspapers and saw that the US Securities and Exchange Commission (SEC) had charged Stanford with fraud and multiple violations of the country's securities laws for alleged 'massive ongoing fraud' involving $8 billion in certificates of deposits.

It transpired that the FBI had raided three of Stanford's opulent offices, in Houston, Memphis and also in Tupelo, Mississippi, and ten days later the SEC amended its original charge and now claimed that the alleged fraud was a 'massive Ponzi scheme' (a financial scam named after the Italian-born swindler Charles Ponzi). The SEC claimed that Stanford and his accomplices had misappropriated 'billions of investors' money' and had falsified the Stanford International Bank's records to conceal the fraud.

A spokesman for the SEC alleged that Stanford International Bank's financial statements, which included its investment income, were fictional. It was also simultaneously revealed that the Florida Office of Financial Regulation and the Financial Industry Regulatory Authority had investigated Stanford's wholly-owned company Stanford Financial Group.

FBI agents tracked Stanford down to his girlfriend's home in Virginia, where he was promptly served with legal documents issued by the SEC. Stanford's assets, together with those of his companies, were frozen and placed in receivership and he was ordered to surrender his passport. Unconfirmed reports claimed that Stanford had tried to flee the country to Antigua in a private jet, but the airplane company refused his credit card.

A former executive in Stanford's empire was alleged to have told SEC investigators that Stanford had presented hypothetical investment results as factual data while making sales pitches to clients. With Stanford's reputation as a philanthropist and trustworthy financier in abject meltdown, there was a swift reaction among those who had worked closely with him, especially where it involved direct business and monetary dealings. Eastern Caribbean Central Bank (ECCB) quickly took over the local operations of the Bank of Antigua, and the Venezuelan Government took over the Stanford Bank Venezuela.

The FBI arrested Stanford four months later on 18 June 2009, but even then he adamantly denied that he had done anything wrong, and claimed that his companies had been well run until the SEC came along and 'disembowelled' them. A week later, on 25 June, Stanford appeared in a Houston court where he pleaded not guilty to charges of fraud, conspiracy and obstruction, and his expensive team of lawyers revealed that he had resorted to 'liberal alcohol' as he fought to deal with what was happening to him.

A US tax court claimed that Stanford and his wife, Susan, had under-reported their 1990 federal taxes by $423,531.36 while running his bank in Montserrat, and public records later allegedly showed that he owed $212 million. It also emerged that the FBI, and other agencies, had conducted investigations into Stanford for possible money-laundering for Mexico's Gulf Cartel, but no charges were brought against him.

Troubles continued to escalate for Stanford, and while being driven from a private prison in Huntsville, Texas, to the federal courthouse in Houston, he complained of a racing heart. He was admitted to the Conroe Texas Regional Medical Centre where doctors checked him over and discharged him with the ironic words 'you have nothing to worry about'. But he would need medical attention again on 26 September, when he was admitted to the Joe Corley Detention Facility with injuries reportedly sustained in a fight with another inmate.

In the twinkling of an eye, Stanford had plummeted from the height of luxury to the depths of despair, and he was admitted to hospital yet again on 8 November 2010 with more injuries, sustained in yet another fight with an inmate in a private prison near Conroe. Distressing photographs showed him with his neck in a brace, one eye half shut, a bandage wrapped around his head, and shamefully shackled hand and foot. In addition to his painful physical beatings, Stanford took a hefty psychological blow when Stanford University protested that he had damaged its name by claiming that his great-great-grandfather was a relative of the founder, Leland Stanford.

He had funded the restoration of Leland Stanford's mansion in Sacramento, California, and hired his own genealogists to prove that he was a member of the Leland Stanford family, 'to help preserve an important piece of Stanford family history'. But the university refused to accept his personal claims, and brushed him aside in a brusque statement: 'We are not aware of any genealogical relationship between Allen Stanford and Leland Stanford.' The university then filed a trademark infringement suit against Stanford, claiming that the school's name was being used 'in a way that creates public confusion, and is injurious'.

According to the Federal Aviation Administration, the ubiquitous Stanford had six planes registered with them, and it was generally observed that he had used his aircraft to build relationships with politicians. Official records showed that four Democratic congressmen flew in a Stanford jet to Montego Bay for talks with Jamaican leaders in a Ritz-Carlton hotel, and various political committees paid for at least 16 flights on Stanford jets.

Once the fraud allegations against Stanford were made public, red-faced officials at the ECB rushed to distance themselves from their flamboyant benefactor and his offer to fund quadrangular tournaments at Lord's for the ensuing three years, and three days later announced that they had cancelled every contract with him.

In the briefest statement possible, the ECB said: 'Following allegations made today by the United States Securities and Exchange Commission, and their decision to apply for a temporary restraining order, the England and Wales Cricket Board and the West Indies Cricket Board have suspended negotiations with Sir Allen Stanford and his financial corporation concerning a new sponsorship deal.'

Ironically, ECB Chairman Giles Clarke was told of the crisis while watching England in a Test match against the West Indies on

Stanford's home island of Antigua. Hapless Clarke was immediately blasted, and ridiculed, for having become involved with the silver-tongued Texan, and Lord Marland, who had unsuccessfully opposed Clarke in his re-election as Chairman, gleefully led the charge.

A furious Lord Marland said: 'The ECB has walked into the arms of a man who has been accused of a massive fraud, and who, through his actions during the Stanford Super Series, brought the game of cricket into disrepute. The ECB has failed in its due diligence, and was negotiating with him up to the eleventh hour to strike a new deal. At any other organisation those responsible for this [type of thing] would resign. Those pictures of Giles Clarke and Stanford posing behind that chest of money will haunt English cricket for ever.'

Former England pace bowler Jonathan Agnew, now a leading BBC cricket correspondent, steamed in and facetiously reflected on the day Stanford was greeted with naïve adulation when he whirred into Lord's in his black helicopter, and blew them all away.

Agnew groaned: 'Even now, there's an air of disbelief about the whole thing. Did it really happen? Did this man, this Texan, who basically said our cricket was rubbish, land his helicopter here on the Nursery ground? We thought our administrators had completely lost the plot. What were they doing associating with a man like Sir Allen Stanford who'd already been turned down by South Africa, India and Australia?'

The Stanford Group also sponsored the Stanford St Jude Championship, a PGA tour golf tournament in Memphis, and a polo competition in Palm Beach, Florida. One of the world's top golfers, Vijay Singh, had also signed an endorsement deal with Stanford, the serial deceiver.

Having been extravagantly described in the *Houston Chronicle* as the 'leading benefactor, promoter, employer and public persona' of Antigua and Barbuda, all the praise collapsed into a pile of rubbish in October 2009 when the island's National Honours Committee unanimously agreed to strip Stanford of his knighthood. This order was duly carried out in April 2010.

All those thousands of people who had so proudly gone out of their way to inform friends, family and business associates of their personal contact and affection for the 'wonderful' Stanford were now suddenly stampeding into the distance, angrily chastising themselves for being so gullibly seduced by him.

Stanford was given the names Robert Allen when he was born on 24 March 1950. He grew up in Mexia in Texas with his father James, a one-time mayor in the town, and his mother Sammie, a nurse. He lived with his mother after his parents divorced, and then rejoined his father when they both remarried. Eastern Hills High School in Fort Worth provided Stanford with excellent educational grounding before he moved on to Baylor University in Waco, where he graduated with a Bachelor of Arts degree in finance.

Stanford's first foray into the competitive business world was a string of health clubs situated near Waco, called the Mr and Mrs Heath Studios. It turned out to be a disastrous venture and was declared bankrupt in 1982. Two years later Stanford followed in the same way, declaring himself bankrupt with debts of around $1.3 million. Any doubts that he might have held about being a born 'failed businessman' were blown away when he teamed up with his father, and they made a fortune by reselling property – bought into when real estate was at rock bottom – in a thriving market.

Stanford took full control when his father retired in 1993, and headed a company with 500 employees. As time went on, Stanford's popularity grew as he gave generously to charities and good causes, and in February 2009 – the dreaded month when the police pounced – the Stanford Financial Group's website ironically crowed: 'Sir Allen supports charitable, cultural, educational, social and sporting events, and organisations throughout the world.'

He had also written in the *Stanford Eagle*, his company's glossy magazine, that: 'St Jude Children's Research Hospital has been Stanford's corporate charity of choice for three years, and our partnership has raised more than $15 million for the hospital during that time.' Yet on 19 February, a spokesman for the hospital disputed Stanford's figures, and said that only $8 million had been received during 2007 and 2008.

After becoming a founder of the Bauer College in Houston, the apparently indefatigable Stanford chose to speak about leadership and ethics at its first undergraduate intake, which seemed appropriate for him at the time.

Stanford's grandfather started out as a barber, but quit to be a small-time insurance salesman, although Stanford later falsely claimed that he had started the worldwide Stanford Financial Group, which boasted assets of $8 billion and clients that included affluent investors, institutions and emerging growth companies. US court records left no one in doubt that the Stanford offshore bank was formed in Montserrat in 1985, and moved to Antigua in 1990.

When the FBI knocked on Stanford's door in February 2009, the Stanford Development Group owned a luxury home with 14 rooms that covered 7,000 square feet, surrounded by palm trees and rows of bright flowers on a quiet street in Houston, just a mile from the Stanford Group's headquarters, an imposing three-storey building. While he was being feted in the West Indies, the mesmeric Stanford owned *The Sun* newspaper in Antigua and Barbuda, as well as *The Sun* in St Kitts and Nevis, but both were shut down in April 2010 after their owner's reputation had been destroyed.

For someone who was so naturally alert and organised, Stanford's private life was in a disastrous mess. Those who knew him well even joked to his face that he had become the philandering philanthropist, having fathered six children by four different women, and some found it hard not to smirk when told that he had a daughter named Randi. The sexually rampant Stanford also reared two other daughters and three sons, and over the years he somehow found the energy and time to juggle three mistresses, whom he proudly referred to as his 'outside wives'.

Memories of those rousing escapades were about all that Stanford had to keep him sound while detained at the Federal Detention Centre in Houston where he waited for his trial – and the next chapter of his extraordinary life.

Early in 2011, a judge declared that Stanford was 'mentally incompetent' and not fit to stand trial on charges of running a pyramid scheme that swindled investors out of £4.5 billion.

United States District Judge David Hittner agreed to delay the start of proceedings so that the disgraced Texan could be treated for his medical problems. Three psychiatrists testified that Stanford was not competent, partly because of a brain injury that he sustained during a fight in prison in September 2009.

Stanford and three former executives of his now defunct Stanford Financial Group stand accused of advising clients from 113 countries to invest more than $7 billion at the Stanford International Bank in Antigua, promising enormous returns.

Lawyers for Stanford said that he ran a legitimate business, and that he did not misuse bank funds to pay for a lavish lifestyle, as claimed by the prosecution.

CHAPTER FOURTEEN

LAWYER BLASTS WARNE AND WAUGH FOR HELPING INDIAN BOOKIE

While he was director of cricket's Anti-corruption Unit, former Metropolitan Police chief Lord Condon released a comprehensive summary of several major international inquiries, along with their findings, which included high-profile cases of some of the world's most prominent cricketers.

AUSTRALIA 1995: Australian Cricket Board

During the Singer World Cup series in Sri Lanka in September 1994, two of Australian's star players, Shane Warne and Mark Waugh, accepted money from an Indian bookmaker known to them as 'John' – one of several names used by Mukesh Gupta – for providing 'weather and pitch' information regarding matches in which Australia took part. Warne accepted $5,000, and Waugh pocketed $4,000.

Teams from Sri Lanka, India, Pakistan and Australia took part in the tournament, and the Australian team stayed at the Lanka

Oberoi Hotel in Colombo, a short distance from the city's popular casino. Both Warne and Waugh visited the casino, and 'John' – who was also staying at the Lanka Oberoi – spoke to them while they were at the gambling tables. He openly told Waugh that he was a bookmaker, and asked him if he would be interested in providing pitch and weather information for matches that involved Australia, as well as inside knowledge about the team, tactics, and the names of those who had been selected to play.

'John' told Waugh that he would be paid $4,000, which Waugh accepted, and he also agreed to introduce the bookmaker to Warne, but stressed that he would not divulge anything that involved team tactics, or the names of players who had been selected for matches. According to official inquiries, Waugh was alleged to have given 'John' information 'about ten times over five months', and that this included matches played by Australia in Pakistan, the 1994/95 home Ashes series, matches in New Zealand, and matches in the West Indies.

'John' allegedly gave Warne an envelope containing $5,000 as a show of appreciation for meeting him, and Warne said that he provided pitch and weather information to 'John' before three matches during the 1994/95 Ashes series – a One-day Test against England in Sydney; the Second Test at the Melbourne Cricket Ground; and the Fifth Test at the WACA in Perth.

This clandestine contact that Warne and Waugh had enjoyed with the Indian bookmaker came to an abrupt end when a journalist told Ian McDonald, who was then the Australian team manager, what he believed was going on. Officials from the ACB interviewed Warne and Waugh who handed over unsigned handwritten statements concerning the acceptance of money from 'John'. After attending a further interview with ACB officials, both Warne and Waugh 'made admissions', and Warne was fined A$8,000 and Waugh A$10,000.

AUSTRALIA 1998: O'Reagan Inquiry

After the Warne and Waugh allegations were revealed in the media, the Australian Cricket Board came under heavy attack from an angry public for the way in which it had handled the affair, and it responded by appointing lawyer Rob O'Reagan QC to head up a Player Conduct Inquiry to cover six years from January 1992 to December 1998.

O'Reagan's duties included: 'To investigate whether any of Australia's contracted players had engaged in conduct that related to betting, bribery, match-fixing, the unauthorised accepting of money or other benefits, and related matters. Also to investigate the disciplinary processes that were available to consider such conduct.'

Because the inquiry was totally private, O'Reagan could not compel potential witnesses to give evidence, was not protected by absolute privilege, and crucially did not offer a complete defence against an action for alleged defamation. O'Reagan focused on events that had surrounded Australian players in respect of:

- allegations that the second match of the 1992 World XI versus an Indian XI was rigged
- allegations that Allan Border was approached to fix the final Test during the 1993 Ashes tour of England
- acceptance of $4,000 by Mark Waugh and $5,000 by Shane Warne during the 1994 Sri Lankan/Pakistan tour
- alleged approach to Ricky Ponting for match information in 1997
- alleged approach to Mark Taylor for 'weather and pitch' information during the 1998 Pakistan tour.

During an extensive investigation, O'Reagan's assistants conducted 60 interviews, while he handled ten, and he eventually released his hugely critical report on 28 February 1999. O'Reagan slated the

ACB for the way in which it had dealt with the Warne/Waugh case, and described the fine each player was given as 'inadequate, as their size did not reflect the seriousness of what they had done'.

He believed both players should have been given a lengthy suspension, and in a scathing summary, O'Reagan concluded: 'They must have known that it was wrong to accept from, and supply information to, a bookmaker whom they also knew bet on cricket. Otherwise they would have reported the incident to team management long ago, before they were found out in February 1995. In behaving as they did, they failed lamentably to set the sort of example one might expect from senior players and role models for youngsters.'

O'Reagan recommended that the ACB should review the way in which it dealt with serious disciplinary proceedings, publicity of such proceedings, penalties to be imposed, and counselling for players with gambling interests. Warne and Waugh said that they had been 'naïve and stupid', though neither of them used the word 'greedy'. Former Australian batting legend Neil Harvey said that, if it had been up to him, they would have been banned.

PAKISTAN 1995: Justice (retired) Fakhruddin G Ibrahim

An inquiry was initiated by the Pakistan Cricket Board, under Chairman Justice Fakhruddin G Ibrahim, to look into allegations by Australian players regarding the First Test between Pakistan and Australia in Karachi in 1994, and a One-day International in Rawalpindi.

Some months after the Test match, a newspaper alleged that Salim Malik (a leading Pakistan player) had offered Australian trio Shane Warne, Mark Waugh and Tim May $200,000 to manipulate the game on the final day. Waugh also alleged that Malik offered him $200,000 for four or five Australian players to under-perform during the One-day International in Rawalpindi. The inquiry team became frustrated when the Australian players did not travel to Pakistan to give evidence, and the team was forced to rely on statements and the cross-examination of Malik.

In February 1995, the International Cricket Council urged the Pakistan Cricket Board to be discreet, 'always bearing in mind the damage to the image of cricket if allegations were made in public in any way'. Justice Ibrahim concluded the proceedings in October 1995, stating: 'The allegations against Saleem [sic] Malik are not worthy of any credence, and must be rejected as unfounded.'

INDIA 1997: Chandrachud Inquiry

Following revelations in *Outlook* magazine, the Board of Control for Cricket in India appointed Justice Y V Chandrachud to inquire into allegations of betting and match-fixing by Indian cricketers and/or management. The magazine had alleged that Manoj Prabhakar (a prominent Indian bowler) had been offered approximately $53,000 by an Indian team colleague to under-perform during the 1994 Singer Cup match between India and Pakistan, in order to favour Pakistan.

Justice Chandrachud concluded his thorough investigation in November 1997, when he stated that although he had accepted that large-scale betting occurred in India, he was unwilling to accept, upon the information provided to him, that there was proof that any Indian player, official or journalist had been involved in such activity. The result of this inquiry remained undisclosed for a further two-and-a-half years.

PAKISTAN 1998: Qayyum Inquiry

Pakistan set up a one-man judicial commission to investigate allegations that members of the national team had been involved in betting and match-fixing, and Mr Justice Malik Muhammad

Qayyum was appointed to the commission. The term 'match-fixing' was defined as 'deciding the outcome of a match before it was played, and then playing, or having others to play, below their ability to influence the outcome to be in accordance with the pre-decided outcome... and undertaken primarily for pecuniary gain'.

Justice Qayyum considered two offences – match-fixing, and bringing the team into disrepute – and it quickly became apparent that Pakistan's star batsman Salim Malik was the focal point of many of the allegations. Australian players Mark Waugh and Mark Taylor appeared as personal witnesses, and alleged that Malik had approached them shortly before a One-day International in Rawalpindi on 22 October 1994, and asked Waugh if he could persuade the Australian team to throw the match.

However, neither of them mentioned the undisclosed ACB 1995 finding that Waugh and Warne had accepted money from an Indian bookmaker, a fact that Taylor was also very much aware of, though not involved in. The ACB finding was only revealed in December 1998, after Waugh and Taylor had given evidence before Justice Qayyum. As a result of this subsequent disclosure, the Qayyum inquiry switched to Australia, where a special hearing was convened under Pakistan law, and they heard directly from Waugh and Warne.

Justice Qayyum eventually reported that: 'The allegation that the Pakistan team as a whole is involved in match-fixing is just based on allegation, conjecture and surmises, without positive proof. As a whole, the players of the Pakistan cricket team are innocent.' But Justice Qayyum had not finished. He followed up with a stinging knockout blow, concluding that the evidence against Salim Malik was sound and acceptable, and recommended that this national hero should be banned from cricket for life, and that there should be an inquiry into his assets.

He further recommended that Ata-ur-Rehman should be similarly banned for life. Additionally, Wasim Akram, Mushtaq Ahmed, Waqar Younis, Inzamam-ul-Haq, Akram Raza, Basit Ali and Saeed Anwar were all subject to various penalties, including being warned, censured, further investigated, or kept under observation.

Justice Qayyum also recommended that the captaincy of Pakistan should be removed from Wasim Akram. Fines were recommended for Salim Malik, Wasim Akram, Mushtaq Ahmed, Ata-ur-Rehman, Waqar Younis, Inzamam-ul-Haq, Akram Raza and Saeed Anwar.

Justice Qayyum's devastating conclusions represented an unprecedented exposure of international cricket wrongdoing, with so many icons being found guilty of on-field offences. It was a terribly sad day for world cricket. Deeply concerned by all that he had ascertained, Justice Qayyum advised the Pakistan Cricket Board to order the players to declare their assets and, if necessary, to investigate their accounts.

A series of recommendations was also made to try to prevent future match-fixing incidents, which included:

- character of captain and manager
- independent team ombudsman on foreign tours
- new code of conduct
- increase to players' pay and conditions
- educate players about entrapment by bookmakers
- enforce strict discipline with zero tolerance.

ENGLAND 1999: Metropolitan Police investigation

Stephen Fleming, captain of New Zealand, was approached by two Indian gentlemen in his team's hotel in Leicester and asked if he would 'fix' the Third Test against England at Old Trafford, Manchester, on 5 August 1999. Fleming emphatically rejected what the Indian pair had proposed, and referred the matter to his team manager.

A day or two later, former England all-rounder Chris Lewis was similarly approached by two Indian gentlemen, who also wanted him to 'fix' the Third Test or, alternatively, other matches involving England. He, too, flatly rejected the offer and the incident was reported to the England and Wales Cricket Board and the Metropolitan Police, which launched an immediate criminal investigation and exchanged information with New Delhi Police and the Central Bureau of Investigation in India.

The result of the investigation was passed to the UK judicial authorities for consideration, but no action was taken against anyone, and the case was completely dropped.

INDIA 2000: New Delhi Police investigation

It was while the New Delhi Police were monitoring telephone calls made by an Indian national that they accidentally overheard a conversation in which the name of Hansie Cronje, the highly respected captain of the South African cricket team, was mentioned, and, having been alerted, they subsequently listened to him discussing details of match-fixing.

New Delhi Police promptly launched a full-scale investigation, primarily centred on the association between Cronje and other South African players, London-based businessman Sanjay Chawla, and two Indian bookmakers. In May 2000, the police charged Cronje and several of his South African colleagues in their absence with cheating, fraud and criminal conspiracy. At the time of writing, the case is still unresolved.

SOUTH AFRICA 2000: King Commission

After the sensational revelations of substantial match-fixing involving Hansie Cronje (see Chapter Nine) and his subsequent unforced confession to officials of the United Cricket Board of

South Africa (UCB), the country's President set up a major inquiry into match-fixing, chaired by Judge Ewin King and later referred to as the King Commission.

Among the terms of reference for King's preliminary investigation was that Cronje had confessed to accepting approximately $10,000 from a bookmaker during the triangular tournament between South Africa, England and Zimbabwe in January and February 2001. The UCB revealed that it had first become aware of allegations that Cronje had been involved in match-fixing on 7 April 2000.

Cronje adamantly denied the allegations at first, but then confessed to accepting money from bookmaker Sanjay Chawla for being involved in cricket malpractice with the South African team. It was irrefutably established that South African bookmaker Hamid Cassim had introduced Cronje to Chawala, and further evidence revealed that Cronje had approached several South African players in a light-hearted and jocular manner, suggesting that money could be made by fixing the results of cricket matches. This was perceived as Cronje's way of testing the interest of players.

In the main, the players literally laughed it off, but batsman Herschelle Gibbs and bowler Henry Williams were later named in Cronje's elaborate web of corruption. It was during the Central Bureau of Investigation (CBI) investigation in India that the country's iconic batsman Mohammad Azharuddin had admitted to introducing Cronje to bookmaker Mukesh Gupta.

Wasting no time, Gupta then propositioned Cronje, who accepted $30,000 to ensure that South Africa lost the Third Test starting the next day, which they did, but Cronje insisted that he did nothing to influence the result. Around this period, Gupta made an offer to Cronje for South Africa to lose a One-day International match which was initially played as a benefit game for Mohinder Amarnath, but subsequently revised to qualify as an official international fixture.

Cronje approached several South African players to make them aware of the huge offer, reportedly around $250,000, for them to play badly in the One-day match. Cronje later indicated that the offer was increased by a further $100,000, but after meetings that involved senior players, and the team as a whole, Gupta's proposition was rejected.

The highly lucrative Gupta/Cronje partnership ended abruptly in November 1997, apparently after Cronje had turned down certain undisclosed Gupta proposals. With Gupta off the scene, it was alleged that Cronje still influenced the result of the Fifth Test against England at Centurion Park, Pretoria, in January 2000. South Africa had scored 155-6 at close of play on the first day, and the second, third and fourth days were all washed out by rain.

On the eve of the final day's play, Cronje spoke to Marlon Aronstam, an expert in sports betting, who urged him to 'make a game of it'. South Africa batted on during the last day until Cronje declared at 248-8. Both teams forfeited an innings, which left England to score 249 for victory, which they achieved with two wickets and five balls remaining in the match.

Aronstam had reportedly agreed to make a donation of 200,000 rand to a charity of Cronje's choice if he could ensure a victory to either side. Cronje later said the offer was 500,000 rand ($60,000 at the time). Aronstam also testified that he paid Cronje 50,000 rand as an 'advance' for future cooperation about pitch reports.

The UCB banned Cronje for life, and Gibbs and Williams were both banned from international cricket for six months but allowed to play in domestic matches. Gibbs was also fined 60,000 rand and Williams 10,000 rand for accepting a $15,000 bribe offered to Cronje to under-perform in a One-day International.

CHAPTER FIFTEEN

TAX PROBES AND 'FIXING' IN THE IPL

There can be little doubt that the most exciting introduction to world cricket in modern times is a new format of the game that has infuriated the dogmatic purist, but has brought thrills and spills to those who relish being spectacularly entertained – not to mention bagfuls of money through the turnstiles to bolster battered balance sheets and fend off quibbling bank managers.

Capturing a viable cricket audience had become a seriously tough challenge, with fewer and fewer people wanting to spend a whole day sitting patiently watching what many disparagingly referred to as 'paint drying on a wall'. Chief executives of professional cricket clubs were feverishly pulling their hair out – some of them literally, it seemed – to find ways of increasing income to stay in a sport that desperately needed a strong and vital financial injection.

The game appeared to be plunging into a crisis – cynics would say oblivion – when up popped the proverbial Aladdin with a magic lamp and, suddenly, before our very eyes, there was a new game that was still to be played generally to cricket's laws and regulations, and would be known as 'Twenty/20'. This new game was keenly promoted as a guaranteed panacea for the ills that were threatening to cripple the sport.

As predicted by the marketing moguls, crowds packed into cricket grounds to witness this pulsating contest in which each team was allowed just 20 overs to bat and bowl. New laws were introduced to limit where fielders could stand at different stages of the match to encourage players to launch daringly into big hitting to keep spectators on the edge of their seats with excitement.

Measured in income and attendance, Twenty/20 was a revelation that attracted men, women and children in many thousands, including hordes who had never attended a cricket match before, and huge numbers who admitted that they had absolutely hated the game.

A truly competitive Twenty/20 match will equal just about anything in sport for tension and spectacular rivalry, but it also provides the simplest opportunity for crooked players to under-perform deliberately to pocket bribes from bookmakers and gamblers, and with no fear of questions being asked.

For instance, all batsmen are expected to take wild slogs at some point in Twenty/20 matches, and many are dismissed this way, but no one watching it live at the cricket ground, or on TV, can possibly know whether it was a genuine mistake or one that had been pre-arranged for betting purposes. Still, spectators will look sceptically at catches fielders drop, especially the easy-looking ones, as well as wides and no-balls from errant bowlers, missed stumpings by wicketkeepers, and strange decisions by captains.

Lord Condon made no secret of his concern for potential fixing in Twenty/20 matches shortly before he stepped down from his position as head of cricket's Anti-corruption and Security Unit, when he said: 'Twenty/20 is just ripe for corruption, as the shorter the game, the more influence each particular incident can have. So I think it opens up a great deal of opportunities for bookmakers to try to corrupt players into providing various different outcomes in the game, even the result itself. Cricket needs to be very, very careful.'

England's magical off-spinner Graeme Swann shared Lord Condon's fears, and said: 'It probably does go on in some form with some players. You can never know who it is, but I certainly don't think anyone in this England team has done it.' To be told that England's players were probably totally clean was indeed reassuring, although even Swann, who knew them all personally, had to admit that no one could 'be sure' – as we all remember so well from the seismic shock of the Hansie Cronje scandal.

Both Lord Condon and Swann were perfectly placed to assess the potential of corruption in Twenty/20 cricket, but even they could not have predicted the serious allegations that were to be levelled at players and officials of the Indian Premier League (IPL), where bribery and corruption appeared to exceed everything that the game had suffered before.

The Board of Control for Cricket in India (BCCI) introduced the IPL as a professional Twenty/20 tournament in April 2008. It involved 59 matches played over 46 days, and was won by the Rajasthan Royals, who beat Chennai Super Kings on the last ball of a gripping encounter. This was a tremendously exciting new venture, akin to a commodity market in which the players, who came from various cricket-playing nations, were the commodity and were bought and sold for enormous sums through bids at auction by the corporate-owned teams.

One unknown Indian bowler earned as much as $959,000 in a three-year deal for potentially sending down just four overs a match in an estimated 16 games a year. Million-plus bids were made for India's popular big-hitting captain Mahendra Dhoni and Australia's swashbuckling Andrew Symonds.

As the 2009 IPL tournament coincided with India's general election, serious worries arose about the safety of players, so the event was moved to South Africa, where the Deccan Chargers defeated the Royal Challengers Bangalore in the final. The third IPL season opened in January 2010, with the traditional auction for star players, this time with 66 on offer, although only 11 were sold. In a thrilling final, Chennai Super Kings beat Mumbai Indians by 22 runs.

After just three years of existence, the IPL brand value had soared to a dazzling $4.09 billion, and the average annual salary of an IPL player had rocketed to around £2.5 million. Huge money was cascading into the tournament from franchises, television rights and sponsorships. Greedy businessmen, and even politicians, were seeking ways of sticking at least one finger in this prodigious 'stake pie' to generate an even bigger fortune for themselves.

When scheduling began in March 2010 for the 2011 tournament, it was announced that two new teams – from Pune and Kochi – would be added to the eight that had competed the previous year, but the Kochi proposal soon became the centre of a Government of India investigation into the financial dealings of the IPL and other existing franchises, and one of its ministers, Shashi Tharoor, mysteriously resigned from office.

By the third year, the burgeoning IPL had matured into a $4 billion package of sponsorships, broadcasting rights, franchises, fees and various other extra takings. Powerful organisations frantically battled to head the queue to grab a share in an IPL team, and allegations of money-laundering, tax evasion, illegal betting and bribery and corruption strengthened and escalated.

Rumours grew that bent politicians had worked their way into the League, and that some especially astute individuals were hiding their ill-gotten gains under false names in countries such as Mauritius. Entertainment giant Sony became part of the vast ongoing IPL investigation after it signed a ten-year, $2 billion contract to broadcast IPL matches to countries all over the world, and Google was brought into the same inquiry after paying an undisclosed sum to show highlights of IPL matches on YouTube.

It was impossible to predict what IPL would do next, and so it proved when the BCCI suddenly removed the League's Chief Executive, Lalit Modi, who had signed the Sony and Google contracts. Modi was charged on 22 counts of corruption and bringing Indian cricket into disrepute.

Modi braced himself for a barrage of questions in a major inquiry about all the contracts he had negotiated, which included auctions for the franchises of the IPL's teams.

While announcing that an inquiry had been launched, BCCI President Shashank Manohar said: 'The alleged acts of individual misdemeanours of Mr Lalit K Modi… have brought a bad name to the administration of cricket, and the game itself. Mr Modi was suspended from participating in the affairs of the Board, the IPL, the working committee, and any other committee of the Board of Control for Cricket in India. The IPL is a great property, and commercial aspects in certain events are an important thing. However, ethics and transparency are more important.'

With so many big names and vast international organisations caught up in the escalating drama, the IPL was crammed with potentially damaging allegations, and India appeared to be on the brink of its worst scandal in modern times.

Modi strenuously denied that he had done anything wrong, including allegations of irregularities on franchise bids and broadcasting rights, and he insisted that the IPL was 'clean and transparent...' Yet despite his shaky claim that all was well, he admitted that: 'There have been some unpleasant off-field dramas based on the unknown, half-truths, and motivated leaks from all sorts of sources. I reassure you that if there has been any flouting of the rules and regulations, or if there have been any irregularities, I shall take full responsibility.'

After a crisis meeting in Mumbai, the BCCI enlarged on why Modi had been removed, and disclosed its main allegations against him, stressing that they related to original bids for franchises for the

Rajasthan Royals and Kings XI Punjab, plus the IPL's broadcasting deal, IPL's internet rights, the bidding for two new franchises, and Modi's 'behavioural pattern'. The BCCI also expressed concern that a number of documents requested by tax officials had vanished from the IPL office.

A team of revenue inspectors and enforcement officers widened their inquiries and examined mobile phone records linked to a number of franchises and to 'several personalities who had access to VIP enclosures' during matches. Some serious public guessing began after the Income Tax Department, allied to India's Finance Ministry, claimed that a 'famous' Australian cricketer and a leading Indian player were both involved in match-fixing during the IPL tournament that was moved to South Africa in 2009. In an alarming report, the Income Tax Department alleged that 29 players and one official had been involved in IPL match-fixing and betting in 2009, and that the problem had 'scaled new heights'.

England's straight-talking all-rounder Paul Collingwood, who played for Delhi in the tournament, said: 'I've never been offered anything. I would hate to think I have been in a team that has been involved with that [type of thing]. I guess where there's money, there are problems. We want to keep the game as clean as possible. We must keep our eyes open as players.'

With the IPL reeling from allegations of mammoth corruption and players being investigated, Lord Condon stepped in and fought hard to restore confidence in the competition. On the day he retired as chief of the ACSU and handed over to Sir Ronnie Flanagan, a calm Condon stated: 'IPL Three [third year in existence] seems to have been a very clean event. There were rumours and vague allegations about match-fixing in IPL Three, but no one has come forward from within the Indian Board, the IPL or franchises, or journalists, players or team managers with any specific allegations about match-fixing in the IPL. All there has been is a generic rumour.'

In a separate statement regarding reports of 29 international players under investigation, a spokesman for the Anti-corruption and Security Unit said: 'The media is trying to fish for information without any basis for doing so. Had there been such investigations in process, the ICC would have notified the relevant Board. Kindly dismiss such queries, and if in doubt please refer any media inquiries to Colin Gibson, head of ICC media and communications.'

On the face of it, what the Indian Cricket Board and the Income Tax Department were claiming was a total contradiction of what the ICC was asserting, although Lord Condon did leave a little room for manoeuvre when he made the point that no one had *come forward* from within the Indian Board.

Maybe if someone *had* spoken out, Condon's report might have been different. It is also reasonable for any government or tax authority to want to keep such sensitive inquiries strictly confidential at all times, so on this occasion the ICC could well have been left out of the loop, as they say. For whatever reason, the Anti-corruption Unit did not monitor the first two IPL Twenty/20 tournaments, having presumably decided that all those taking part would have too much on their minds to contemplate bribery and corruption, and would not be tempted.

Multi-screen Media, an international television channel, said in a statement: 'MSM wish to state that payments made to BCCI and WSG Mauritius [a television broadcaster] have been in accordance with applicable laws, and as per established international cross-border banking norms and procedures. MSM received tax advice from external tax experts that the transaction with WSG Mauritius did not attract India taxes, and MSM has accordingly not withheld any India tax. MSM has accounted for the payments in its financial statements which have been audited and filed before statutory authorities.'

A Google spokesman was equally firm, stressing: 'Our agreement to stream IPL matches on YouTube is with Global Cricket Ventures – who own the mobile and web rights to IPL – [and] as per terms of the agreement we have exclusive access to rights to stream matches on YouTube everywhere except the United States, where matches were time-delayed, and available 15 minutes after the match ended.

'The deal is for two years, covering seasons three and four, and we will jointly share revenues from sponsorships and advertising on the official website of IPLt20. This deal was recently extended to include streaming of the semi-finals and finals in the United States, but we have not been contacted by any investigating authorities regarding our agreement with Global Cricket Ventures.'

As the private storm reached hurricane proportions, Rajasthan Royals and Kings XI Punjab both had their franchises terminated for 'breaching ownership rules', and the new Kochi franchise was forcibly warned to resolve its ownership disputes. Australian legend Shane Warne had captained Rajasthan Royals, co-owned by Bollywood actress Shilpa Shetty, and Sri Lanka's skipper Kumar Sangakkara had led Kings XI Punjab. Neither player was involved in, or responsible in any way for, the two teams being excluded.

England's star duo Andrew Flintoff and Kevin Pietersen were reported to be the most expensive players in the IPL, and that they were each pocketing $1.55 million. It was predicted that the IPL would earn the BCCI in excess of $1.9 billion over a period of five to ten years, a mind-boggling sum that would be directed to a central pool, with 40 per cent going to the IPL itself, 54 per cent to franchisees, and 6 per cent as prize money.

Kingfisher Airlines was signed up in a £15 million deal to be the official partner to all umpires in the tournament, and in return for this investment its brand title would appear on all uniforms used by on-field umpires, and on giant screens around the grounds when the third umpire was called upon for a decision.

Sony Entertainment Television signed a contract with BCCI that guaranteed it handing over an astronomical $1.97 billion for the broadcasting rights to show IPL matches all over the world for ten years. Once the ink was dry on the deal, Sony re-sold parts of the broadcasting rights to other companies, including those based in Australia, New Zealand, Pakistan, Hong Kong, Malaysia, Central Africa, South Africa, United Arab Emirates, United States, Canada, the Caribbean and the UK.

India's biggest property developer, the DLF Group, dished out $50 million to be the title sponsor up to 2013, and other hefty sponsors included Hero Honda, Pepsi, and Bandelier, the Swiss watch manufacturer. Investments in the IPL were completely justified when the tournament was rated the top programme on Indian television. Pakistan also reported a 'massive' reception for it. Substantial interest had come from South Africa; the UK's figures had shot up sharply in the third season; and the organisers boasted that a mammoth 48 million people had watched the 2008 final.

England's most vocal supporters, the 'Barmy Army', echoed the worries of Lord Condon and Graeme Swann when they revealed that they believed that any number of One-day Test matches and Twenty/20 games had been rigged, or had included moments when players deliberately under-performed in spot-fixing arrangements with bookmakers and gamblers.

Co-founder Paul Burham, who has led the 'Army' for 15 years to many countries where the game is played, sadly admitted: 'All cricket played on a One-day format is an absolute gift for spot-fixers. The Barmy Army is not a fan of any format of the One-day game. To be honest, there's an element of mistrust in them.

'We are convinced that some matches have been fixed, and that particular players have deliberately under-performed for rewards from gamblers and bookmakers. The One-day formula, especially for Twenty/20 matches, makes it easy for batsmen to take a big slog, miss the ball, and be dismissed without suspicion or questions being asked.

'It can be done in a way that no one could possibly know whether a batsman has deliberately thrown his wicket away or been dismissed fairly and squarely. It's the same with bowlers, who send down wides and no-balls. You cannot be absolutely sure that it's a mistake done under pressure, or been done deliberately.

'Just two per cent of the Barmy Army who watch Test matches attend One-day games, which tells its own story. The proof is in the pudding. Spectators get peed off with suspicious goings-on in One-day matches. At the Barmy Army we are Test match followers through and through, where spot-fixing and match-fixing are more difficult to do, though it was at a Lord's Test in September 2010 that two Pakistani bowlers were caught in a newspaper sting deliberately bowling no-balls, and that appalled us.

'Having watched Test matches all over the world, I can truly say that no one has ever come up with the name of an England player who was suspected of being involved in spot-fixing, or tied up with a bookie or punter.

'The Barmy Army was at The Centurion ground to shout England home, and we were ecstatic, but we learned later that South Africa's captain Hansie Cronje manipulated the last day's play, and picked up money from a bookmaker for doing it. We were all puzzled and suspicious at the time, and sensed that something was not quite right, though it was only when Cronje admitted to "organising" the result for a South African bookie that everything fell into place.

'In reality, that match had also become a One-day contest because of bad weather, which again supported the Barmy Army's doubts about the overall honesty that exists in the short form of the game.'

There is not a single member of the Barmy Army who will deny that flying around the world to watch Test cricket is something they do for pleasure and a good time, but it is rare that anyone from this battalion of jolly soldiers will blow the trumpet to let the world know about all the enormous work they do for good causes.

At least 14 charities have benefited from the Barmy Army's immense money-raising activities, and have so far shared around £100,000 that has been raised by its 3,000 paid-up travelling members, and its 25,000 online supporters. Burham has no desire to crow about their colossal charity work, and he modestly insisted: 'It's a great delight to help those people who are not as lucky as we are.'

A large donation was handed over to those who survived the horrendous Sri Lanka tsunami, but Burham flatly refused to talk about it, and had no wish to explain how his members had rallied round to make it possible. The most he would say was: 'Yes, we took our buckets around and everyone dug deep. People were extremely generous.'

He went on: 'To be honest, we've probably not done our members justice by keeping quiet about all their wonderful work for charity, but we do it without expecting a pat on the back. That's not our scene. Wherever we are, at home or abroad, members and supporters of the Barmy Army are always ready to raise money for those who genuinely need it.

'We've collected well over £100,000 in total, and quite a large chunk of that has gone to Leukaemia Research, for which Sir Ian Botham has done so much good work. It's a fact that lots of people think we're just a group of loyal England fans who drink ale all day and sing badly, but the truth is, we are a large number of responsible people who feel committed to supporting our national cricket team and to raising money for good causes whenever we get the chance.

'We have a strict code of conduct, and our members know that they will be automatically expelled for excessive abuse or bad language. England players have always appreciated our support and regarded us as their twelfth man. When Michael Vaughan was captain, he often came over to us at the end of the day and thanked us for our rallying calls.

'On one occasion, England were in deep trouble, and Michael came across and made a special request for us to get behind Steve Harmison, who was down in the dumps, so we got ourselves organised and we stoked him up like he'd never been stoked up before, and he responded brilliantly. It was another Michael Vaughan masterstroke, and Harmison and the public never got to know about the invaluable part that we had played in helping to see England over the line.'

An unexpected moment of light relief eased the scandals emanating from around the IPL when former England off-spin bowler Shaun Udal advised the billionaire franchise owners not to knock on his door, as he had no interest in making a few hundred thousand pounds for doing virtually nothing. Some cynics saw Udal, at the age of 41, as cricket's equivalent of the *Antiques Roadshow*, especially as he was struggling to retain his place, even as captain, in the 2010 Middlesex team that wallowed near the foot of Division Two in the English championship.

Udal rarely took wickets, his batting was less than average, and he was constantly having treatment for a dodgy knee. One outspoken Middlesex fan also unkindly posted on the club's unofficial website that wherever Udal went after his days with the London club, bar takings would soar through the roof.

Explaining why he didn't want a call from the IPL billionaires, Udal said: 'I've decided that after some soul-searching, and for a variety of reasons – one of the main reasons being the Middlesex captaincy, which is something that I really treasure. If you [sic] did get taken on by one of the IPL franchises, I would have been coming back after a month or so of the season, and it would have an unsettling effect on the squad. I've always preached loyalty, and hopefully I've shown it by not going down the IPL route.'

A few months later Udal quit as Middlesex captain and then retired from championship cricket altogether, and subsequently signed to play for Berkshire in the Minor Counties in 2011 – quite a distance from the IPL and its myriad of world-class superstars like Shane Warne and Kevin Pietersen.

It's not everyday that a creaking 40-year-old cricketer turns down the lucrative IPL and then signs for Berkshire!

CHAPTER SIXTEEN

PETRIFIED STAR FLEES
FOR HIS LIFE

When Zulqarnain Haider stroked the winning runs for Pakistan against South Africa in a One-day Test match at the Dubai International Cricket Stadium in November 2010, he had every right to be ecstatic. His 19 not out in the fourth of a five-match series had very definitely secured a place for him in the national side, and enhanced his dream to become a wealthy and feted superstar.

This talented 24-year-old all-rounder, who had emerged from a humble family home in the dusty backstreets of Lahore, could now feel confident of establishing a permanent place in the Pakistan team. Above all else he was thrilled at hitting those winning runs because he knew his friends back home would be proud of him for putting his family name high in the sporting headlines.

But behind all his extroverted leaping and bat-waving, Haider was riddled with personal turmoil, as he was concealing a secret that would soon catapult him back into the headlines – only next time a great deal bigger, and certainly more sinister, than before.

Within a few hours after Pakistan's stunning victory it emerged that on the eve of the match Haider had asked a management official for his passport, claiming that he needed it to buy a SIM card for his mobile phone. The official readily handed it to him, and he had no cause to doubt that the reason Haider had given him was the truth, but it soon turned out that he desperately needed his passport, not for a SIM card, but to fly to the UK where he would frantically seek asylum.

Everyone in the Pakistan tour party was understandably staggered when it became known that Haider had quietly slipped away from under their noses at the team's hotel shortly after their brilliant victory, taken a taxi to the airport and boarded a flight to London. According to Haider, he had borne his terrifying secret all through his match-winning innings, and it was only after he had landed in England that he felt safe enough to talk about it.

From a room in a hotel close to Heathrow airport he broke his silence in a disturbing statement to an Asian newspaper: 'I received death threats to lose the fourth and fifth One-day Internationals against South Africa, but I could not compromise the dignity of my country. I would rather flee away than sell out the dignity and respect of my motherland, and I cannot talk about the kind of threats that I have received because my family is in Pakistan.'

Haider, whose wife and two young children were at home in Lahore, burst into tears when asked about his family and claimed that he did not alert the Pakistan Cricket Board about the alleged threats because 'it would have worsened the situation'. It was not clear what Haider meant by this cryptic comment, although it did remind me of the former Pakistan batsman Qasim Omar, who blew the whistle on bookmakers and corrupt cricketers. He was banned for seven years and had his career destroyed by officials who took exception to his desire to want to clean up the game.

Another well-known fact was that ruthless bookmakers and gamblers preferred to target young players and those new to international cricket, as they were more easily intimidated and less likely to turn down an offer of big money and other attractive perks. In this respect Haider, a wicketkeeper and top-order batsman, was highly vulnerable, having played in only one Test match, four One-day Internationals and three Twenty/20 games, though it was commendable that such a novice in world cricket was able to handle his horrendous experience with such courage and maturity.

Millions of sports fans would have been aware of Haider on the subcontinent because of their fanatical interest in cricket, and through the extensive television coverage that the game is given throughout Asia. Haider's only Test match was against England at Edgbaston in the summer of 2010, when he was dismissed first ball but scored an aggressive 88 in his second innings. He then broke a finger and had to miss the rest of the series.

At a second news conference in west London, shortly after he had landed from Dubai, a frightened Haider recalled the moment when a man from a gambling gang, whom he had never seen before, approached him before the One-day match and allegedly said: 'If you work with us, we will give you a lot of money. If you do not, we will kill you, and your family.'

With his voice distinctly cracking, an emotional Haider made it plain that he did not tell a single colleague or official of the threat, or his plan to flee, because he feared that if it leaked out that a particular person knew of his proposed getaway and why, and had said nothing, the game's top brass would make life hell for him.

Haider said: 'I felt very nervous, and I thought England was the best place to come to. I just felt that if I told anyone about the threat – senior players, my manager, the Pakistan Cricket Board – maybe if they were involved in the situation, that they too would be in trouble. If your family was threatened, you would think like me.'

He said he was approached with the bribery offer when he left the team hotel for dinner, and he recalled that horrific experience to a large Pakistan television audience after landing in the UK, saying: 'I received death threats to lose the fourth and fifth One-day Internationals. One person asked me to fix those two matches and [said] there would be a problem for me if I did not do it. I was told to cooperate or I would face lots of problems.

'I couldn't be part of any corruption in the series or go against my country. My only concern now is the safety of my family in Lahore. I have decided it is best for me to retire from international cricket since my family and I are constantly getting threats. I can assure you that I am safe and sound, but I cannot say where I am hiding for the sake of my life.'

Haider was understandably eager for his family to be allowed to join him in the UK, and disclosed that immigration officials in London had advised him to appoint a lawyer to plead his case, but he claimed that he had no money to hire one, and that he was forced to do it all himself.

Before boarding his flight from Dubai, the fleeing Haider managed to find a minute to update his Facebook page to read: 'Leaving Pakistan cricket because get bad msg fr 1 man fr lose the match in last game.'

Haider's brother, Aqil, said on a television news programme that the 'man who apparently approached Zulqarnain in Dubai seemed to be of Indian origin, and he threatened that if my brother didn't take money, and play accordingly, not only would his life be in danger, but they would also kidnap his family'.

The longer Haider remained in London over the next few days, the more talkative he became about his fears for the integrity of cricket in Pakistan, and he specifically recalled being the target of threats when captain of his club side, Lahore Eagles. He said: 'Yes, I got threats that I should select such-and-such a player, or not pick a certain player…'

Haider referred in particular to a Royal Bank of Scotland Cup match between Lahore and the National Bank of Pakistan that was played in the spring of 2009. He had successfully led Lahore right through this One-day series, but the captaincy was suddenly taken from him for this match because he refused to pick at least one player whom he had been told had to be in the team. What followed in the course of the match was highly suspicious. National Bank was one of the strongest domestic teams in Pakistan, but needed to win this particular match and improve their run rate to be sure of qualifying for the final stages of the RBS Cup tournament.

Lahore batted first and scored 122 in 40.3 overs. Haider was dismissed for a duck. But it was what came next that caused Haider the greatest concern, and it was such an unusual sequence of events that any fair-minded person would have shared his doubts and worries.

National Bank raced to 123 in just 6.1 overs without losing a wicket, which was a phenomenal response and comfortably raised their overall run rate for the tournament. Even more extraordinary, Lahore's opening bowler conceded a mammoth 78 runs in just three overs! And it came as no surprise to learn that Haider had expressed 'serious reservations' about having this so-called bowler in the team.

This bowler was a modest right-arm paceman who had never played for Lahore before that match, and has not appeared in a List 'A' game since then. So why did he play on that occasion? A further interesting aspect of that match was that Salman Butt, the Pakistan captain who was banned over the 2010 spot-fixing allegations, hammered 92 runs from only 25 deliveries, with 16 fours and five sixes.

Pakistan wicketkeeper Kamran Akmal, Mohammad Amir and Wahab Riaz, who were all questioned by British police along with Butt in the spot-fixing probe, also played for National Bank in that match. Media commentators led the way with inevitable questions about the astonishingly unlikely circumstances of the match, but the Pakistan Cricket Board found no evidence of any wrongdoing.

While still urgently seeking asylum in the United Kingdom, a visibly stressed Haider called a media conference in the relative safety of a curry house among the heavily-populated Asian community in Southall, west London, and pleaded with the International Cricket Council to bug the telephones of players who were suspected of match-fixing.

Earlier in the day, Haider had learned that the PCB had appointed a three-man committee to investigate why he had left the team hotel in such a frenzied dash; and officers of the UK Border Agency had interviewed him to begin inquiries into his application for asylum. In a message to the ICC, troubled Haider said: 'The best way is for them to record all the players' phones, and their activity. I've heard back in Pakistan that a lot of people are involved in fixing, but I think the ICC are doing a good job.'

By now, the PCB had withdrawn Haider's central contract of 50,000 rupees (£365) a month, and he insisted that he had only £500 in his pocket, having arrived in London with just £900, which was his daily wage. Despite his prodigious problems, Haider remained resolutely undaunted, and said: 'God will help me somehow. I am not worried about losing the central contract because only God gives you food. I will leave these decisions to cricket.'

Around six months after landing at Heathrow, and while still waiting for news of his asylum application, Haider revealed that his wife Shazia and daughters Zahra and Fizza were planning to fly to London to be with him, which would ease his worries about their safety at home in Lahore.

Yet at the same time as his spirits were being raised at the prospect of a joyous family reunion, Haider bitterly complained that the Pakistan Cricket Board was withholding up to £16,000 in wages from him, and he was also threatening to sue them for 'character assassination'.

PCB Chairman Ijaz Butt refused to confirm or deny that wages were being kept from Haider, but the Board's senior lawyer Tafazzul

Rizvi was adamant that any legal action by him that alleged 'character assassination' would be defended strongly.

At this point, Haider was looking for every opportunity to plead his case for asylum in the UK, and was desperate to assure the Home Office that he 'wanted to pay tax and play [cricket] normally here'.

It took Haider just four days after the three Pakistan players were banned for spot-fixing in February 2011 to lay down a tantalising challenge to the International Cricket Council.

Right out of the blue, he daringly invited investigators from the ICC headquarters in Dubai to fly to meet him, probably in London, and he positively promised to make their journey worthwhile by naming and shaming the 'big names' who were corrupting world cricket.

Sticking his neck out, Haider insisted that Mohammad Asif, Mohammad Amir and Salman Butt were 'just the tip of the iceberg', and he assured everyone that 'there are some very big names involved in these illegal activities, but they are getting away [with it], as thorough investigations are not being carried out,' which appeared to represent a hefty swipe at the ICC and sleepy officials high up in cricket's national boards.

With absolute confidence Haider predicted that: 'Players are going to be even more careful now, and I know that they are watching their backs and attempting to make it even more difficult for the Anti-corruption Unit to catch them. I am ready to name and shame them, if asked by the relevant authorities.'

It must be assumed that the ICC and its Anti-corruption Unit made immediate contact with Haider to grab this gilt-edged opportunity, and if they didn't it could be fairly classed as gross irresponsibility and a dereliction of duty. They would have let the game down in a very big way. The ICC declined to comment on whether it had taken up Haider's offer.

Haider was also especially keen for the ICC to expand its areas of investigation, which would allow it to take a closer look at the personal finances of international cricketers and find ways of examining their bank accounts and financial dealings.

Above all else, he believed that the personal contracts these players signed with their boards should include a clause that would compel them to disclose every financial transaction and bank account detail to board officials and the ICC when required.

Stressing his determination to help lead the fight against international cricket corruption, Haider said: 'I sacrificed a promising career and my mission now is to clean up the game. I am prepared to do anything to help [those in authority to achieve this aim].

'This is just the start. The net has to be widened, and it has to be widened across other countries in addition to Pakistan.'

On hearing of Haider's dramatic arrival in London, and the alarming allegations that he had made, Wajid Shamsul Hasan, the Pakistan High Commissioner to the UK, said: 'We will give him any consular assistance that he requires.' It was just the type of warm welcome that Haider needed in his hour of anguish, but this upbeat tone did not last long before a depressingly cold reaction blew in from Pakistan's Sports Minister Ijaz Hussain Jakhrani, who blasted Haider for what he had done.

'If he is such a weak and scared person, he should not have played cricket in the first place,' said Jakhrani firmly, with no sympathy whatsoever. 'We don't support his actions, and we believe he should have come to us if he was under threat from anyone. He didn't have confidence in the national team management or Pakistan Cricket Board.'

These were bizarre comments coming from someone so high up in the Government, and it seemed that he had ignored completely the dangerous predicament of Haider and his family, who struggled to stay strong when under threat of serious physical injury and abduction. Jakhrani's insensitive remarks clashed badly with the

Pakistan Government's more reasoned view of the dangerous situation for Haider's immediate family; the Government had backed its support by arranging for armed police to stand guard outside their home in Lahore.

Former Australian spin bowler Tim May, now the highly respected head of the international players' union, insisted that cricketers everywhere were shying away from reporting corruption because they did not trust their own national board, or the ICC. May stressed that he 'admired' Haider's 'courage' and was sure that 'some players have concerns about reporting [corrupt activities] because they fear the confidential nature of them reporting it will be breached'.

Straight-talking May was in no doubt that Haider had done international cricket a substantial service by drawing attention to a problem that needed to be stamped out speedily and thoroughly. He said: 'If what he says is true, what he's done is not cowardly. It has taken a significant amount of courage, because no one has ever done that before.

'I am certainly not surprised that there are players out there who have been threatened, their families have been threatened, and they are fearful for their lives. I think you'll find that there is general knowledge around the Anti-corruption Unit that these threats have been used before. The damage to our sport is not immaterial. Every spectator and every player wants to know that every contest they play in is a vital and real contest, not one that has been affected by corruption.

'The culture of cricket needs to change from top to bottom, from administrators to grass-roots level. That culture needs to be one of zero tolerance of corruption. Cricket cannot just sit by the wayside, and think that this thing is going to go away. Whatever we have done in the past is obviously not working as well as it should be. We need to review our ways.'

Tim May made it clear that he was convinced that there were any number of players who had no faith in their national cricket boards or in the Anti-corruption Unit, and he said ominously: 'This problem is not an issue that is just confined to Haider. In the past, certain players have gone to the Anti-corruption Unit, and details of their talks with the Unit have reached the media. Whether those talks have come from the ICC, or whatever, it still gives the players the question over whether they can trust the Anti-corruption Unit.

'We've said to the ICC that we need to get the reporting processes streamlined far better than what they are at the moment. We have put forward a couple of options to the ICC in a meeting we had with the Anti-corruption Unit for a change in the reporting system. We have not heard from them since that meeting, but we hope they will look at those options in a positive manner.

'These [options] involved the players reporting to a trustworthy body in the players' eyes, a place where they believed their anonymity could be protected. In most cases, in most countries, we believe that the players' association has a vital role to play.'

May's outspoken views, especially his verbal assault on the Anti-corruption Unit, provoked a stinging reaction from ICC Chief Executive Haroon Lorgat, who branded him 'ignorant or irresponsible' and was livid about allegations that confidential details that were reported by players had been deliberately leaked to the media.

In a fierce outburst, Lorgat declared: 'He [May] said that the players have no confidence in approaching the ACSU [Anti-corruption and Security Unit]. I felt it quite strange that Tim May was making these comments. He either made them out of ignorance or, I hope, he is not being irresponsible. Those comments are certainly not justified in my view.'

Lorgat claimed that many cricketers had gone to the ICC to report being offered money, and that not one of those confidential visits had been reported publicly. He assured everyone: 'We have never made any disclosure about which player came and spoke to

us. We don't say who has come, because we protect their identities.'
Yet another former Australian bowler, paceman Geoff Lawson, fully
endorsed what Tim May feared about corruption and kidnapping
being a real and positive threat to international cricketers.

He also wondered whether certain Pakistan players had been
compelled by outside forces to take part in the 2010 spot-fixing
scandal that ended with three of the team being suspended, and
several others being interrogated by the police and the ICC.
Lawson was coach to the Pakistan first team for 15 months between
July 2007 and October 2008, and believed that criminal gangs
deliberately targeted certain players, and that they had sinister ways
of making sure that matches proceeded in a specific way to a pre-
arranged plan – and this did not necessarily involve money.

In his *Sydney Morning Herald* column, Lawson wrote: '[The
allegations] could be related to extortion, threats, and the well-
being of [the players'] own family members. It would not surprise
me if illegal bookmakers have told players that if they do not
perform x and y, their families will be kidnapped or harmed.'
Lawson recalled being summoned to a meeting in the captain's
hotel room on the eve of a match, and was shocked to find that a
selector was also there waiting to speak to him.

A particular player had been dropped from the team for the next
day's match but the selector insisted that someone had to be
removed from the chosen side for the other player to be brought
back. Lawson alleged that the selector was terrified, and said: 'I
have been told that if he is not in the team tomorrow my daughter
will be kidnapped, and I will not see her again.'

In addition, Lawson believed that there were many other factors
that could potentially cause an international cricketer to become
involved in shady practices, and he explained: 'I will never condone
any form of fixing, yet we should consider that a cricketer might
not be thinking of personal gain but of getting money to buy a
generator for his village because it doesn't have electricity.

'I had a lot to do with Mohammad Asif, and he was always missing training sessions to look after his sick mother. He has spent a lot of his money on looking after his family. And if Salman Butt is involved in any match-fixing I would be absolutely stunned. He is a very intelligent, polite guy, and has done well since taking over the team.' The ICC suspended Asif and Butt, as well as 18-year-old Mohammad Amir, following investigations into the 2010 spot-fixing scandal.

According to certain players and commentators, kidnapping and intimidation have been poisoning Pakistan cricket for at least 25 years. Wasim Akram, one of the finest left-arm pace bowlers ever to perform in Test cricket, revealed in a Channel Four documentary that his 65-year-old father was kidnapped, and that the callous perpetrators had ignored his age and had beaten him up.

Akram's voice trembled with anger when he recalled: 'My brother rang me to say that my father had suffered a heart attack, and I believe the reason behind it was that he had been kidnapped for a day. The people who kidnapped him thought a match was fixed, even though someone else [and not I] was captaining the side at the time. They held him captive for a day, and they hit him all over – and he is 65 years old. If we don't get justice in our country, where are we going to get justice?

'After everything I have done [as a player for Pakistan], and I don't get justice, what happens to other people out there? You can imagine what they go through. No one is more patriotic about Pakistan cricket than me. I've given so much to my country, and I don't deserve this.

'I don't know what to do to get justice for my family or me. Someone has to help me! At times I feel at a loss, and at other times I am very down. It's difficult to explain what I am going through, but I try to put on a brave face, and hopefully that will help me.'

Despite Akram's enormously successful Test career, it did not guarantee that he would be immune from disciplinary punishment should any issue be proved against him, which was the case when he was censured by a Pakistan judicial inquiry into match-fixing, and his vociferous plea of innocence was rejected.

Judge Malik Mohammad Qayyum ordered that Akram must never captain Pakistan again, and ordered that his bank accounts should be audited. The incensed Akram raged in vain: 'I'm respected all over the world apart from in my own country.'

Shortly after the 2010 spot-fixing scandal, a chilling death threat was made against beautiful television star Veena Malik (32), a former girlfriend of Mohammad Asif, who had been identified as one of the players caught up in the scam. According to Veena, the threat followed her call to the ICC about Asif's alleged link to an Indian bookmaker. She was reportedly threatened in person, and also in an e-mail message, which warned: 'Don't talk to the media. Keep your mouth shut. I'll kill you. Watch what I do.'

Veena told the media that the man who had approached her had warned that someone would be going after her, and she broke down, sobbing: 'I can't sleep at night. I fear for my life.' Her sensational claim was that she had discovered that boyfriend Asif was 'throwing matches' when a particular number appeared on a phone bill, and believed that it belonged to another woman, and that he was having an affair.

Veena claimed that cheating was rife among players, and continued: 'I knew that he had women all over the world, so I rang this number thinking it was another of them, but a man answered, and he claimed that they were working on commercial campaigns together.'

According to Veena, the much-travelled Asif also slipped off secretly to Thailand, and he admitted that he struck a deal with an Indian man while there. She also alleged that she listened to Asif on the telephone when a man was supposed to have said: 'We spent a lot of money on you, and you've made a commitment to us.'

Making a specific allegation, Veena added: 'They were paying Asif £25,000 to play badly, but he said he needed £128,000. It was a couple of weeks before Pakistan's tour of Australia. One day I told him I was praying for them to win, and he replied: "Why are you wasting your time? We're not going to win anything until December 2010." I told him not to be involved [with bookmakers], but he did not listen.'

Veena and Asif separated sometime in 2010, and she later claimed that he had made calls to bookmakers on telephones belonging to servants. She said she knew the name of a well-known Indian bookmaker who allegedly paid Asif for spot-fixing in matches. She also said that she had advised the PCB about the places that Asif had visited.

Betting is officially banned on religious grounds in India and Pakistan, but those who wish to be involved just carry on with impunity, totally disregard ethical laws, and set up gambling dens in front rooms, back rooms, garden sheds, offices – and even in a room at a Karachi hospital. Illegal gambling generates a turnover of around £2 billion a year in Asia, and betting on international cricket plays a principal part in this enormously lucrative industry.

CHAPTER SEVENTEEN

COCAINE COMMENTATOR ACCUSED OF BRADMAN SCAM

D ermot Reeve was a charismatic first-class cricketer who
played for England in three Test matches before he retired
to become a television commentator for UK TV station Channel
Four. During his controversial career, Reeve played championship
cricket for Sussex and Warwickshire, was awarded the OBE, and
was once voted Wisden International Cricketer of the Year.

Many will also remember him for selling alleged fake Don
Bradman signatures in a lucrative business venture, spending £200
a week on cocaine, and fanning a feud with West Indies batting
legend Brian Lara.

It was in May 2005 that Reeve, who had built a sizeable
reputation for being erratic and unpredictable, stunned the cricket
world when he revealed that he had worked as a commentator on
a Test match for Channel Four while under the influence of
cocaine. He immediately resigned from the company before he was
fired, and then admitted that he had also used marijuana during his
playing days with Warwickshire, although he insisted that he did
this for one season only.

Finally ripping off the mask that had hidden his drugs horror, Reeve confessed that cocaine had undermined his television career and his family life for two years, and he blamed it entirely for destroying his marriage. He sheepishly looked back at his horrific stint in the Channel Four commentary box during the Lord's Test between England and New Zealand in 2004, and admitted: 'I had no recollection of seeing the ball on Saturday or Sunday. I had to watch the video to hear what I said. Apparently I was very chirpy, and I kept doing silly impressions of Imran Khan when I was not on air.'

Stung by Reeve's sensational disclosure, the England and Wales Cricket Board warned him that a full-scale investigation would be launched into his cocaine habit should he ever try to work in English cricket again. Reeve was the third member of Warwickshire's 1994 treble-winning side to admit to taking drugs. All-rounder Paul Smith had already confessed to taking recreational drugs, and wicketkeeper Keith Piper had tested positive for cannabis.

Smith was highly critical of how Warwickshire had deftly sidestepped the drugs problem, and strongly insinuated that the club had preferred to look the other way and pretend that none of it was happening. He said: 'The club could have informed the Professional Cricketers' Association and organised proper treatment [for those on drugs] but it was easier not to bother. I requested an interview with the club's Chief Executive, but he didn't get back to me. I didn't go home for two years. Success attracted the wrong people for the wrong reasons.'

Smith was profoundly sorry that he didn't do more to fight his drug habit, and he admitted that he was always 'on and off cocaine' during his 12 years with Warwickshire. Random drug tests never really bothered Smith, as he made sure he also took 'blockers' which hid all the illegal substances that he had taken, and the authorities were kept in the dark.

He said he believed that it was a sporting scholarship to

Johannesburg that put him on the road to ruin, and candidly recalled: 'In South Africa drugs were a whole new ball game. Soon I was downing 15 cans of lager, and tipping it off with grass [cannabis]. I was introduced to drugs like cocaine and "speed", and I found that they were commonly used in sports out there.'

Smith told a Sunday tabloid that he had seen international stars taking drugs at parties all over the world, and that cannabis was the most common. Stating the ridiculously obvious, he continued: 'Well-known personalities who were into cocaine, and heavier gear, didn't go around broadcasting it because the penalties were high if they were caught.'

Following his confession, the ECB banned Smith for two years, even though he had already retired from the professional game, and he was later reported to be doing 'valuable charity work' in Los Angeles and with the Prince's Trust in Britain, but had not found a job that provided an income.

Keith Piper was the third Warwickshire player caught on drugs, and he was fatuously banned for just one match after failing an internal test, which fully reflected how pathetically lenient the club was with offenders, and confirmed Smith's opinion that not enough was being done to deal with the problem.

It probably came as no surprise when Piper was caught again several years later, and this time given a longer suspension. It also posed many serious questions: Where were these players getting the drugs? Were other players taking them and not being caught? Even worse, was there a dealer on the staff?

Club officials closed their eyes, and stuck their fingers in their ears. For them it was a subject to ignore. It appears to have been a gross abrogation of duty to young men who desperately needed firm discipline and positive guidance.

Dermot Reeve popped up again in a fresh scandal in 2009 when he stood accused of selling fake signatures of Sir Donald Bradman on limited-edition cards, which the Bradman Museum in South

Australia claimed were poor copies. An international expert on Bradman memorabilia had prompted the doubts after he examined the autographs for which Reeve had issued 'authenticated' certificates to 'guarantee' that Sir Don had signed them personally.

But the expert the Bradman Museum was using to protect against counterfeit was sure that Reeve was selling 'non-genuine' items, although Reeve denied that this was the case. Prices for Bradman memorabilia were at their peak at that time. Even single signatures were fetching around 200 Australian dollars, while the baggy green cap that Bradman wore in his final Test match was on sale for a massive 400,000 Australian dollars.

Reeve was also selling his disputed Bradman autographs on eBay, the online auction site, and he added a personally signed certificate that they were 'genuine originals of Sir Don Bradman'. A highly respected collector bought these autographs on eBay, and he promptly sent them to the expert at the Bradman Museum for him to examine them, and to confirm that they were authentic, or not.

Once he had analysed them, the expert said: 'I am certain that these Bradman signatures are just not genuine. In fact, they are very poor simulations of a genuine Bradman signature.' Despite this formidable professional adjudication, Reeve still refused to back down, and he angrily responded: 'I'm giving my opinion. These autographs are real.'

Reeve's defence was always confident and solid, and when he was asked whether what he was selling represented fraud, he snapped: 'Of course it's not! That's ridiculous!' Reeve claimed that the Bradman signatures were from the mid-1980s, and insisted that he would 'never knowingly pass on an item if I did not believe it to be authentic'.

Amid all the mayhem, Reeve did admit that he had not seen Bradman sign the autographs, and that he had no way of proving that the great man had done so. Reeve's best answer was: 'In the legal world of memorabilia, an authentication is just a person's opinion. That's all it is.' When asked whether he considered himself an expert on Bradman's signature, Reeve replied: 'Yes, but without wanting to sound arrogant.'

Meanwhile, the collector who contacted the Bradman Museum after buying the signature from Reeve on eBay said: 'I took one look at it, and thought: "There's no way in this world that's Don Bradman's." I wanted to get one to have it analysed, so I bought it for 150 dollars.'

In a straightforward explanation, the museum expert said: 'They are not written with the same speed and fluency as the Bradman signature. There are pen lifts in places where there shouldn't be. A number of letter formations are totally wrong, with one obvious example – the letter "B" in Bradman. And the "man" part of the name is illegible, though it is usually a very legible part of the Bradman signature.' The museum expert also claimed that Reeve's authorisation certificate was 'not worth the paper it was printed on'.

When sales were at their best, Reeve charged between 100 and 1,500 dollars for various Bradman memorabilia, and insisted that he had bought the signatures from a source in the UK. Reeve stopped selling on eBay after an avalanche of doubts and questions had poured in on him, but he flatly denied that he had taken this decision because he was dealing in fakes, and said: 'I've stopped, partly because I have only a few signatures left of Bradman. I'm a very busy man. I don't need to defend myself.'

In addition, he was 'happy to refund the guy's money if the leading Bradman expert was not comfortable with them'. He would also destroy all the autographs he held, should it become necessary, and insisted that he had every right to authenticate the Bradman signatures. Reeve contended: 'If you had collected Bradman's signature for 15 years, and had letters written by Bradman – handwritten letters – would you not consider yourself to be a good judge on whether something was authentic?'

Defiance, tenacity, ego, intolerance, stamina, and certainly arrogance, all in equal proportions, described the enigmatic Dermot Reeve who, despite his penchant for recklessness and daring escapades, was very much a 'thinking' cricketer with considerable strengths in batting and bowling.

Reeve was born in Kowloon, Hong Kong, on 2 April 1963. Those who intensely disliked him believed that he should have entered the world exactly 24 hours earlier, so that he could have been officially registered on All Fools' Day. His career began when he was selected for coaching and training with the MCC Young Cricketers, an academy for above-average young players between the ages of 18 and 20, based at the Nursery End of Lord's cricket ground in St John's Wood, north London.

Natural talent and hard work combined to put him on track for a professional career with one of the country's 18 championship clubs, and it was thought that he could have ended up playing for England had he fulfilled his youthful potential.

Reeve represented Hong Kong in the 1982 ICC Trophy, boasting an average of 34.50 with the bat, and 15.71 with the ball. A year later he left the MCC Young Cricketers and signed for Sussex, where he made an instant impact with his medium-pace bowling, taking 42 championship wickets, although he failed to reach a score of 50 in 20 innings.

Reeve served Sussex as a reliable all-rounder for six seasons, and in 1987 averaged more than 40 with the bat and took 42 wickets, but he felt it was time to move on and signed for Warwickshire in 1988. It proved to be a brilliant career switch, and he excelled at Edgbaston, especially in 1994 when he amassed 1,412 runs at an average of 54, which included his highest first-class score of 202 not out, and two other centuries.

Reeve had been appointed club captain in 1993, which he totally justified a year later when he led Warwickshire to an unprecedented domestic treble, winning the county championship, the AXA

Equity and Law League, and the Benson & Hedges Cup, as well as being losing finalists in the NatWest Trophy.

Brian Lara, the ebullient West Indian run-machine, played a major part in Warwickshire's colossal success, though he and Reeve were never the best of mates, which prompted supporters to wonder how the team could have done so well with such a major rift and acrimony in the dressing room.

When questioned about his feud with Lara, the straight-talking Reeve replied: 'It was no secret that Brian and I did not see eye to eye. Dealing with him, and the whole situation, was very difficult because the club tied my hands behind my back.

'There was a separate rule for Brian because he was tired, so he could get to the ground late. I didn't like it, and I lost quite a bit of my self-esteem through having to captain him in a way that I didn't really want to. Having said all that, Brian was the best batsman I have ever seen. I would have run things differently, but the club said "let's get by", and we must have done that because we won three trophies that summer and finished second in the other competition.'

It was also the season when the prodigious Lara established his world record innings of 501 not out for Warwickshire against Durham in a massive score of 810-4 declared. Reeve remained with Warwickshire in 1995 when they again won the championship and the NatWest Trophy, but left midway through the following summer and became coach of the first team at Somerset, where he also played in several One-day matches during his four years at the club.

Peter Anderson, Chief Executive of Somerset at the time, said: 'Dermot has found it difficult to be a professional broadcaster and to pay due diligence to his coaching duties here.' Somerset and England star batsman Marcus Trescothick publicly praised Reeve as the best 'technical' coach that he had ever worked under.

Reeve's burgeoning broadcasting career crashed in a haze of

drugs long before he could reach his potential, and he vanished off the cricket radar until July 2008, when Central Districts in New Zealand announced that it had appointed him first team coach. Yet again, Reeve did an excellent job and helped Central Districts win the 2009/10 highly competitive Twenty/20 tournament.

By now, just about everyone in international cricket knew that controversy stalked Reeve no matter where he went, or what he did. Having settled down in distant New Zealand, it seemed Reeve had finally said goodbye to trouble, but that notion was quickly exposed as faulty when he recklessly accused England's young all-rounder Ravi Bopara of tampering with the ball.

Having been dropped from the Ashes squad, Bopara had decided to join Auckland as its overseas player, and he hit a brilliant hundred in a One-day victory over Central Districts, plus taking 1-51 in ten overs. But straight after the match, tetchy Reeve charged off and accused Bopara of using his nails on the ball to make it swing. 'I had the binoculars on him,' said Reeve, 'and I saw his nails on the ball on several occasions.'

Bopara was furious, and stormed: 'He must be going mad. Nothing untoward took place either from me, or from any of our other bowlers. All that happened was that it was a windy day, and we managed to get the ball to swing against the wind. He couldn't work out how we got the ball to swing in those conditions so, without checking the facts, he accused me. We did nothing wrong, but whatever he said is in the past now. He was entitled to his point of view, but he should have checked first.'

Reeve ended his coaching spell with Central Districts in April 2010 to spend more time with his family, and they crossed the water and settled in Sydney. On the credit side of his incredibly chequered career, Reeve pocketed a handsome £500,000 tax-free bonanza from his Benefit Year at Warwickshire, was Wisden's Cricketer of the Year in 1996, as well as being awarded an OBE for services to cricket during the same 12 months.

Drugs in cricket were certainly not confined to Warwickshire's trio of Reeve, Smith and Piper. It was secretly common throughout the game in the late Nineties and into the new millennium, and several prominent players were caught, and punished.

A banned diuretic was found in a test taken from Australia's spin wizard Shane Warne, who amusingly insisted that his mother had given him the substance so that he could look good in front of television cameras, as its manufacturers were claiming that it could help people to lose weight. It was also confirmed that this same drug could be used as a masking agent for other drugs, and the authorities concluded that Warne had used it for that reason. They rejected his 'caring mother' defence, and banned him from all cricket for a year.

England and Middlesex left-arm spinner Phil Tufnell was fined £1,000 and given an 18-month suspended ban for failing to appear for a random drug test after a championship match. Earlier in the year he had denied smoking cannabis on England's tour of New Zealand after waiters at a restaurant in Christchurch had allegedly seen him hurrying from a toilet in a haze of marijuana smoke. One of England's greatest all-rounders, Ian Botham, was not so lucky when the ECB banned him for 63 days for smoking cannabis during a tour of the West Indies.

New Zealand trio Stephen Fleming, Dion Nash and Matthew Hart were all banned for smoking cannabis at a barbecue, and the three were fined $175 each. Fleming and Hart admitted they were guilty, but Nash denied that he was involved.

Fleming, who captained New Zealand for many years, said that this fine was only a small part of the punishment, as his mistake had also cost him a lot of money in legal fees and lost sponsorships. He later claimed that more than half the squad was dabbling in cannabis, but sportingly did not name any of them.

West Indian wicketkeeper David Murray was such a serious victim of drugs that it destroyed a career that was crammed with potential. In the end, Murray admitted that he had smoked marijuana since he was 12, that he had used it before, and after, a day's play, and that he later moved on to cocaine. Murray was caught with drugs during the West Indies tour of Australia in 1975/76, and was on the point of being sent home when sympathetic colleague Lance Gibbs stepped in and persuaded the people in charge to give him a second chance. A life ban was imposed on Murray after he toured South Africa with a rebel West Indies side, and he was later reported to be living in poverty in Barbados.

Five of the South African tour party that won the 2000/01 Test series in the West Indies were each fined $1,300 when caught smoking cannabis in Antigua, where Andre Nel, Justin Kemp, Roger Telemachus and Herschelle Gibbs, as well as physiotherapist Craig Smith, all admitted the charge. Gibbs was already serving a suspended three-month ban for breaching a team curfew in Australia a year earlier.

One of the world's finest fast bowlers, Wasim Akram, was on his first tour as captain of Pakistan when he was caught with marijuana during the team's stopover in Grenada en route to the West Indies. Three colleagues – Waqar Younis, Aqib Javed, and Mushtaq Ahmed – and two British women tourists were also charged with having marijuana in their possession. The Pakistan management claimed that the players had been 'set up' to unsettle the squad.

Charismatic Ed Giddins, a seam bowler in the summer and a Christmas tree salesman in the winter, won four caps for England between 1999 and 2000. In a remarkably controversial career, Giddins was no-balled for throwing, suspended for five years for betting on his team to lose, and sacked by Sussex for using cocaine, although he insisted he was innocent and that someone had spiked his drinks at a party. English cricket's rulers didn't swallow the drinks defence, and they banned Giddins for 19 months, and later rejected his appeal against the length of the ban.

Giddins was randomly tested while playing for Sussex against

Kent at Tunbridge Wells on the day after the late-night party, and traces of cocaine were found in the sample that he provided. A close friend of Giddins said: 'There was a night when substances were flying around, but Ed is not a user of narcotics. He had never taken this, or any other drug, before.'

Bosses at the Test and County Cricket Board accepted that Giddins was caught experimenting with cocaine rather than being a habitual user, but suspended him because players under the influence of drugs 'had the potential to put at risk the safety of fellow players and officials'.

Colleagues, and opponents, later ribbed Giddins about the incident, and he recalled: 'I was batting against Surrey when a bowler called out "Can I have a snort-leg for this guy, please?" And at Sussex there were cracks like "Keep a tight line, Ed!" But the best one came when I was taking a bit of stick with my bowling, and someone called out "Don't let them get up your nose, Giddo!"'

Sussex sacked Giddins after the ban was announced, and club secretary Nigel Betts said: 'We were satisfied that this was a rare experiment with cocaine rather than a habit, and I would say the punishment is about right.' Giddins said that during the ban he would recover some of his lost wages by selling Christmas trees.

CHAPTER EIGHTEEN

ICC PLANTS 'MOLES' TO SNARE CHEATS

Whenever a major problem arises in world cricket, especially in identifying and punishing corrupt players, the tendency is to blame the international governing body and accuse its officials of being weak and inept. No doubt on some occasions certain allegations made against the International Cricket Council (ICC) have been justified, after all, no sports organisation this large can make the correct decision every time. It inevitably claims to be policing the sport efficiently and fairly, but does that self-proclaiming boast really stand up to scrutiny?

At no time in the history of cricket has the need been so great for authoritative control of the game to combat the appalling surge of wilful cheating and deception, gamblers and bookmakers, match-fixing and spot-fixing, and lack of integrity and credibility. The prying lenses of television cameras have infuriated the game's cheats, especially those who had enjoyed universal acclaim as great bowlers capable of making the ball swing like a pendulum, only to be caught and exposed scraping it with fingernails and metal bottle-tops, and making it glisten with Vaseline and hair gel.

253

Even worse has been the arrival of ruthless gamblers and illegal bookmakers who have threatened players' lives if they refused to bowl a no-ball or a wide at the precise time they requested so that a huge bet could be landed. Equal pressure has been applied on batsmen, who have been compelled to give their wickets away at pre-arranged times, in pre-arranged ways, and for a pre-arranged score. To be run out in the first over, for instance, can earn a player, and his bookmaker, a large sum of money.

Assembled together it makes a mockery of international cricket, and leaves millions of dedicated, and trusting, spectators wondering what is actually genuine, and what is false. That is the scary challenge facing the ICC in a new and frightening era, as scandal follows scandal, and which has caused what happens off the field to be of as much importance as what happens on it.

With all these difficulties and worries swamping the game, I set off in search of the ICC bosses at their headquarters in Dubai to learn as much as they would reveal about what they were doing to beat the cheats.

Sir Ronnie Flanagan had now succeeded Lord Condon as Chairman of its Anti-corruption and Security Unit, taking to the post the immense experience he acquired while Chief Constable of the Royal Ulster Constabulary, and the Police Service of Northern Ireland. For some time he was also Chief Inspector of Constabulary for the United Kingdom, excluding Scotland, and was later appointed to review the police arrangements in Iraq, before he spent two years as strategic adviser to the Abu Dhabi police force.

It is an extremely impressive CV, but it came with no guarantee that he alone could solve problems that would be entirely new to him in the complicated world of sport, and it was blatantly imperative that, if he were to lead the way successfully, then he should receive maximum support and cooperation from colleagues – especially the national cricket boards that operate within the ICC, which covers a vast total of 104 countries.

Representatives from England, Australia and South Africa originally formed the ICC as the Imperial Cricket Conference, which was renamed the International Cricket Conference in 1965, and became the International Cricket Council in 1989. It is wholly responsible for the organisation and governance of cricket's major international tournaments, appoints Test umpires and referees, enforces the ICC code of conduct, and coordinates action against corruption and match-fixing through its Anti-corruption Unit.

Interestingly, it does not govern domestic cricket in member countries, and does not compile the laws of the game, which are controlled by the Marylebone Cricket Club (MCC).

My first question to those at the top of the ICC, in view of the ongoing bribery scandals, was what message could the ACSU give to those many millions of cricket followers all over the world who feared that corrupt and cheating cricketers could not be stopped.

Its response was clear and firm: 'So long as human greed exists, then corruption in any sphere of society, including sports, is going to be a possibility, and it is, therefore, vital that we remain vigilant. Notwithstanding the current allegations [about three Pakistani players linked to spot-fixing at Lord's cricket ground in 2010], and media attention, the significant progress made against corruption by the ICC means that corruption in the game is not widespread, and probably is as low as it has ever been.

'Anything that tarnishes the image of the game is simply not acceptable, because the integrity of the game is absolutely fundamental. But it is important not to overstate a few incidents, as we do have in place robust anti-corruption protocols that prevent dishonest behaviour.'

These reassuring comments were made shortly before Pakistani wicketkeeper Zulqamain Haider fled from his Dubai hotel – ironically a short distance from the ICC offices – and landed in London seeking asylum, claiming that death threats had been made against him and his family because he refused to fix a match against

South Africa, the situation being made even worse for him when he hit the winning run.

Referring directly to the three Pakistani players named in the spot-fixing scandal, the ICC candidly said: 'This is about spot-fixing rather than match-fixing. Instead of the entire match being fixed, which would clearly be devastating, this seems to be isolated parts of the match being fixed by a few dishonest individuals.

'Regardless, we still take this very seriously. We do have a stated zero-tolerance approach to any sort of corruption. Our Anti-corruption and Security Unit is the most advanced, and successful, of its sort in the world. We will stop at nothing to make sure cricket is protected against those who seek to damage it in this way.

'Another factor in our fight against corruption has been the deterrent effect. Players know the penalties they face if found guilty under the ICC Anti-corruption Code. They are considerable, ranging up to, and including, life bans.

'But most important is the education of players, the role of Member Boards, and team management. The ACSU also has a visible presence at every Test match, One-day International and Twenty/20 International that is played, so players and player-support personnel know that any suspicious activities will be monitored. The more effective our policing and monitoring of international cricket have become, the more effective the deterrent.'

The ICC officials also revealed that a wide network of undercover informants was now actively assisting in the fight to stop the cheating. This is a major step forward and it reminded me of another sports governing body that paid a handful of trustworthy players from a private fund to act as 'moles' to pry on and report unsuspecting colleagues who sat next to them in the dressing room. I also discovered that security chiefs at the Jockey Club had placed undercover investigators in a large north of England racing stable to gather information on a trainer suspected of cheating.

The ICC understandably would not talk precisely about its intelligence-gathering, although, with so many former high-ranking police officers in its elite squad, it would be disappointing to find that it fell short of the best investigatory standards. Above all else, the ICC was keen to stress that the ACSU had stepped in and actually prevented cheating from taking place, though again it firmly declined to divulge where and when, and gave no clue as to whether it had acted on advice from one of its cloak-and-dagger informants.

A senior ICC spokesman – who also asked to remain secret – said: 'It is impossible to say how many times the ACSU has prevented any sort of corrupt practice. Through its education programme, which every single international player must undergo before taking to the field, the ACSU has prevented corruption at an early stage, and from taking hold.

'Every time a player, or wider squad member, reports a suspicious activity to the ACSU, as they are required to do, then a potential fix has been thwarted. In addition, the ACSU investigators prevent fixing by their presence at all international matches. We also are able to prevent corruption by stopping known corruptors from entering stadiums, and advising team managements to keep their players away from such individuals.'

To monitor, let alone control or destroy, the odious cheating in cricket is clearly a mammoth task. It is nothing short of a war, which the ICC bosses would like everyone to believe that it is winning; that would be truly fantastic, but we have to ask, where is the evidence to support this statement?

Many highly respected cricket commentators and international players, past and present, have publicly ridiculed the ACSU by claiming that it is an expensive waste of time and money, with no decisive powers to punish the guilty. The anonymous ICC spokesman hit back fiercely, insisting: 'That is clearly not a fair and informed view. We have arguably the most proactive and effective anti-corruption unit of any sport, and this is widely acknowledged by other sporting codes. It is important to note that we can only do what the law allows us to do, and what our members mandate us to do.

'We do not have powers to arrest, we cannot conduct sting operations, we cannot seize possessions, and we cannot get a warrant to search players or premises. But we do have robust, cutting-edge anti-corruption protocols, which other sporting codes acknowledge to be the best, and seek to learn from.

'If any player is guilty of corruption, we will not hesitate to take severe action. Also, do not underestimate the success we have achieved to date through our awareness and prevention initiatives. The ACSU in its current form is well placed to fight the battle against corruption. What is more, it is winning that fight. The number of suspicious approaches reported to us, and the information we hold that we know prevents corrupt practice, is hugely significant.

'Unless every single player, or official, behaves with absolute integrity, it may never be possible to remove the threat of corruption altogether. We must, therefore, always be vigilant to the threats.'

The ICC spokesman was particularly adamant that international cricket is not infested with crooks and cheats, but in reality his emphatic, and heartening, claim seemed at odds with the frequency of allegations, and with the evidence of serious wrongdoing.

The ICC will always need to keep well clear of spotlighting the number of corruption allegations levelled against players of particular countries, as this would land the Council in a disastrous political minefield. Extreme circumspection is called for, and the ICC has managed that side of the problem extremely well, even though it must be tempting at times to respond to their 'it's not that bad' assertion by releasing a list of known perpetrators, and the countries they come from.

The ICC spokesman insisted: 'What we do know through the ACSU protocols is that corruption is not widespread in the game.

Also, let us not underestimate the role of the players. They have equal responsibility to uphold the integrity of the game and, fortunately, the vast majority of them do just that.

'It is true that the ICC and ACSU are acknowledged worldwide as the leaders. We would not presume to speak for other sports, but it is clear that the issue of corruption is not unique to cricket. Some sports have taken measures to combat it, while others have not.

'In the past ten years or so, cricket has certainly taken a lead in this area, and it is telling that many other sports are now coming to us for advice on how to deal with the issue. Because of its nature, which is a series of mini-events, cricket could be seen as being more susceptible than some other sports, but it would be foolish of any sport not to be aware of the potential for corruption.'

The ICC, along with the governing bodies of many other sports, has formed a strong, and direct, link with British bookmakers and large betting exchanges by setting up a Memorandum of Understanding (MoU), which amounts to a guaranteed promise that confidential information received about a possible corrupt action, or evidence of suspicious betting on an event, would be relayed to the governing body immediately.

In particular, this close and positive arrangement works well for the British Horseracing Authority by spotlighting gamblers who might be linked to licensed individuals – such as jockeys and trainers – who are passing on inside information for betting purposes, but the help it could provide to those investigating cricket corruption could be much less effective.

International cricket is bedevilled by illegal bookmakers and gamblers, which must not be confused with bona fide betting firms such as William Hill, Ladbrokes and Coral. Indeed, many of cricket's illegal bookmakers are wealthy businessmen, or well-paid employees in vast companies, and are generally based in Asia and the Far East.

Although the ACSU had tracked down and interviewed

bookmakers in India and Pakistan, the ICC spokesman confirmed that this was a highly frustrating problem, and said: 'There are MoUs in place with relevant bodies. However, in some countries where betting on cricket is extremely popular, such as India and Pakistan, most gambling is illegal, so it is not easy to set up protocols, or agreements, like it is elsewhere.'

He also frankly admitted: 'As long as people are weak, and there is a thing called human greed, it may never be possible to remove spot-fixing from the game entirely. We, of course, depend on the integrity of individual players.'

For the ICC's strict code of conduct to function properly, it is imperative that the boards of every country that participates on the international cricket scene are fired with the same interest, energy and enthusiasm about identifying the cheats, and are prepared to charge players, and apply the correct punishment, when they are found to be guilty.

However, there are numerous cases of lengthy – even lifetime – bans being overturned and quickly reduced to a minimum penalty, or in some instances to nothing at all, by a lenient national board, which makes the so-called punishment system a complete laughing stock. Too many times, players who have been found guilty of taking drugs or under-performing in suspicious circumstances have escaped with pathetic penalties that fall way below what was required for the offence in question.

Cooperation with the ICC is vital, but its spokesman went on to admit that at least one board had not followed up on advice that it had been given about a player who might be cheating. Condoning offenders like this is outrageous, but it comes as no surprise. The player, and those who shield him, should be named and shamed, but the ICC spokesman found himself in a difficult political position, and was forced to honour the code of confidentiality, although he did admit that the ACSU had been 'disappointed' by the lack of cooperation.

In conclusion, the ICC spokesman said: 'The success of the ACSU in educating players, preventing corruption and, where necessary, prosecuting cases against players means they are much less likely to risk fixing matches these days and, when they do attempt it, it is much more difficult to get away with.

'The entire landscape is different, and the problem is much less widespread than in the past. A major part of the ACSU's work is in the form of education and awareness programmes in order to prevent corruption, so no player can claim ignorance. The role of Member Boards, team management and players – along with the ACSU – should not be underestimated.'

Typical of the abuse that the ICC has received was that which came from Pakistan's captain Salman Butt and their 18-year-old left-arm seamer Mohammad Amir, after their appeals against suspension over the 2010 spot-fixing scandal were thrown out by Michael Beloff QC, who chaired a disciplinary hearing in Dubai.

Butt ranted on television: 'They [the ICC] listened to us, but it felt that their decision had already been made from before. It was not based on a single piece of evidence.' Butt, Amir and Mohammad Asif, who had also been suspended by the ICC but withdrew his appeal, had been banned from using training facilities at the Pakistan Cricket Board academy, as its administrators reacted to mounting private criticism from the ICC over the way in which it was handling anti-corruption measures.

Rumours were rife that 'strong voices' at cricket's highest level were urging the ICC to take over the running of the Pakistan Cricket Board, and that the PCB was fighting for its future. As the strident 'wake-up' call echoed around the panicking PCB offices, a letter was hastily signed and sent to the ICC pledging a series of steps to improve the way in which it dealt with corruption issues.

By now Giles Clarke, Chairman of the England and Wales Cricket Board, had entered the conflict, specifically stepping in as

Chairman of the ICC's special Pakistan Task Force, and he needed very little time to convince the PCB that it should agree to a special eight-point anti-corruption initiative, which included measures that would bring it in line with the rest of the cricketing world.

Without delay the PCB agreed that it would implement an anti-corruption education programme for players and officials, which was just as well, as the ICC had strongly hinted at sanctions against the PCB should it fail to conform to new international guidelines.

Sharad Pawar, the ICC Chairman, stressed: 'We will not tolerate any form of corruption in cricket, and we will work tirelessly to root out those who have acted in a way that brings cricket into disrepute. The matter of integrity is non-negotiable. Integrity and honesty are the bedrock of our game, and the ICC will protect that foundation stone with everything at its disposal.'

It was a resounding supportive statement, even if long overdue, and it left the hitherto hapless PCB doing everything in its power to remain in position. Pakistan players were instantly instructed to sign a new code of conduct – crucially before they left for Test matches and a One-day series against South Africa in the United Arab Emirates. They were also told that the new code would be introduced into Pakistan domestic cricket.

National team manager Intikhab Alam, a former Pakistan captain and coach, confirmed that this new code of conduct would bring in stricter standards of behaviour, and that players would be barred from addressing the media directly. Further restrictions included a clause that no player should carry a mobile phone into the dressing room, and that all unauthorised people should be prevented from entering the dressing room at any time before, during or after a day's play.

Intikhab fully recognised the importance of the fresh measures, and said: 'The new code of conduct is the first step towards fulfilling the ICC's recommendations. There is a lot more stress on creating awareness among players about anti-corruption laws and regulations. We hope the new code will help us in dealing with the disciplinary and corruption problems.

'The players have been briefed about their responsibilities, and about corruption in the game, as well as doping and discipline. I hope they will be responsible enough to show good conduct on tour and in home matches. The Board has made it clear in the new code that the manager will waste no time in stamping out indiscipline in the team. We do not want a repeat of what happened in England.' (Here Intikhab was referring specifically to the 2010 spot-fixing scandal that involved two Pakistan bowlers and their captain.)

A few days after Intikhab's stirring battle cry, the PCB announced that it had provisionally agreed not to select five named players for the World Cup tournament in 2011 as part of its 30-day pledge to clean up its image and cooperate with the ICC.

Three of the five – former Test captain Salman Butt, and bowlers Mohammad Amir and Mohammad Asif – were already suspended while the Lord's spot-fixing probe continued, and wicketkeeper Kamran Akmal and leg-spinner Danish Kaneria were added to the blacklist, but the Pakistan Cricket Board quickly changed its mind, as it tends to do in cases of discipline, and cleared Akmal for selection, although there was no such reprieve for Kaneria.

Akmal had been under investigation for his part in Pakistan's controversial defeat by Australia in Sydney in January 2010, and it is interesting to consider the extraordinary circumstances and facts of that match. Australia won the toss and chose to bat, but could manage only 127, having found Mohammad Asif (6-41) too hot to handle. Pakistan responded with 333. Australia rattled up 381 in their second innings, powered by Michael Hussey (134 not out) and Shane Watson (97). Kaneria ended with 5-151.

At one point, Australia were tottering at 257-8, a meagre 57 ahead, and seemed doomed to a huge defeat, but Pakistan captain Mohammad Yousuf decided to place eight men on the boundary when Hussey was on strike, and wicketkeeper Akmal dropped the incredibly 'lucky' batsman three times off Kaneria's bowling, and also missed a straightforward run-out opportunity.

Hussey and novice batsman Peter Siddle added an unlikely 123 for the ninth wicket, and Australia had built a lead of 175 when dismissed for 381, though this was still too much for Pakistan, who were shot out for 139, leaving them 36 short of victory. An illegal bookmaker was reported boasting that 'We made a real killing on that one.'

Pakistan lost all nine international matches in that dreadful series in Australia, which prompted a snap Cricket Board inquiry once the players had returned home. A disciplinary panel decided that Mohammad Yousuf and Younis Khan should be banned indefinitely for 'in-fighting, which brought down the whole team'.

Rana Naved-ul-Hasan and Shoaib Malik were each banned for 12 months and fined the equivalent of £15,900 in rupees. Shahid Afridi, Kamran Akmal and Umar Akmal were also fined and warned that their conduct would be strictly monitored over a six-month period. At one stage the former PCB President, Tauqir Zia, alleged that the ICC had six Pakistan players under suspicion for fixing the Sydney Test, and that all six needed to be watched closely.

Zia had assumed that the ICC had gathered information on the six players by intercepting text messages, and he confidently added: 'I know the ICC had told the PCB this year to monitor these players because it had got hold of some SMS messages that these players exchanged with suspected bookmakers. The ICC approached the PCB after the Australian tour and warned them to keep a watch on these players, as they went for the Twenty/20 World Cup and Asian Cup.'

Zia was in no doubt that match-fixing had existed for a long time, and he recalled the day when an illegal bookmaker asked him to select a particular player for a certain match. Although he refused to respond to the bookmaker's request, he was satisfied that this approach indicated that the player had been involved in something shady before, and he was never selected for Pakistan again.

Despite taking this extreme action, it was followed by a disgraceful cover-up in which no information was released about whether the player had even been questioned and, worst of all, he was not identified. Zia attempted to explain why he, and the PCB, did not name and punish this player, saying: 'We did not make a big deal out of it, as that player had been hauled up earlier.' This admission made matters even worse, suggesting that the player had been grilled over a separate issue, and on that occasion allowed to remain in the Pakistan team.

World cricket has absolutely no chance of ridding the game of the appalling excrement that stains it from grass roots to the highest level when serial offenders like this anonymous character are allowed to stay unnamed. It is quite disingenuous for the ICC – the game's ultimate police force – to sit back and allow these national boards to make seriously damaging decisions without stepping in and punishing them.

Anyone remotely passionate about cricket – from the school playground to the vast Test arena – is compelled to ask the vital question: 'Is the International Cricket Council letting the game down?' There appears to be a serious lack of leadership. Too often sleaze occurs without questions being asked or proper penalties being imposed. Name and shame must become a major policy if the battle against corruption is to be won.

Senator Enver Baig did not hold back while addressing a Pakistan government committee, when he said, scathingly: 'The main problem in the Pakistan team is gambling and match-fixing. Most of the Pakistan team are involved in it.' This devastating indictment by a front-line Pakistani politician emphasised the scale of what the ICC, and its ACSU, faced in their efforts to put a stop to a nation's cricketers who, too often, could not resist saying 'yes' to a bribe.

Enormous psychological damage has already been done to public perception by perpetual Pakistani misdemeanours, so cricket fans no longer know whether a wide or no-ball is an accident, or if it has been perpetrated deliberately to satisfy a bookmaker or gambler.

CHAPTER NINETEEN

COOL COOK PLAYS DOWN ASHES 'CHEAT' STORM

Former England captain Ian Botham branded Australia's opening batsman Phil Hughes a cheat on air while commentating for Sky TV during the third and final Ashes Test at the Sydney cricket ground in January 2011. In his usual up-and-at-them style, Botham accused Hughes of deliberately claiming a clean catch even though he knew that the ball had bounced in front of him.

England's prolific Ashes opener Alastair Cook was on 99 when he delicately turned a delivery from Michael Beer towards Hughes at short leg. Hughes leapt high and claimed the catch. Umpire Billy Bowden immediately consulted TV umpire Tony Hill who, using vital close-up video footage, followed the ball from Cook's bat and was satisfied that the ball had bounced before it had finally settled in Hughes' hands.

Botham was furious, and he railed: 'Terrible. Cheating. How much do you want it to bounce in your hands? He knows he hasn't caught it. There's no appeal. Someone else says something, then he goes up.' All through the drama, Cook remained Mr Cool, and continued slaying the Aussies until he was dismissed at 189 to become only the sixth England player to score three centuries in a series in Australia.

Once the day's play had ended, Cook and Australia's acting captain Michael Clarke hit back at Botham, strongly defending Hughes as a player of integrity. Cook said: 'Obviously it was very close, and to be fair to Phil Hughes, he said straight away "I wasn't sure". I was obviously going to hang around. On 99, you don't walk off quickly. You want to be dragged off. He said he wasn't sure, so it went upstairs, and I think the right decision was made.'

Clarke fully agreed, and said: 'I can guarantee one thing, and that is Phillip Hughes is not a cheat. He is a wonderful young guy. The end result was spot-on. Hughes wasn't sure, and Brad Haddin [the wicketkeeper], who saw the ball clearly, wasn't sure, and we made that quite clear to the umpires, who referred the catch, and the right result was made.'

World cricket's worst ever year for multiple scandals, skulduggery and depressing misconduct had continued right into the 2010 festive season, when two of the game's most experienced captains paid no heed to sharing the goodwill of Christmas with those around them. Australia's desperate Ricky Ponting and South Africa's abrasive Graeme Smith both lost their cool at precisely the same time in different matches thousands of miles apart – and both while staring defeat in the face.

In Smith's case he was badly taunted by lippy pace bowler Shanthakumaran Sreesanth, the renowned Indian serial sledger, but there was no cause whatsoever for Ponting to go berserk and set about two highly respected umpires, who were doing their job admirably. They did not deserve the type of aggressive grilling that sports fans have come to hate from arrogant, overrated footballers intimidating referees in the English Premier League.

Ponting and his battered Australian team-mates were chugging aimlessly to yet another Ashes contest defeat against their brightly polished England opponents at the Melbourne Cricket Ground (MCG) when he suddenly overheated like an old banger, blew a proverbial gasket, and plumes of personal hot air spewed into the arena.

Kevin Pietersen, one of a number of England's top performers, with a distinctive South African accent, was at the crease and gingerly poked at a quick delivery from pace bowler Ryan Harris. He saw the ball zip past his bat and straight into the gloves of wicketkeeper Brad Haddin.

Harris and his Aussie colleagues were plainly satisfied that Pietersen's bat had not made contact with the ball, and they did not appeal for a catch, but Haddin very definitely thought otherwise. He leapt and shrieked and implored umpire Aleem Dar to raise his finger and send Pietersen to the pavilion.

But the placid Pakistani official stood firm, rejected Haddin's frantic pleadings, and was ready to get on with the game when Ponting strode forward and asked for the incident to be referred to the third umpire, Marais Erasmus, for him to decide finally whether Pietersen had hit the ball and been caught legitimately.

Again the decision was 'not out', and it was at this point that Ponting exploded into an eight-minute rant at Aleem Dar and his umpiring colleague Tony Hill, repeatedly wagging his finger and remonstrating in a manner that belied the respect that he held in the game. Match referee Ranjan Madugalle fined Ponting a paltry 40 per cent of his match fee ($5,400) for dissent towards the umpires, which the Australian captain thought was fair. In truth, it should have been much tougher.

Legendary Australian batsman Greg Chappell believed Ponting's prolonged ugly tirade deserved a ban, and let fly at the ICC for not punishing him more severely. Chappell said: 'If I were adjudicating, I think a suspension would be in order. The International Cricket Council has to get tough on this sort of thing. I'm not sure it's a sign of [Ponting] cracking. I think it's just a bad habit that Ricky has. He likes to argue judgement calls with umpires, and it should have been stopped long ago.'

Chappell felt it was time to remind the public that the ICC had fined Ponting four times in four years for dissent and, as this action had clearly failed to deter him, a heavier penalty was justified. However, once he had cooled down, Ponting apologised for the way that he had lashed out at the two innocent officials, but still desperately tried to justify that video umpire Marais Erasmus was wrong to rule that Pietersen had not touched the ball with his bat as it went through to wicketkeeper Haddin.

Ponting protested: 'I had a chance to look at it again last night, and I still, in my heart and mind, believe that he inside-edged that ball. If you look at the replay properly, in the way that it needs to be looked at, I think everyone will understand that the hot-spot mark wasn't a long way from where the ball passed the bat, but that's irrelevant now. The decision was made, and I have to get on with it.

'I got caught in the heat of the moment and went on too long with that chat. I know that we've kept some footage through this series of different decisions that have been made, as far as the use of technology is concerned, and that's taken up at a higher level. Maybe that's how I should have handled it yesterday.'

Ponting believed it was a blatant flaw that all replays were shown on the big screen, and remained convinced that from what could be seen on the screen, there was a 'pretty obvious hot-spot mark on the inside-edge of his bat'. He wanted to make it clear that all he wished to do was clarify what had caused the third umpire to make the decision, which was what started the discussion between him and Aleem Dar.

Ponting rather reluctantly conceded: 'There's no doubt that my actions have caused a massive public reaction. I just wanted to put my points across about it. I understand that I overstepped the mark, and I was charged with dissent for having a prolonged discussion with the umpires.

'When I looked back at it last night, I realised that it didn't look good. The umpires vouched for me in the meeting [with the match referee]. They said that at no time was I actually aggressive, or showed any malice towards them, just that the discussion went on longer than it should have done. I understand that I set a bad example for other captains and young people who look up to me as the Australian captain.'

Ponting accepted that judgements were being made about him, and conceded that a lot of those views were because he hadn't scored the runs that he needed to score.

With an unusually urgent ring to his voice, he said: 'I understand that, and I understand the criticism that is coming my way at the moment is pretty much warranted. I just have to find a way to get myself out of that.'

Ponting was confident that the incident would not affect his future dealings with Dar or Hill, and said: 'It wasn't the on-field umpires, anyway, that made the decision. I was just having that discussion with the guys that were in the middle. I really like the two guys. I think they are two of the better umpires in the world. The relationship that I have had with Aleem Dar over the years has been first-class, so nothing has changed.'

Pietersen was on 49 when Ponting's appeal was turned down, and he added only two more runs before he was dismissed, which made Ponting's absurd blast even more pointless. It got even worse for Ponting when England later cruised to a scintillating victory by an innings and 157 runs to retain the Ashes, and within 24 hours he was being medically ruled out of the final Test at Sydney, having caused further damage to a broken finger.

Less than 24 hours after England's colossal win, Pietersen was at his boastful worst when he attempted to claim that the team's enormous success had resulted directly from him engineering the removal of previous coach Peter Moores in 2008.

With no sign of tongue in cheek or mischievous twinkle in an eye, Pietersen appeared to be totally serious when he said: 'I got rid of the captaincy for the good of English cricket. We wouldn't be here today if I hadn't done what I did then. There is no way in this world that we would have continued under that regime and won the Ashes again in Australia.'

Pietersen was fired after only three Tests following major rows with Moores in India in December 2008, and the ECB reacted swiftly to Pietersen's claim that Moores was holding England back, sacking both of them and handing the captaincy to Andrew Strauss.

England's magnificent MCG triumph was their biggest win over Australia since they trounced them by an innings and 170 runs at Old Trafford in 1956, when the furious Aussies bawled 'cheats' for allegedly fixing the pitch on which Surrey's brilliant off-spin bowler Jim Laker captured an incredible 19 wickets in the match.

The pitch was unusually dusty for Old Trafford, and after England had amassed 459 when batting first, Australia were shot out for 84, with Laker picking up 9-37, and he quickly followed up with 10-53 in the Australian second innings. Australian opener Colin McDonald was livid, and raged: 'England cheated – if by cheating you include the practice of preparing wickets to suit your own purpose.'

Former Australian spinner Bill O'Reilly went further, writing in his newspaper column: 'This pitch was an absolute disgrace. What lies in store for Test cricket if the groundsmen are allowed to play the fool like this again?'

In Durban, over Christmas 2010, South Africa's captain Graeme Smith was at the centre of a bust-up with firebrand Shanthakumaran Sreesanth in a bad-tempered Second Test, which India went on to win. Shortly before he was dismissed for 37, a riled Smith had exchanged words with Sreesanth and appeared to point his bat at the bowler in a moment of anger and frustration.

But when asked to explain what had taken place, Smith stayed tight-lipped, saying: 'I'm not going to get into that. It's between Sreesanth and me. I've played enough Test cricket to know what I can handle and what I can't handle.' India's captain M S Dhoni was far more forthright: 'There are guidelines that need to be followed. You need to be yourself, but you shouldn't get into the other person's space. You shouldn't cross the limit.'

Dhoni revealed that he had spoken to Sreesanth about the time he took to complete an over during the previous Test match, when India fell behind the required rate, and he explained: 'One thing I told him is that, if it takes six or seven minutes to bowl an over, it can be very difficult. In the last Test we were five or six overs down, and we had to use part-timers a lot. He did well in this game. The over rate was good and he bowled well. You always need to have him under control. It's good for everyone – for him, our side, the opposition, umpires, and spectators.'

Trying to shed light on the blazing row, South African spinner Paul Harris said: 'I know Sreesanth has said a few personal comments on the field, which is not great. Graeme doesn't usually react in that type of situation. We want to see it played hard on the field, but not getting personal. It's a fine line, and we don't want to see players cross that. If it was personal, and I've heard it was, I think we should stamp it out of the game.'

Sreesanth has been warned several times for indiscipline, both on and off the cricket field. In October 2009 the Indian Cricket Board issued a final warning to him to mend his on-field behaviour or he would be banned from domestic matches. He was also involved in an ugly incident with Indian colleague Harbhajan Singh after he had taken two wickets to help Kings XI Punjab beat the Mumbai Indians, captained by Harbhajan, in an IPL match in Mohali.

It was alleged that Sreesanth had approached Harbhajan at the end of the match and said 'hard luck', and that Harbhajan had lost his cool and struck Sreesanth in the face. Earlier in the match Sreesanth had exchanged words with batsman Robin Uthappa, who was leading Mumbai's run chase. The fast bowler's extravagant celebrations after dismissing Shaun Pollock also angered the opposition.

Sreesanth denied that he had exchanged words with opposing players on the field, but was 'shocked' by the reaction from Harbhajan, who declined to answer questions at a subsequent press conference. Sreesanth's captain Yuvraj Singh refused to let the issue pass without comment, saying: 'This was an ugly incident and totally unacceptable.'

Former Australian captain Ian Chappell once described Sreesanth as 'an accident waiting to happen'.

CHAPTER TWENTY

ENGLAND WIN WAS RIGGED, RANTS ACE BOWLER

A major bribes scandal erupted after England had trounced Pakistan in a lopsided One-day International at Trent Bridge in 1992. Former Pakistan pace bowler Sarfraz Nawaz, who had also played for Northamptonshire in the English championship, was in no doubt that the match was rigged.

Without publicly revealing any known incriminating facts, Sarfraz boomed: 'Pakistani players were bribed!' And he caused even greater mayhem by alleging that several other international matches involving Pakistan had also been fixed over the previous 14 years.

Having been a vital member of the side right through those controversial years, it was highly likely that he knew precisely whether match-fixing or spot-fixing had taken place, but he clearly felt that it was not his duty to name the guilty ones, no matter how much he might have hated what he witnessed, but that it was for the Pakistan Cricket Board and the International Cricket Council, and even the police, to investigate.

Sarfraz also claimed to have received death threats in late 2010 because of his persistent fight against cricket corruption in

Pakistan, and he lodged a complaint with the police in the capital Islamabad. He claimed the threats came shortly after he had stated that he had known for some time that certain Pakistan players would be involved in spot-fixing in England in 2010, which was highlighted by three players being banned in a major scandal after a newspaper sting that exposed the deliberate bowling of no-balls in a Test match at Lord's.

Sarfraz told the police that, while he was walking in a park in Islamabad, two men shouted at him from behind that he should stop giving public statements about match-fixing by Pakistan cricketers, and threatened to kill him if he turned round and looked at them.

He said: 'I have lodged a report with the police and they are investigating. I have never cared for these threats. I will continue my fight against the corruption, and I am ready to contribute in efforts to free our beloved game from all such corruption. Pakistan cricket has suffered badly, and the only way to eradicate this malpractice is to take stringent measures, otherwise it will continue to haunt us.'

After he retired from cricket in 1984, the frank and fearless Sarfraz had set out to climb the tricky political ladder as a member of parliament, and had become an outspoken sports adviser to the Government, always doing his utmost to assure the nation's fair-minded people that he was on a mission to root out corruption in cricket, and to urge heavier penalties to deter the cheats.

Sarfraz announced that the country's Secret Service was trawling through the bank accounts of leading Pakistan cricketers in a meticulous and concerted operation to secure enough evidence to nail the guilty men.

After winning the toss, Pakistan asked England to bat in that controversial 1992 Trent Bridge contest, and then suffered absolute humiliation in the field as they conceded a massive 363 runs in the allotted 55 overs, the highest team score, or total, in One-day games between the two countries.

Robin Smith hammered 77 runs in 72 balls, while Neil Fairbrother (62) and Graeme Hick (63) also helped to destroy a bowling attack that included Mushtaq Ahmed (0-58), Wasim Akram (1-55), Aaquib Javed (2-55) and Waqar Younis (4-73). Pakistan used seven bowlers in total.

Pakistan began badly in reply when star opener Rameez Raja was dismissed without scoring, caught by Graham Gooch off the bowling of Phillip DeFreitas, and were shot out for just 165 in 46.1 overs, with skipper Salim Malik hitting his side's top score of 45. DeFreitas took 3-33 in his allotted 11 overs, and Ray Illingworth 3-34.

Sarfraz was a pioneer of reverse-swing bowling, and in one Test match in Melbourne he dismissed seven startled Australian batsmen for just one run off 33 immaculate deliveries. In a career that lasted from 1969 to 1984, Sarfraz played in 55 Test matches and 45 One-day matches for Pakistan.

One of cricket's most fascinating scams, which is perpetrated at all levels of the game, from a village green 'friendly' to international Test matches, takes place even *before* the first ball is bowled.

Suspicion grew on the Test match circuit in the late eighties that cheating had become so bad that certain captains were even fixing the toss of the coin while they stood in the middle preparing to decide which side would bat or bowl first.

Officials were urged to be more vigilant and a blacklist of names was reportedly drawn up of those suspected of pulling off the sting. Eventually it became an important part of the match referee's duties to accompany both captains to the middle and to look closely when the coin was spun in the air, and even more closely when it hit the ground.

Captains who cheated this way had mastered the conjuring skills of

TV magician Paul Daniels, so that when the coin came down as 'tails' they would scoop it up and claim that it was 'heads'. To 'win' the toss by these foul means enabled the successful captain not only to ensure that his team had the best of the day's playing conditions, but even more importantly for his gambling accomplice to land a whopping bet for predicting which of the two skippers would call correctly.

The best exponents of coin-fixing will flip the coin in a particular way so that it wobbles rather than spins, and by watching it closely the captain can tell whether it is going to be heads or tails before it finally hits the ground in front of him.

Magician Gary Kosnitzky produced a booklet in which he teaches how the toss of a coin can be controlled, and there is every chance of it proving more profitable for a captain to spend more time practising this at the expense of honing batting and bowling skills.

Officials at the ICC have admitted that their investigators uncovered evidence of bets being placed on captains calling the toss correctly, and even bets on the number of players who would wear sunglasses, caps or sweaters before and after lunch.

British bookmaker William Hill might be many thousands of miles away from where a Test match is taking place, but its security team is always watching closely for cricket cheats. Secret systems are in place to detect a crooked bet and, although the company is in serious competition with other major UK bookmakers (such as Coral, Ladbrokes and Stan James), messages are instantly flashed to one another when a dodgy cricket bet is suspected.

William Hill's spokesman Joe Brilly stressed: 'In terms of security, there is nothing more important than for all of us to stay in contact, because if one of us is caught up in a cricket betting scandal, it would do the industry enormous damage and have our names in the headlines.

'Cricket is one of our top earners, behind horse-racing and football, and we operate online to more than 100 countries. We must be on guard every minute of the day. Illegal betting in India and Pakistan has been linked to cricket scandals in a big way, but we have no outlets in those countries because they have laws against gambling, though we do take online cricket bets from clients in both those countries.

'We also take in-play bets like "who will be the next batsman out" but we don't offer odds on wides or no-balls being bowled by a particular player at a specific time, which was the central issue in the scandal involving certain Pakistan players at Lord's.

'Every person who works in our UK betting shops has been trained on what clues to look out for when punters put their money down. You can imagine the suspicion a stranger would create if he walked through the door and wanted to bet anything from £1,000 to £10,000 on a Test match batsman or bowler doing something specific at a specific moment in the match.

'We do take bets on the Indian Premier League despite all the talk of cheating, and we do good business on it. In a case like that, we put our trust and confidence in our security office, and our online security systems which pick up on anything that might look fishy. There are cheats everywhere, not only in world cricket, who might think that bookmakers are an easy target, so it's important that we don't drop our guard. We need to be sure at all times that no one places an online bet with us unless we have that person's account number and bank account details.'

Gamblers and fraudsters will try every trick imaginable to beat the bookmaker, and the one that was tried in a Liverpool betting shop some years ago has no equal. The bookmaker couldn't believe his eyes when, standing behind his counter, he suddenly saw the name of a horse gradually appearing on a betting slip in the tray in front of him.

It had been written in invisible ink, and as the writing became stronger, the bookmaker could read the name of the horse that had already won the 1.30pm race at 50-1. Within a minute, the word 'double' had also appeared. The bet was time-stamped 1.40pm, so the slippery punter had written the name of the winner once it had passed the post. But this was the bookmaker's lucky day, as he was there to see it all happening. Moments later the bogus betting slip would have been buried under many others, and the brazen cheat would have walked off with a wad of dirty money.

Don Topley first came to the notice of British cricket fans when he was hastily brought on as a substitute fielder for England against the West Indies at Lord's in 1984. Young Topley was a member of the MCC ground staff, and lived with 15 other talented and ambitious cricketers in a north London hostel. Every day during the summer months he attended the nearby indoor school, alongside the Nursery ground at Lord's, for specialised coaching.

When an England player was injured and had to leave the field during that Lord's Test, a message was swiftly sent to the Nursery ground for someone to hurry to the main pavilion to be kitted out in an England sweater, and then to go straight on the field as a substitute and face the 20,000 spectators and millions more watching on television.

Malcolm Marshall was at the crease on that day in 1984 and he hit the ball with tremendous force, high in the air, towards the boundary where substitute Topley was fielding. As he saw the ball rocketing towards him, Topley dived to one side, thrust out a hand, and incredibly caught it close to the ground.

Spectators went wild with delight – until television replays showed that Topley had accidentally put a foot over the boundary rope as his hand grabbed the ball, and his 'catch of the season' had to be disallowed. There was considerable consolation, as the name Don Topley was now very much in the public domain and, though not a star cricketer, his fleeting moment of brilliance had left a favourable image.

Little was seen or heard of him after that stunning moment of glory until around ten years later when the name Don Topley hit the headlines again, just as suddenly as it had done before, though this time for all the wrong reasons.

Topley had long left the MCC ground staff and was now playing as a professional for Essex as a medium-pace bowler and middle-order batsman, and was generally referred to as a 'journeyman' cricketer, which usually means being dependable without being something special.

In addition to his skills as a cricketer, Topley had always come across as someone who was deeply conscientious and honest, and he proved this to be the case when he stepped forward to claim that a crucial championship match had been fixed – which left the game's rulers seething.

Topley alleged that a deal had been done to allow Essex's opponents, Lancashire, to win their Sunday match at Old Trafford on 25 August 1991. In return, Lancashire would make it easier for Essex to win their half-completed three-day match, which would strengthen their bid for the championship.

As it happened, Essex did win the championship match, collecting 21 points to secure the title and picked up £44,000 in prize money. Lancashire were just as pleased when they beat Essex by five wickets on the Sunday, and although it didn't take them to the top, it guaranteed second place and £13,000.

One national newspaper correspondent, completely unaware of Topley's allegation, wrote that he could not understand why Lancashire's captain Neil Fairbrother had asked Essex to score 270 runs to win on an excellent pitch, and with a modest bowling attack. Topley has always remained adamant that what he claimed at the time was wholly true, and has admitted to being 'ashamed' of his bowling in the One-day match, which was so bad that even one of the umpires told him it was 'awful'. Topley confessed: 'I had to keep telling myself that winning a Sunday match wasn't that important, but I didn't like what was going on.'

Guy Lovell, who usually bowled for the Essex second team, was promoted to first-team duty at the last minute to replace the experienced England spinner Peter Such, and he totally backed up what Topley had alleged.

'It was in the pavilion around lunchtime on Sunday,' said Lovell, 'after coach Keith Fletcher and secretary Peter Edwards had left the room that someone came in and announced: "We have done a deal. If we lose today, we will win the three-day game tomorrow." I was shocked, but I didn't protest, and our senior players didn't seem fazed. I was told to keep my mouth closed, and not to tell any official, or bet on the result.

'It is true that Don Topley began to bowl some very bad balls – wides – that gave the batsmen an easy job. I gathered that at one point one of the umpires even remarked how bad he [Topley] was.'

Former England all-rounder Derek Pringle, who captained Essex in the Sunday match, later said he was 'surprised' at Topley's claims, but he had no further comment to make. Foster denied any knowledge of a private arrangement between the two clubs, and said: 'Any such thought would have been completely contrary to my feelings for the game.'

Team captains have always preferred to set up a contrived finish to a championship match in order to get a positive result rather than end three, and subsequently four, days of hard competition with a drab draw. Spectators in the main would also rather be 'entertained', even if it meant that players who rarely bowled in a match came into the attack and lobbed up juicy long hops and full tosses.

Genuine cricket fans, of course, loathe contrived finishes. I fully understand why, and I support them. Although a contrived finish does not strictly come under the heading of 'cheating', it could, nevertheless, have a serious knock-on effect on other clubs who might be challenging for the championship, or battling to avoid relegation, and could be a gift for gamblers or bookmakers if information about a contrived finish got into their hands.

The greatest danger would come from clubs doing a reciprocal deal, which Topley highlighted so effectively. Most championship cricket grounds now have at least one onsite betting shop which, along with the mobile phone, makes it simple for punters to place bets at all times during the hours of play.

Contrived results might be fine to keep bored spectators interested, but in truth this practice brings with it far too much scope for deliberate wrongdoing, and the England and Wales Cricket Board might be wise to recognise the potential dangers and make a statement to stop it before the game is hit with another unnecessary scandal.

Many years after Topley had retired from professional cricket to be a physical education teacher at a boarding school, another Essex pace bowler, Mervyn Westfield, was charged in May 2010 with conspiracy to defraud after being arrested on allegations of match-fixing in a One-day Pro-40 match against Durham.

Crown Prosecution Service lawyer Antony Swift said: 'I advised that Mervyn Westfield should be charged with one count of conspiracy to defraud for intentionally playing other than to the best of his ability, contrary to his contractual obligations.

'It is alleged that he dishonestly agreed to bowl his first over to allow the scoring of a certain number of runs in a match between Durham and Essex on 5 September 2009. I have made this decision after careful consideration of a file of evidence from Essex police. There is sufficient evidence to prosecute Mr Westfield, and it is in the public interest to do so.'

Old Bailey judge Justice Saunders told Westfield in March 2011 that he would stand trial over two weeks in January 2012. He was granted legal aid.

Essex sacked Westfield shortly after the police had interviewed him, although the club insisted that it had taken this action because the player had not fulfilled his potential, and it made no mention of the match-fixing allegations.

Club coach Paul Grayson said: 'It is a huge disappointment that it has come to this. For the past few years we had high hopes for Mervyn to become a big name in cricket. He has received a lot of guidance from our players and coaches, but he has not progressed as we had hoped.' Westfield was born in Romford, Essex, in May 1988, and has played in seven championship matches and eight One-day games, and has taken 11 wickets.

Sussex and England fast bowler James Kirtley was furious when players from opposing teams labelled him a 'cheat' for the way in which he released the ball, claiming that he broke the rules by throwing it, and branded him a 'chucker'. So much fuss blew up that the ECB was forced to call in experts in 2005 to decide whether Kirtley's unusual bowling action came within the laws of the game, and he feared that he could be kicked out.

When I spoke to him for a Sunday tabloid about his harrowing experience, he said: 'I was feeling absolutely terrific after taking six wickets in a Test match for the England A team in New Zealand until someone came up and ruined it all, claiming that I had been reported for throwing. It knocked the stuffing out of me, and my immediate thoughts were that my career would soon be over, especially as the New Zealand Cricket Board had become involved, and I knew that I would have to be cleared by an ECB panel.

'Certain people had decided to knock me personally, and to take credit away from what I had done. I obviously realised that what they were doing could put me out of the game, but Mike Gatting, our manager, and Martin Moxon, our coach, were fantastic. They stressed that I had to stay positive, and they assured me that I was technically sound, and not to worry. I had played in 100 first-class matches up to then, and nothing like this had happened before. I was sure it was people who didn't like it when the heat was turned up.'

Kirtley returned home from that tour after taking 19 first-class wickets, and went straight into a career-threatening ECB inquiry that had been arranged to study his bowling action in minute detail. Slowly and deliberately, Kirtley recalled those anxious moments: 'I was filmed from all angles while bowling at different speeds, and I knew that my future was on the line. Even though Mike Gatting had told me that I'd be fine, I still had butterflies in my stomach.

'I knew there was no way that I could relax until the ECB had announced that my action had passed the test and was legal, which they did. To be honest, even though I knew I wasn't a chucker, and that I had been completely cleared, I was still sure that certain people would continue to point a finger at me. So it was up to me to stay strong, and shut it out of my mind, and get on with my game.'

It was a solid and positive statement from Kirtley, whose spirits were brilliantly boosted a few months later when he flew off to help spearhead England's bowling attack on a tour of Zimbabwe. Sadly it did not turn out as well as he had hoped. What had promised to be a stress-free tour disintegrated into panic and doubt as his controversial bowling action was again questioned and reported.

After an impressive two-wicket debut in the first One-day International, match referee Colonel Naushad Ali reported Kirtley's action to the ICC. It also emerged through a mischievous leak – maybe from one of those 'certain people' Kirtley had referred to – that a first-class umpire had reported him in the English championship in the previous summer.

For reasons exclusively known to itself, the ECB had chosen to keep this incident totally under wraps, as well as the umpire's identity, and it prompted a storm of protest from the media, which condemned it as a 'cover-up'.

To Kirtley's credit, he refused to capitulate under persistent whispering by players and officials at other clubs, and he worked tirelessly to adjust his action with specialist help from the ECB and continued to bowl successfully for Sussex right up to his retirement in September 2010, at the age of 35.

In his troubled, stop-start career, Kirtley still took more than 600 first-class wickets and a total of 19 in his four Test matches, which led his Sussex cricket manager, Mark Robinson, to shower him with praise, saying: 'The dedication and sacrifices that James Kirtley made for his career were a constant source of inspiration and an example to any player fortunate enough to play alongside him. He will go down as one of the all-time greats of Sussex cricket.'

CHAPTER 1

EPILOGUE

When the proud founder of England's unique Barmy Army confessed that only 2 per cent of its members watched international One-day matches because they feared some form of fixing, it left me in no doubt that cricket corruption around the world had hit a new low.

These are loyal and knowledgeable supporters who spend a fortune to travel thousands of miles to attend a major cricket contest, yet it is only now that they have divulged that extreme care is taken about where to go and what to watch. Not because of the teams who are taking part, but because their trust and confidence in the integrity of One-day tournaments have been shattered, especially in Twenty/20 competitions.

It is a sad fact that no one can be absolutely sure any longer whether a dropped catch in the outfield was a bad piece of misjudgement or a deliberate mistake to fulfil a bribe with a bookmaker. Or a chaotic run-out, a first-ball duck, a wide in the opening over, a no-ball in a batting powerplay...

Spot-fixing and blatant cheating have become a menace in

modern cricket to such an extent that I witnessed it personally during a Saturday afternoon club match when a bowler asked me to conceal the metal bottle-top that he was using to damage the ball to make it swing more because he feared the umpire had spotted it in his hand, glinting in the sunshine.

Financial greed has replaced in abundance the honesty that once made cricket such an honourable game. During my extensive investigations and collating of information for this book, it became worryingly clear that cheating and corruption are not confined to one country in particular, as many would like us to believe. I discovered that just about every international cricket nation at one time or another has experienced cheating of some kind.

Too many of the game's head-in-the-sand leaders have made absurd claims that players who cheat in cricket do so because they are badly paid and want to boost their income to match that of team-mates around them. Truth is, some of the worst culprits have been world superstars on vast fees, endorsements and sponsorships who have found it impossible to curb their insatiable financial greed.

It has now reached that woeful stage where no one can be shocked any longer by reports that *any* player or official, no matter how big in the game, has been caught providing 'inside' information and taking bribes from bookmakers.

Personally, I have very little faith in most of the boards of control at the head of the main cricket-playing nations to expose and stamp out corruption, which is their responsibility, and I find it depressing that the International Cricket Council, the game's governing body, is so impotent when it comes to locating and punishing properly the guilty fixers.

Enormous gratitude must be extended to those investigative reporters at the *News of the World* and at other newspapers, and to those television camera operators who spot and report players illegally tampering with the ball, who misguidedly think that they are safe from detection. Big Brother is definitely watching!

As a passionate lover of cricket at all levels – the greatest sport ever devised – I have found it hard while writing this book to believe and accept that the game has been bedevilled by so many devious people who masquerade as righteous yet are crooks who make a laughing stock out of paying customers, as they voraciously fill their pockets with dirty money. That is the biggest scandal of all...

Shortly before I completed this book, three Pakistan players had each been banned for five years by an ICC tribunal panel that had found them guilty of spot-fixing for a bookmaker in a betting scam during a Test match against England.

There was an outcry from many of the game's top players, officials and parts of the media, all claiming that the ICC had allowed the disgraced trio to escape lightly. A 'slap on the wrist' was what they called it. The more extreme believed that all three should have been banned for life.

I was more concerned that, but for the skills of a Sunday tabloid, the ICC would not have had the opportunity to impose punishment of any kind, and it left me desperately hoping that the Anti-corruption Unit will now do its job better in future and root out and name the guilty itself, rather than leave this crucial job for journalists to do.